Highly Functional

Craig DeRoche

Mysong Media Publishing

Mysong Media Publishing Ltd
Coleraine
Northern Ireland
UK

Extracts from *The Big Book*, 1939, 55, 76, 2001 © World Service Inc., used by
permission.

A CIP record for this book is available from the British Library.

First paperback edition 2015

ISBN: 978-0-9932845-0-2

Cover design by SpiffingCovers, Colchester, UK – www.spiffingcovers.com
Typeset by CRB Associates, Potterhanworth, Lincolnshire
Printed in the United States

Prologue

The sun radiated warmth through the tall windows extending some twenty feet up toward the ornate, hand-painted ceiling. Outside, I could see the familiar Romanesque gray buildings below surrounded by narrow patches of rich, green grass. A thick row of traffic sat silently, four cars wide, extending out of view. The beautiful sunlight spilled into the hushed room, past the majestic drapery and rich carpet and over the heads of a couple hundred people seated before the stage.

As I took in the scenery, the United States Attorney General, Eric Holder, was finishing his speech and United States Senators Rand Paul and Mike Lee had just entered the room. The guests kept their eyes forward as the Attorney General made a ground-breaking speech on his support for the restoration of rights of citizens who had paid back society for the crimes they had committed.

This was happening in Washington, D.C. in the spring of 2014.

The same year that leaders would be noted for agreeing on almost nothing and be described as creating a toxic and partisan environment in the nation's capital. In fact, just a few months later the government would be shut down because of their inability to compromise on the budget.

This day was something different though. The leaders were there to agree with each other without any mention of compromise or cutting a deal. Three of the most visible and powerful leaders in

American government would share the stage and talk about criminal justice reform and . . . they would do this alongside me.

Me of all people.

A pretty startling development if you knew who I am or what I have done in my life. How I got here is the interesting part I suppose. It isn't a story I thought I'd want share until something happened that day.

I had written the story down before. I had to for the benefit of my lawyers.

I also wrote about it for my three daughters. They are still young, but with the internet being such a part of education and life today, they are nearly old enough to see all the good things their dad did . . . and the bad.

On that particular day, I wasn't giving a thought to the supernatural story that had landed me on stage. I was just there to do my part and offer advice, suggestions and support as I had done so many times before. It wasn't until I left the grand stage and walked past the windows to the back of the room that things changed.

A young lady reporter pulled me aside for an interview. I was happy to oblige. The interview was brief. When we finished, she folded her notepad cover back on top of the scribbled pages and said, "Can I just ask you something? Off the record?"

"Sure," I replied. I was puzzled by the abrupt change in her posture.

"I just want to say that what you said up there means a great deal to me. Actually, what you went through means more to me. I mean I . . . it's just my dad, you see. He is like you, only he hasn't gotten sober even though he needs to. He doesn't know how to do it and he thinks he's better than other people and, well, your story is so amazing. I wish you'd share it. I wish you'd write it so people like my dad could see it and maybe know that if it can happen in your life, it can happen in theirs."

And with this little seed, the idea of writing this book—and sharing it—has grown. I wrote this book to bear witness to the gift I received. The greatest gift I will ever have or know. A gift I wish I could bottle up and ship to you today. Maybe this book will help you or someone you know or love in some small way I can't predict.

This book is written as a true account of who I was, what happened and what I am today. The circumstances and my experience described here are authentic and real. This said, to tell the story completely would require me to encumber several living people with families, careers and lives of their own. In my desire to be accurate without being unnecessarily selfish, I have had to change the names and descriptions of most of the characters in this book outside of my family. In addition, I changed some sequencing of events and dialogue. In this book you will read of the many paradoxical things I have learned in order to grow personally and I will preface the story with an important one: to tell the truth it is necessary to fictionalize some attributes of characters to grant the real people increased privacy.

For anyone reading this who was so inclined as to read this book along with the multitude of related news stories and sworn testimony, you will find that I have stayed very close to the facts and amazing truth of what I experienced. This was the whole point of writing the book in the first place. I avoided using fiction to add in scenes, embellish or minimize my extraordinary encounters in every case.

Craig DeRoche
May 2015

Dedications

For my wife Stacey, and our daughters,
Carley, Zoe & Phoebe.
In Memory of an American Hero
Kirk DeRoche and for his wife, Kim, and their kids,
Ella, Wyatt & Erin

With thanks to
Paul & Anne DeRoche, Paul Marc DeRoche
Marsha & Tom Zoellner

And Chuck Colson for his dream and vision and the "living monuments" he has created in his work.

Chapter 1

I was the one dispatched to Mick's house. My wife, Stacey, sent me. It was Friday evening, about eight, and already Mick was blotto drunk. His wife, Mim, was away at a grad school class, but she knew about the problem and called Stacey, asking if I could go by and look in on him and their kids.

When I got to his house, he had a raging fire going in one of those tin-can fire pits they sell to suburbanites like us at the local big-box hardware. The split wood was stacked in a pyramid right up to the edge of the tin, with more piled on top.

Mick was busy throwing two last splits of wood onto the blazing pile. The bonfire popped and crackled, sending smoke and embers up into the night sky. From the other side of the fire, Mick grinned and nodded at me. He slid his hand along the ledge behind him until he found a full longneck among the dozen or so empties already lined up.

"What brings you by?" Mick said.

"Nothing. Wanted to see what you were up to."

"You know me and fire: the bigger the better. Want a pop? I bought your kind. They're in the fridge."

"Nah, I'm good. I can't stay long. Just wanted to see what you're doing."

"Drinking." He pushed his hair back. Actually I a-am drunk. *Phew* . . . Mim has these classes. Leaves me here and there isn't anything to do. I don't know how you go without. I mean, I know you haven't been perfect about it, but I couldn't even go a week. I'd never make it."

Mick stammered a bit and slurred his consonants while he spoke.

"You always seem s-so happy," he said. "What are you doin' different this time? You mussa los' thirty pounds."

"Forty, actually. I give Richard Simmons all the credit. Besides, things are going great. But I haven't figured *anything* out. I'm in no better shape than you—just sober tonight, is all."

I had lost forty pounds through a lot of hard work and by no longer using food as a way to cope with the stress of the past four months. The truth was, I no longer wanted to be recognized, not after my public flogging by the media for a drunk-driving arrest.

"Mim and Stacey say you're learning shtuff I should know," Mick said. "What're you learning about?"

"God—things like that."

"Oh, here we go. *God's* helping you now? S'pose God could help me?" His movements were more animated now. Mick wasn't angry with me, but he was winding up to put on a show.

"Where wash your God when I was growing up? Y-you tellin' me you believe a guy raised from the dead way back when's gonna h-help you or me today? I'll tell you who gets me what I need: me." He paced from side to side, with the blazing fire between us. "This house, the money I've m-made, the life I h-have. *God's* doin' all that for you?" He paused, looked across the smoke, and took a long drink from his beer. "Stupid . . . Serious, though, who can you count on?"

"I'm just saying I—"

"Dude, lemme tell you how it is. You wanna talk supernatural stuff? Well, how'z iss: I can see the future, and it's d-dark."

Mick was in full stride now. Chin up and using his free hand for dramatic effect, he raised his voice, declaiming up into the billowing smoke, "I keep having this dream, and in it I die." He looked down. "It'll happen. I know it'll happen. It w-will h-happen in the nex' five years. That's why I'm gonna live *now*."

Having completed this profound thought, he looked at me, full of energy tinged with anger. "You think there's a God. I know I'm gonna die and go nowhere." He stumbled forward, and I jerked, thinking he might fall headlong into the fire. "Here, you don' believe me? Shake," Mick said, righting himself and sticking out his hand.

"I'm not going to shake your hand, man." I said. "You're crazy and you're drunk. You're stupid, too," I said now raising my own voice. "Whether you believe in God or not, you should know, the things you think about tend to come true. So stop wanting to die."

"I don't. I've spent my life trying to be different from my dad. Do you know what it's like to have your dad taken away from you when you were a kid? He screwed up his world completely. He died last year, 27 years later, broken and alone without anyone left for him in his life. I don' wanna go out like that, but where was God for *him*? Where was God for me when I was growing up? Everything I got, I got myself."

This conversation was grim, nonsensical, and pointless. I wanted it to end now. I was sober and didn't want to be where Mick was tonight. I just needed to go home and go to bed. No drinking, no problem.

"Well, listen," I said. "I'm going home and try to be good. I'm still on probation for that drunk-driving ticket for another couple months, and I don't want to end up having to serve that ninety-three-day suspended sentence."

"They g-gave you a *jail* sentence?"

"No. Probation. First offense. Six months and I am done. If I drink, I go to jail."

"AA meetings?"

"Yep. I have to go to twelve, but I'm going to a church group instead. Counselor, too. Expensive ticket."

"I had to do that, too. It sucks. Buncha losers. Very humiliating. 'S anyone recognize you?"

"Not yet. I'm just keeping my head down, though. Hey, listen, I'm gonna run. I'll see you over the weekend."

"All right, DeRoche. See ya."

I returned home and told Stacey I had tried to help Mick but that he was having none of it. She thanked me for trying and told me she appreciated that I wasn't drinking anymore.

Stacey is the most beautiful woman in the world to me, and really the only long-term relationship I have ever had. Those green-blue eyes and that smile can light up any room, and she has always loved me through our ups and downs. More than anything, I didn't want to lose her.

That little acknowledgment from her meant a lot to me. It made me feel that I was making some headway in restoring our broken relationship. I really hoped I was, in fact, doing better, and wondered if I just might be on the right path after all.

Amazing, the difference a week can make.

*　*　*

The following Saturday evening, the phone jangled me awake.

"You okay?" Mick said.

"Tired—you woke me up," I said in my best fake-sober voice. It was June, and the sun was just setting. It had been eight days since I dropped in on Mick as a favor to his wife. Now the tables were turned.

"Stacey says you've been drinking. I can tell you have, too. She's pissed. I told her I'd come talk to you and try to help. I'm comin' by."

"Don't bother . . ." I paused and let out a long breath. "I'll talk to her when she gets home tomorrow. The kids are in bed, and I am going up now."

"I'm comin' either way. I told her I would. Dude, I'm not lettin' you off the hook here."

"Fine—for a minute." I tried to snap loose from the gravity holding my body down and from the sleepy fog that made my mind feel like Styrofoam. I hadn't slept much the night before, drinking vodka well into the morning. Now I had one last conversation to deal with, and then I could crash.

Damn it! How had I gotten in this situation again? What was I going to say this time? *Think.*

I was lying on the couch in the great room of our house, in an upscale suburban neighborhood near Detroit. Both Mick and I lived in what people call "McMansions": bigger houses than our young families really needed, churned out by developers in a way that makes them look and feel the same no matter where you are.

I peered up at the second-story rooms and the catwalk connecting them and listened to make sure the kids were still asleep. No noise or movement from any of my three daughters. I paused to evaluate my physical state.

To be this tired and out of sorts surprised me, even after the thousands of days I began with a vow to stay sober, only to crash into bed drunk that same night. I was 14 when this occurred to me for the first time. Even at such an early age, I had done enough embarrassing, awkward, or downright stupid things to draw the conclusion that alcohol and I didn't get on well together.

Nothing had ever worked to solve my drinking issue, and clearly, nothing was working at this moment.

I just needed to get through this visit from Mick and prepare to face the music from Stacey tomorrow. Mick's coming by wasn't the worst that could happen, anyway. He was one of the only people in the world who knew how bad my drinking actually was—and his wasn't much better. Hell, only a week ago, he was the one in hot water with his wife.

The doorbell rang, and I looked out to see Mick standing in front of the picture window. I opened the door, and he walked past me into the house and asked if I had a cigarette.

Mick is a tall, handsome, athletically built guy. With his chiseled features, ripped muscles, and blond Gordon Gekko do, he always had a way with the ladies and could always translate his charm into big sales and a big salary. Since Mick and his family moved up from Texas, we had shared a lot during that time, including vacations together, concerts, nights on the town. Lately, though, Mick's behavior had grown erratic and had become quite bothersome to many people, including his wife and neighbors. I could see his bicycle in the driveway through the front window.

"What's up with the bike?" I said.

"I'm too drunk to drive," he replied, "but I came to bring you to my house."

"Dude, you're crazy."

"Dude, you're screwed! Stacey is off the charts m-mad. I've been t-talking with her. You'll be lucky to stay married. You need to come over. Your neighbor's gonna watch the kids."

"You just decree all this and I'm supposed to go along?"

"It's for the best."

Within moments, my neighbor Michele came over. One of Stacey's best friends, she is a professional soccer coach and has a way of dealing out discipline. It was easy to see she couldn't care less about either Mick or me and would just as soon be somewhere else.

"Mick, why don't you go home?" she said in a stern voice. "Craig, why don't you go to bed?"

"S-Stacey wants Craig to come to my house," Mick said.

"Whatever. Both you guys are a train wreck. Craig, make a decision. Todd will drive you over there. Craig, Stacey's mom is coming by, too. She's on her way, so you may as well go. Where are the kids?"

"U-upstairs," I muttered.

So Michele's husband, Todd, was going to drive Mick and me, and Stacey's mother, Marsha, was coming by. Stacey had really called in the troops this time.

Michele looked straight at me and seemed to size me up.

I factored in that Todd and Marsha, as well as Michele and Mick, were now involved in the effort. I knew I had screwed up royally this time, and cooperating might win me some points.

"Fine," I said. "I'll go and talk with Mick for a while. When Marsha—Stacey's mom—gets h-here, please tell her I'm s-sorry for this and I'll be home later," I said.

On the ride over, Todd didn't say a word. I sat in the front seat, and Mick sat in back.

Todd's a real straight arrow. He doesn't create a lot of controversy and avoids it where he can. He was already way outside his comfort zone, and any words I could conjure up seemed more awkward than the silence, so I just sat still. I thought I had successfully made Todd as comfortable with the drive as I could, and didn't see what was coming.

When we arrived at Mick's house, Mick jumped out from the back seat and opened my door while I was thanking Todd for the ride. Mick's entire posture had changed. He stood upright and stalwart, with the pugnacious bearing of a drill instructor.

"Get out of the car," Mick said.

He didn't wait even a second.

"I said get out of the damn car."

I looked up.

"Get out of the car now, loser," he barked, grabbing my right arm and pulling me as hard as he could.

"Whoa, what the hell!" I said as I swung my legs around and put my feet on the ground.

My body clicked to high alert immediately, and I think Mick sensed it. Todd certainly did.

"What are you doing, Mick?" Todd said.

"Nothin'," Mick replied. "He's staying here."

"Craig . . . ," Todd started.

"I-it's all right, Todd," I said. "Calm down, Mick. What's going on?"

Mick scowled at me and then shook his head at Todd as if he had just caught his own kid doing something bad.

"Are you sure?" Todd said quietly to me as Mick walked away toward the back of his house.

"It'll be fine," I said. "I-I can get home from here. I really a-appreciate this. I'll let you know how it goes with Stacey tomorrow. Thanks for the ride."

I could see the concern and shock on Todd's face. He looked at me for an extra moment before backing the car away and driving off.

I walked past the end of the driveway and onto the grass that led around Mick's garage to his back yard and the fire pit we had kibitzed over the week before.

"What was th-that all about?" I said.

Mick looked down and appeared to be gathering his thoughts. He rubbed his sweaty forehead as he raised his head to eye level with me. He had a look of wonder that changed even as I watched. The corners of his eyes tightened, and he jabbed a finger across the patio to where I stood.

"You're done. You're a loser. Stacey doesn't want to be married to you anymore. She wants a divorce. You're s-sleepin' on the couch tonight. I'll do ya this favor, but you're outta here tomorrow. I don't want you around. Tomorrow y-you can pack up your s-s-stuff and move out. You're not allowed to go to your house anymore; that's wh-why you're here."

His posture, tone, and energy were no longer intoxicated with drink, but with power. He relished barking commands at me. The alert that my body sends me from the vibrations, actions, or words of those around me could be dumbed down with alcohol, but on this night, the message came through loud and clear.

I had spoken with Stacey. My neighbor Michele had spoken with Stacey. She was mad, but I was asleep at home on the couch, and the kids were in bed. Stacey was three hours away on a girls' weekend with Mick's wife and four other wives. What Mick was saying didn't make any sense, and his violent stance and words made me think the worst immediately. I had been drinking, but I was nowhere near the level of intoxication I was used to, and was actually much soberer than I had been the night before.

"Mick, wh-what the f . . . is wrong with you?" I said.

"You . . . you f . . . . . *loser*," he said.

"Dude, you're way out of line. I'm goin' home. My kids are there in bed. Stacey isn't coming home till morning."

"No, you're not," he proclaimed with disdainful emphasis. "You're n-never goin' set foot in that house again!"

"What on earth are you talking about? Did you take my name off the deed today?"

"Don't mock me, jackass," Mick shouted.

"I'm not mocking you. You're acting like an idiot!" I shouted back.

"Don't talk that way when my kids are here," Mick said, glancing toward the window, where I could see his boy looking out at us.

"Screw you, then. I'm going home," I said.

"No, y-you're not. You s-stay here," Mick declared. He then added, with a logic that someone like me could understand, "I'm goin' ta get another beer. You can't have any, though. You're staying here and you can't drink."

He then turned and walked back toward his garage. I stood in amazement, interpreting the discussion. And in that instant, I understood it in light of the conversation from a week ago.

All at once, my body had pivoted in place, and I was walking away from Mick's house, toward the exit to his subdivision and the road back to my house.

It was a hot summer night, and I was wearing a thin T-shirt, cargo shorts, and flip-flops. I was still a little drunk, but the cobwebs were mostly gone. I passed the house of another friend whose wife was on the girls' weekend with Mim and Stacey. As I came around the side of the house and made my way toward the sidewalk, something hit me hard in the back and side and pressed my knees, chest, and, finally, my chin into the grass. I didn't feel any pain at first, just the tremendous impact and weight.

Instantly, the adrenaline fired—fight and flight at the same time. There was no telling what came next after such a violent hit. I didn't even think about any pain as I felt Mick squeeze my ribs with everything he had and throw me back to the ground, with all his weight landing on me a second time.

Intent and focused, I pushed up to my knees and hands without a word or sound. Reaching down to his arms, I twisted and pushed with all the leverage I could muster, and broke free for a moment. I took three steps forward to regain my equilibrium, losing my flip-flops.

Just then, Mick lunged from behind. I twisted to avoid the hit, and he nearly ran me head-on into the brick wall of his neighbor's house. I sat down and looked back up at him, leaning back against the thick hedgerow along the neighbor's wall.

"You're not goin' anywhere," he said. "If you try to leave, I'll call the cops."

Scanning the side yard, I saw no sign of anyone. Oh, well. This was going to come to a head one way or another. I rolled away from the shrubs, got up, and walked to the sidewalk.

Enraged by my defiance, Mick hit me again and brought me down. He hadn't been strong enough to keep me down before, and I tried to get up the same way a third time. This time he used the sidewalk for leverage, using all his weight to push me down into the concrete.

Pressing one foot against the sidewalk, I pushed and rolled and broke free.

We did this same inelegant dance three more times. The skin on the tops of my feet shredded like cheese rubbed across a grater as he dragged them while I used them for leverage against the rough sidewalk. The skin on my knees and shins looked much the same. His grip around my ribs was unlike anything I had felt in my life, and I became convinced he was trying to kill me or, at minimum, knock me out.

I broke free, fully aware of the cost I was paying in skin. I could feel the enormous pressure on my ribs and back, and the scraping and pounding all over me, but the pain was remote, distant. Time slowed down for me as I walked.

My foot came forward, and I felt warm blood rolling down both legs. I couldn't take in a full breath, because my ribs on the left side still felt as if they were clenched in a giant vise. I was thinking now. Thinking was no longer my problem. I had a decision to make.

I didn't have any fear at all about turning around and facing Mick. I was in the best shape of my life, and he was arguably drunker than I. I could hold my own for sure, but I could see no upside to throwing a punch unless it proved absolutely necessary. In this case, it seemed more trouble than it was worth. Considering what Mick had said a week ago about dying, I didn't want to fight someone who felt he had so little to lose. I just wanted to get as far away from him as I could.

I kept walking.

Some of the pain was starting to register now. I looked down at the blood and was surprised at how deep the cuts on the tops of my feet were. The skin was pulled back in ribbons that remained attached at one end. I felt my ribs, and my entire body flinched with pain.

I moved forward, trying to breathe deeper and calm my senses. I was free of Mick and needed to figure out what had just happened. The air was now cooling off, and the moonless sky was bright with a billion stars.

I was taken by how beautiful the cloudless night sky was and how pleasant the cool air felt after the hellish encounter I had just undergone. I was walking at a good clip, ignoring the pain and wanting only to get home. I even began thinking about what my conversation with Stacey might look like tomorrow.

I had maybe three minutes of peace before I heard a yell in the distance.

"I called nine one one! They're coming and they're gonna arrest you. Better stop now, dude. Don't make this any worse than it has to be."

It was Mick, on his wife's bike. With one hand on the handlebar and the other holding a phone to his ear, he was wobbling from side to side as if trying to keep his balance. He was yelling at me and, I presume, into the phone at the same time.

By now there was nothing I could say to settle Mick down. He was past the point of reasoning with—it would be a waste of my time, and perhaps another escalation of violence.

He was still a hundred feet or more behind me when I started jogging. I had left his subdivision and was now on the main public two-lane road that led to my neighborhood. Off to my left, between me and an apartment complex, I saw a thick stand of small trees. I made a quick calculation and turned left.

I figured Mick was too drunk to follow me into the woods. And sure enough, he stopped his bike and stood straddling it up on the sidewalk. He spoke into the cell phone at his ear.

"Yeah, h-he got away from me. R-ran into the woods . . . No, c-can't see him. D'you send a car?"

Mick glanced around him while he spoke, then snapped his attention back toward the woods. "Never mind, I see your car now. I'll talk to him." He hung up and then looked back to the road.

Crouched low, I had a clear view through the woods. To my right, I saw a Novi police cruiser pull off the road. An officer got out and approached Mick.

This was a discussion I didn't want to miss. I didn't want to join in or anything, but Mick's craziness should provide some entertainment—at least some small compensation for what he was putting me through.

I couldn't believe Mick had called the police, and I couldn't imagine why they would have cared to come out. At the same time, I was on probation for operating a motor vehicle while impaired, and drinking would violate the probation.

I was not prepared for what I heard next.

"You the one that made the call?" the officer said.

"Yeah. Craig DeRoche. Can y-you believe that? You know who he is, right?" Mick said.

"Yeah, everyone in this town knows him," the officer said.

"I w-was just drinking with him at my house and we got in a fight, and he ran away from me into those woods. His wife doesn't want him home, and I'm tryin' ta keep 'im at m-m-my house. She isn't there; she's across the state with my wife. I can't let him go home."

The officer shined the spotlight of the vehicle back and forth across the woods and shouted for me.

"L-listen, I think you're going to need two cruisers out here—one on this side and one on the other side of the woods." He swung his hands left and right from my position, showing his drunken battle plan. "You gonna need a couple of dogs, t-too. We could get 'im if you had dogs."

"I don't even think we have a canine unit on tonight," the officer said. "I think they had last shift. Hold on."

He clicked the microphone on his shoulder. "Do we have a canine unit on tonight, or any other cars that can come by and sweep the area? I have a situation here . . . No . . . Roger that."

The officer adjusted his posture and moved back toward Mick. "We don't have anything else we can do right now, but I will head around and look for him and go by his house. You should just go home. How are you doing, anyway, pal? You're pretty drunk."

"Not as drunk as Cr-Craig," Mick slurred.

"I haven't seen Craig." The officer shined a light on Mick. "You're having a hard time standing up. Can you get home?"

"You know wh-what, officer, I am going to walk my bike home."

"Good choice," the cop replied. He leaned his chin toward his lapel-mounted radio, said a few words, then got in his car and pulled away onto the empty street.

I tried to get my mind around what was going on. The police were going to sweep for me—were actually going to set dogs on me—to prevent me from going back to sleep in my own house? Did Mick, Stacey, or anyone else actually know what they had just done by calling the police?

The political calculator in my head was whirring away, as always. I desperately tried to figure out a way to get this situation back into a manageable place.

It couldn't happen, though. I knew this firsthand. Things were already out of control, and there was nothing I could do to stop them from getting worse. I had learned this fact in the little town of Saline, Michigan, just four months before. Once the police were called and they found out who I was, there was a different set of pressures on them, with nothing I could do about it.

You can't avoid, influence, or alter the course of that juggernaut once it gets underway. I had learned this the hard way, and now I knew that my only option was to prepare for the storm. I had no idea how long or rough this storm would be, though recent experience gave me plenty to fear.

* * *

I sat crouched in the thick woods as the police and Mick left. My thoughts returned to the pleasant, peaceful summer night that had just been marred by all the drama and fighting. The night was beautiful, and the air smelled fresh, like spring, even though it was late June. My ears were ringing with tinnitus, and I felt a burning pain from all the woodland dirt and debris getting rubbed into the open abrasions on my knees and feet.

Rolling onto my back, I gazed up at the stars and took in their beauty and peaceful presence. Around me, nothing stirred but the crickets and katydids, and a solitary car every few minutes. I imagined a life different from the one I now had—a life without secrets, fear, and the problems that came with alcohol.

This dream wasn't new to me. Years before, as a young teenager, I had woken unable to remember anything from the night before. I couldn't count all the days I had vowed it would be different and then gone to bed drunk just the same. All those promises, all those attempts, all the pain, and now this . . .

In an improbable sequence of events, it seemed that all my lies were unraveling at once. I had now totally lost control.

Twenty-nine years of addiction, and nearly all of it hidden from those who knew me best. My parents and brothers never knew the lengths I went to, to keep it under wraps, and the trouble it caused. My wife, Stacey, knew of the problem but thought I was clean and sober nine out of ten days. Friends and family thought I could be a big drinker for sure, though most would have said they themselves had gone too far on occasion, and dismissed my behavior when I got thoroughly drunk. No one really knew.

But *I* knew. It was part of me each moment of every day, and it hurt. I wanted it gone but had no faith that anything would work. I had tried everything, it seemed, and nothing worked for more than a few weeks.

I masked the pain with a smile and used the pursuit of accomplishment and good works to paper over my failings. It worked well. I did a lot of good and got to help a lot of people. At the same time, I was hollowing out emotionally and my marriage was failing.

Lying there in the dirt and last year's leaves, I knew what was coming. I had experienced it all before, just four months before Mick called the police.

I wished I could blot out that night four months ago and just make it go away. I couldn't, though. It had happened. It was real. Lying there and listening to the crickets, I let my mind drift back to the first time I was arrested in such a public way.

Chapter 2

It was February, four months earlier, and I was pacing back and forth on a sidewalk during a major Michigan winter storm. I had been drinking all day, and I had drunk a lot the day before. Luckily, a flat tire had prevented me from driving any farther earlier in the day. I had driven the car earlier and was surely above the legal limit, though nowhere near as drunk as when the police arrived.

While talking on my cell phone, I went into a store and, in my drunken state, knocked over a huge stand holding trays of bread. I looked at the owner and saw her expression of amazement. At the time, I had no idea that she was probably the one who called the police in the first place, suspicious of the man pacing in front of her store. Cutting through her store to a mall-like area that had no exit, I returned to the sidewalk and toward the side of the building before the police approached me a second time.

"What are you doing?" a male officer said as he got out of his cruiser.

"No, I'm good. Just trying to get a cab and get to my hotel." I said, still holding the phone to my ear.

I was frustrated. I had been trying to get a cab and a tow, only to learn that both would take an hour and a half. Dressed in a suit and tie and topcoat, I was headed south to Ohio for meetings in the morning, and when my drinking took off at lunch, I decided to get a hotel in Ann Arbor. Thanks to my drinking, I wound up in a small town just to the south, falling-down drunk, with a flat tire, in the freezing cold.

"We got some calls about someone acting funny around here. About *you*. Have you been drinking?" The officer was speaking politely.

"Y-yes."

"How much?"

"A l-lot. I've been drinkin' all day. I'm really drunk."

A female officer got out of the vehicle and joined her partner.

"Have you been driving?" she asked.

"Nope," I slurred.

"Where's your car?"

"Across the street over there." I waved my hand with the cell phone that I had turned off. "It has a flat. I w-was jus' callin' for a tow and a cab. I'm going to stay in town. I was headed to Ohio."

"Where you from, sir?"

When I told them where I lived, her partner said, "So you got about thirty miles and you're drunk. Didn't make it very far, did you?"

"No, sir."

"Listen, I want you to come down here by the car and we're going to do a sobriety test, okay?"

Looking straight ahead through the windshield, I noticed the camera mounted below the rearview mirror. I knew what the device was there for. I remembered seeing the YouTube video of a Michigan legislator go viral. The video showed him clearly drunk and doing a field sobriety test. I thought of what my family would endure if I subjected them to this, if I agreed to be filmed in my present state.

"You don't have to give me a sobriety test," I said. "I told you, I'm as drunk as I have ever been."

"Too drunk to drive?" the officer said.

"Yes—in fact, way past it. I told you, my car is across the street."

"Well, we received this complaint. I can see you're drunk, and I'm going to take you in for questioning anyway. You can do the test or you can blow into the breathalyzer. I'm not going to let you go."

"Fine. You, you know . . . I will blow into the breathalyzer if you let me go in your car. I'm freezin' and I can't get a ride for an hour and a half. If you wanna charge me with something, I don't mind, but I need to get to the hotel and to have my car brought in. I could actually use your help."

In my drunken state, I thought this was quite the pitch. I was impressed by my own BS. The officers didn't look so happy, though.

"What's in the gym bag you left on the side of the building?" the male cop said.

"Clothes and a bottle of booze."

I could see that the odd behavior and responses clearly left the small-town cop scratching his head. If he was irritated, it didn't show. He just kept leading me along very pleasantly toward the inevitable arrest.

"That's fine. I'm going to ask around with the shopkeepers, and we will either charge you or drop you off. Get in."

I sat in the backseat of the car, satisfied that I had manipulated my way around a field sobriety test. The female cop lifted the tube through the small window between their two seats and had me take a deep breath and blow into the machine. Then she shook her head and showed her partner.

"Well, how'd I do?" I said.

"You lit it up," the male cop said. "You weren't kiddin' about drinking a lot, buddy.

"How much?"

"Let's do it again to be sure."

"Okay."

I blew again. Warming to the circumstances, I started rationalizing. I actually thought getting a public intoxication ticket wouldn't be a big deal. Maybe it was just what I needed—just the kick in the pants that would help me change my ways.

The woman looked straight at me. "It reads point two eight nine. This is not good."

"Wow, that is drunk," I said.

"You better believe it. It's a miracle you can stand up. What were you drinking?"

"Shots. Vodka, beer. A lot of stuff."

"What happened to the top of your head?"

"I fell earlier when I was trying to change the tire on my car. I was trying to turn the lug. Lost my footing. Landed s-straight on my head." I gently touched my skull and smiled.

"You think you're just drunk, or did you hit your head hard enough for a concussion?"

"I'm not s-sure."

The male officer had started driving. He had probably made his decision before asking me about my head, but then asked anyway.

As we drove, he said he was going to bring me to the hospital and have them take a look. He wanted to make sure that with my blood alcohol and a probable concussion, I would be okay.

He said, "I'll hold up my end of the deal and either get you to a hotel or bring you back to the station to process you for a ticket if we decide to give you one. The chief is out of town and we can't get a hold of him. Either way, I'm calling for our towing company to pick up your vehicle and they'll put the spare on for you. This is going to take a couple of hours anyway, and I can't really let you go until you're under point zero eight, so you may as well relax."

Small-town police, I thought. *Genuine hospitality.*

A couple of hours later, the doctor and the police had determined that I would live. Despite my arrogance, he and the two cops and those back at the station were nothing but helpful and nice.

When they took the mug shots, they took four and let me pick the one I liked. (Looking back, I think this is a pretty funny trick to amuse the officers and occupy the attention of the drunk in their custody.)

When I was leaving at about six p.m., I caught a hint of something I hadn't expected but was certainly worried about. The officer processing me to leave said that no decision had been made whether to charge me with anything. He said a decision wouldn't be made for a couple of weeks, because I wasn't driving my car.

I asked if I could see what they had written in their report so far, and that's when I tripped the wire.

"The chief said, under these types of circumstances, he wants to get this right," the desk officer said. "You understand. The report won't be ready for a while."

Ouch. They must have figured things out.

"Can I leave a request to get a copy of it?" I said.

"Yes, just fill out this Freedom of Information Act form, and we'll call you when it's ready."

He gave me a contact information sheet and a receipt for the X-ray at the hospital.

"Here's the number for the tow company," the desk officer said. "They fixed your flat and will come pick you up. You can use the phone over there on the wall. You owe him sixty bucks." And he went back to typing and gazing into the computer screen.

It took about three days for me to get a midafternoon call from a journalist I had known from my previous work. We weren't friendly. In fact, on a big story of corruption in the Democratic-minority staff office, he had actually used his cover of working as a journalist to keep the corrupt parties informed of our investigation as it was going on. (A bit of a twist on the famed Woodward/Bernstein Watergate stories, I suppose.)

"Is this Craig DeRoche?" the reporter said when I picked up. When I hesitated, he added, "Mr. Speaker, is this you?"

I cringed. No one used my former title anymore unless they were putting something in the paper.

"You wouldn't remember me. This is Bert Jackson. I used to work at a different place but covered state politics. Now I'm working as a freelancer in Ann Arbor."

"I remember you, Bert. What's up?"

"Uh, great. Thank you. Um, I'm looking at a police report that says you were picked up on suspicion of drunk driving in Saline last week. I'm calling for your comment."

"I don't have a report here, Bert, and didn't know that one was written. What's it say?"

As he started reading the report to me, my stomach soured and my heart raced. What he read was more or less true, though each word and sentence was constructed to take what I had in fact done and couch it in the most ludicrous and blazingly prejudicial language imaginable. I suspected the police of employing some ringers from the *Tonight Show* comedy-writing team as advisers.

Over time, I have learned that police and prosecutor reports nearly universally attempt to skew words and facts to describe defendants in the most depraved light possible. Some of these efforts can be real works of art.

For example, an officer arresting a man just after observing him get up from a sofa, cut a slice of cheese, scratch himself, and slide over the sofa armrest to sit back down would write the sequence of nonevents as follows:

"The subject abruptly left the room, where he was staring with a menacing glare at the television, which alarmed the complainant. He then secured a knife. He wielded the knife back and forth in an intimidating manner. After wielding the knife, he brought his other hand to his crotch area and made a rapid up-and-down motion. When he returned to the couch, he could barely stand and fell over the armrest."

The prosecutor would then call for "an immediate psychological examination, for Mr. Badguy to be held without bail, for all knives and golf clubs to be removed from his house, and for him to face charges on at least three counts."

The newspapers would then write, "Sexual Pervert Arrested Wielding Knife."

In my case, though, I wasn't in the right. I wasn't behaving well. Though I hadn't been caught in the act, I had driven earlier while above the legal limit. Moreover, I had certainly driven drunk in the past. To my surprise, I actually remember everything about the night, and I thought of ways to explain it in the most innocent light.

But there wasn't an innocent way to express the truth. The truth was clearly different from what I was detained for, and the encounter did not happen as it was portrayed, but as I ran through the true story in my head, I came to the same answer each time.

Indeed, an accurate account of my experience would likely sound even more pathetic than the police report! What I did would make sense only if we were describing the actions of a teenager getting drunk with his friends and making bizarre but thoroughly adolescent decisions. I had no excuses. Still, this was the day I got my first lesson in the way the American media culture deals with celebrity police reports.

Bert read the whole report to me. He asked for my version of the story.

I told Bert that I was, in fact, brought in by the police but that I had never seen the report even though I requested it from the police. I told him it wasn't available yet. I asked if I could call the police to try to get a copy.

Bert's reply was simple. "You're right, it's not available yet and probably won't be for weeks. But that's a fair request. You call them and call me back. I'll hold off until I hear from you, but I'm posting the story whether you call me back or not."

"Okay. 'Bye."

Think, Craig. No, don't think. Just dial.

"Hello, this is Craig DeRoche," I said to the desk clerk at the Saline Police Department. "I was in there on the ninth and I have a report number, and I just wanted to see if I could get a copy of anything—if it's been written."

"Hold on."

The wait seemed an eternity. My heart raced. I chewed a fingernail and rubbed my temples. The political calculator in my head plotted angles for me. My political calculator was always running. When I was faced with any problem, it presented me with the list of solutions and their relative odds for success. This time, though, nothing was clear and no viable answers appeared. I had no angles, no solutions.

"Yes, sir," the clerk said as he returned to the phone. "I see your stuff here. There isn't a report available, and there won't be one. I just talked to the chief, and he says it won't be available for probably five weeks—until your blood test comes back."

"Can you tell the chief a reporter called me? And that *he* has a copy of it?" I added in a tone of restrained outrage.

"*What?* Why would the media have a copy of your report? It isn't even ready."

"You know what?" I snapped again. Then I paused and exhaled. "Never mind. I'm sorry. I didn't mean to be rude just then."

"I do see a note that you want a call when it's ready. We have your number. I'll make another note, and we will call you when it's done. I promise."

"Okay. Thanks. I appreciate your help. 'Bye."

I pushed "end" on my phone and stared at it. Craig DeRoche, the youngest Speaker of the House in Michigan's legislative history and the youngest statewide elected GOP official in America, was about to be exposed as a common drunk. There was no way to dispute the charges against me, and I couldn't do anything to stop the reporters from dragging my name through the mud. Finding the willingness to change would take considerably more pain than I could have imagined. Had I known, while standing in the hole I had dug, what rock-bottom would look and feel like, I would have climbed out sooner to avoid it. But I had no idea. So instead of quitting, I just kept digging.

And now this painful process was going to start again. It started the minute Mick called the police, just four months after my first arrest.

* * *

When you lie about a particular thing long enough, it becomes a part of you—as much a part of you as how you walk or the way you talk to people.

There is no way for me to be sure when I first lied about this part of my life, but I'm certain I was doing it frequently by the time I was 10 or 11. By 14, I was into bigger incidents and bigger lies to cover them. At 15 and 16, I had more precarious and consequential misdeeds and misadventures to be untruthful about. At 17, I graduated from high school and left home for college at Central Michigan University. I returned only to repay my dad for a three-thousand-dollar loan he had given me my senior year, when I was too busy to work. I was carrying twenty-eight credit hours, was the president of my fraternity, and drank heavily every single day. Each night, the big drinkers on campus knew they could come to my room in the basement of the fraternity house and finish the night with a blast and blur. I graduated at age 20 on the dean's list and was named one of three "outstanding student leaders" by the university president.

I was an accomplished liar. I had every angle covered, and looking back, I have to say, it always took a lot of work.

God blessed me with the ability to read and learn things almost as fast as I could look at them—a gift wasted on my reprobate extracurricular activities.

For all the trouble I caused, the scrapes I was involved in, and the astonishingly poor decisions I made, to many my life seemed charmed. I am not saying this to be vain. It was what others said of me or to me. For my part, I never believed it, because I had to live the reality.

For me to patch over the incongruity of who I was and what it took to meet or exceed others' expectations each day, selfishness and dishonesty seemed necessary. As I prepared to call Bert Jackson back and face his questions, I was truly weary of my duplicity. Unfortunately, it took me until I was 39 years old and running a failing business to realize this.

I had talked to Stacey about what was happening, and she agreed that I should call the reporter back. She was understandably upset with the shame I was bringing on our family, especially our kids. She told me she loved me and that she just wanted my drinking to be over and done with. I did my best to comfort her. She was such a great friend and supporter through this time, it gave me much-needed strength.

I walked into my home office and sat down at my desk, took a deep breath, and dialed Bert Jackson.

My mind was racing to spin it all into something palatable, to use the techniques I had always used to shut down reporters in the past. But there wasn't anything there. Something new was happening during the call, and it wasn't just lack of devilish inspiration. The fact was, I stopped caring about my lies so much. I wasn't really sure I *wanted* them to work. Of this much I was certain, and this quickly made me lose interest in telling a story in the first place.

I have had interactions with the police plenty of times in my life. And in every attempt to punish or correct my outlandish behavior through the years, I had come away virtually unscathed by authority.

This time, though, was different in many ways. This time, I truly believed I was thinking clearly.

* * *

After I was arrested just days earlier, I checked into an inpatient addiction rehab clinic. It was the second time in my life I had sought help from an inpatient program. I did this for two reasons: first, because I was afraid to sober up and come off alcohol. I'll explain more about this later. Second, I was finally looking for answers, and I thought I might find them there.

All good intentions, and all of them derailed by my pride, fear, and self-righteousness—after just *two nights* in the program. Against the doctor's strong suggestion that I stay, I checked out.

In the clinic's detox unit, I was surrounded by people strung out on a drug they give opiate addicts as a replacement instead of a cure. Every moment was painful. All they talked about was when their next bump was going to be and how much they had manipulated the doctor into giving them. A lot of drug addicts know more about chemistry and dosages than professionally employed pharmacists, and I was in a roomful of them for forty-eight hours. I was better than them. I could figure this out by myself. After the second night, I got frustrated and checked out of the facility. My marriage, business, and many relationships were on the rocks, and the press would be on me soon enough. The fear drove me crazy, and I just up and left.

* * *

As I finally got through the pleasantries with Bert on the phone and we got down to the questions, I had this persistent thought in my head convincing me that being arrested for drunk driving was exactly what I needed. Having my secret out there and being able to have a public reason to become alcohol free might be just the motivation I needed to stick to it this time. That the penalty would teach me a lesson was what I wanted to believe, so I believed it.

I mustered all the courage I could in the span of a breath and endeavored to meet the reporter where he was. He had a police report that, in some parts, made me sound like an escaped zombie, in others, like an adolescent partier, and, sprinkled throughout, like a dangerous criminal. I suppose I was all those things to the police, and all I can do is give the account of what, unfortunately, I remember in living color.

"Well, it wasn't a run-of-the-mill drunk-driving arrest," I said as a transition between two points I was failing miserably to make with my spin baloney. I knew in an instant that I had given him the caricature he was looking for to affix on the policeman's story.

The prospect of the truth emerging about my drinking and my behavior while drunk was truly my greatest fear in life at the time—a fear that scared away any smidgen of courage I had mustered in that moment to face my demons and come clean. Settling back into the well-worn path of dishonesty and dismissal of reality, I immediately shrank from the truth and started saying to people that I had merely had a bad day and was under a lot of stress.

And this only increased my pain. What I wanted was freedom, and what I chose, once again, in that moment was slavery. I was bitter, afraid, and unutterably lonely. This arrest and the stories in the newspapers could have been the fuel to lift me past my addiction, but at the time, I couldn't imagine it, let alone seize the opportunity.

The story was picked up in some 260 papers nationally and was covered *everywhere* in Michigan.

Everywhere was some version of this headline:

"Craig DeRoche, Former Speaker of the House in Michigan, Arrested on Suspicion of Drunk Driving."

"Bizarre behavior" was about the nicest thing the reporters wrote.

The entire media blitz was fueled by what a freelance reporter spun out of a police report that was unavailable to me or any of the other papers. Each day, the story hit me in the gut, twisting like a knife in some new way.

The story wasn't entirely accurate, but even so, the account of my behavior was a spot-on description of too many other days in my life. It was hard to reconcile. Later, my good friend Bob Adams told me that when someone tells you the truth you don't want to hear, it's natural to get mad and resentful. He said people spend their time thinking of how they are going to show that person up or get them back. Bob explained that if someone told an out-and-out lie about you, it wouldn't bother you so much. This was a good teaching. I was mad as hell because what I was reading hit home.

"Give me an example of what you were talking about the other day," I said to Bob. I had been stewing over it for a couple of days.

"Look, Craig," he said, "if you told me a story and I called you a liar and you got mad, it's likely true that you were lying somewhere in the story. But if I called you a *chair*, you probably wouldn't get mad at all, because you'd know it wasn't true. Well," he said, with a little glint of humor in his eye, "the good news is, you're not a chair."

Recalling this little parable has helped me a great deal over the years, but I was in no condition mentally, spiritually, or emotionally to receive it when the story of my arrest broke. The next day dragged as I fielded endless calls and text messages, avoiding anyone I could.

Our home phone was going off every other minute with calls from reporters near and far, and my cell phone was deluged with calls from political friends and enemies with bewildering expressions of support mixed with concern.

The most common refrains were of two types: "Not only have I never seen you drunk, I have never even seen you take a drink"; and "Give 'em hell, Craig. They can't keep a good man down. You weren't even in your car."

Surprisingly to me, even as I wallowed in self-pity over the grand plans in my life that I had so recklessly destroyed, and the pain and humiliation I had inflicted on my family, a great many calls caught me completely off guard. I still remember each one and what it meant to me. What the callers said beneath the surface-level political, press, and marital advice was so genuine, it destroyed the facade of stoical self-reliance that I had practiced to perfection.

"Craig, this may not be the best day to share this with you, but I want you to know that when I was having the worst day of my life, you picked me up and you did this and you did that, and it made all the difference. I'll never forget what you did for me, and if there is anything I can do for you—I mean *anything*—just say the word." I heard this sort of thing from more people than I could have imagined—some whom I didn't even remember helping.

Living my life focused almost entirely on myself, not only had I been deluding myself with my own lies, I wasn't even aware of what I was doing to help other people or what it meant to them. This resulted mostly in general, nonspecific pain that I could not identify or process. The pain then drove me in the wrong direction: back toward my comfort zone. Privately, I began to fantasize about wanting more. I thought about coming clean, turning my life around, and dealing with the mountain of problems I faced. I began talking more openly with Stacey about my life (eleven years into our marriage) and even attended some addiction recovery meetings. Of course, in the church-based recovery meetings I went to, I said nothing about what I did or what my life looked like. Even my reasons for going to a church-based group were shifty. I went there so I could avoid ever having to admit I attended Alcoholics Anonymous meetings. Not that there was anything wrong with

AA—I just worried that this might hurt me should I decide to run for office again someday! I was paralyzed by fear, resentment, and anger and living without any level of emotional maturity, so I simply ducked back into what I knew.

Chapter 3

"You screwed up bad," Harold said.

Harold is a good friend and one of the best lawyers I have ever met. He is also one of the most connected people in the entire country. Harold represents the biggest and the best. And, in many ways, he *is* the biggest and the best—in life, character, and presence and in any courtroom or political theater.

"I didn't even know you drank," he said. "I've never seen you drink."

"Yeah, I've been hearing that from a lot of people," I said.

I told Harold the truth. I figured he could handle it. Between the two of us, we knew enough secrets about political and business figures in Michigan to fill ten books.

"Okay, then. You're saying you are one thing, and I've seen only the other. You need to act like the other—the one that *I* know. Stop talking to the media. I can't handle this for you personally, though; I'm not the guy. For stuff like this, you need the guy who handles these things locally, who the prosecutor and judge have relationships with. I would startle them and draw more attention than . . ." He was looking down at the papers he had clipped. ". . . than what you are already screwing up."

"How much money?"

"I have no idea. You've been out of office for a year; you should have plenty of money. How's business?"

I had too much pride to be honest about this, too. I exuded

confidence and success wherever I went, but my reentry into the business world after six years in office was flailing and floundering. Everything was hit-and-miss, and even the home-run months seemed to barely cover the dog months in between.

"Not great, and now I have to budget for things," I said.

"Okay," Harold said. "Don't worry about it. This guy's a friend, and these types of tickets don't cost much if you don't fight them."

"I don't want to fight it," I said. "I already know what I want to do."

"You're still running the world, eh? Why don't you let me do my job."

"What I mean is, I just want to pay the ticket. Can I do that and avoid going to court?"

Harold paused and looked right at me. His eyes cut through layers of crap I didn't even know were there. The pause was brief, but his manner tightened.

Harold paused again just before I thought he would speak. This time, he edged down, and his blazing focus on me relented.

"This is a criminal offense. It isn't a ticket, and now isn't thirty years ago, when people could screw around with this stuff. By the way, the reason it's so difficult is that you personally and your idiot conservative friends don't have any brains, and you listen to people getting rich running victims' groups, instead of running these things through your head *before* you pass the laws. If this is your first offense, it isn't that big a deal, but you are going to have to appear in court, and that's why I am telling you to shut up and start listening to me.

"Don't talk to anyone about this. Tell people you are sorry and are trying to take responsibility, and then shut up. Can you do that? Can you stay away from a camera, stay away from people?"

"Yes, but—"

"Shut up."

"Okay."

"I'm serious. Do you need help? Are you going to drink?"

"No. This is what I needed: the lesson, the pain—even the humiliation will help. Honestly, I'm good."

Harold rolled his eyes up and off to the side. He didn't do it for effect, and I don't think he intended me to see it. He walked past and gripped my shoulder on his way out.

Chapter 4

The things we build in this world are only as strong as the foundations under them.

The spider web of intricate half-truths connecting the lies to the reality of my situation was holding strong in the windstorm of negative publicity. But the effort was hollowing me out mentally, physically, and emotionally.

After my arrest in Saline, and in the countless interactions with friends, former colleagues, political associates, and my current business contracts, I had patched my sinking ship together with bubble gum. My problems needed daily focus, and this was devouring my attention and energy.

The merriment that the press and the blogs were having with the story made me feel physically sick. I could not bring myself to stop obsessing about all the things people were saying about me. Just thinking about it would get me tied up in knots inside, and I would play back the statements in my head one by one. The news stories were comical and mean, with no regard for me or my family. I was simply the worst guy of the news cycle, and the object of a lot of finger-pointing about politics, drugs, and whatever other ax-grinding the journalists and talking heads cared to finagle into their commentary.

My loyal opposition on the political left took the initiative to rewrite my Web links so that a Google search of my name no longer brought up twenty years of public service. In its place were page after page of disparaging stories. The Wikipedia entry was purged of anything substantive I had done in my career, and carried instead a narrative about my arrest and behavior. Any attempt to change it was reversed, and it made me so mad, I couldn't fall asleep if I had checked it before going to bed.

I rationalized my obsession with image as being the basis for my relevance and how I made my living. My former public relations staff and contractors had programmed alerts to e-mail to me whenever my name came up in the media or on the Web. I saw this checking in and painstaking work to evaluate what it all meant as a professional necessity, and I accepted it as appropriate.

Now, after practicing this vain exercise for several years and believing it to be a healthy thing, I was being cut apart and beaten up by it. This public character assassination hurt me a great deal. It blocked me and consumed my thoughts. I spent so many hours daydreaming about the past and constructing pathways to redemption and success in the future, there was no time left for what was happening *now*—no time for anything except the pain I was going through at the moment. I needed to solve the future, and there my thoughts would race and stay.

I was in a deep hole, and I started planning how to dig out from it. Some of my plans were simple stopgaps, thrown together to get me past my current problems—legal, financial, and marital. I took time to work on what needed to be done each day, but percolating in my mind alongside these necessary expedients were the grandiose schemes—plans by which I would overcome these and my drinking and advance my fledgling insurance business into huge success. My thoughts were always turning and turning. There was no peace in work, family, or even sleep. Amid all that churning mental activity, I no longer thought of honesty. Telling the truth seemed wildly impractical, if not impossible.

I threw myself at a longtime goal of losing weight. This goal was perfect. For one thing, by dropping forty or fifty pounds, I would no longer look like the ridiculous pictures the media ran about my arrest.

Photo editors have one of the coolest jobs in media, second only to that of the editor writing the headlines. Neither editor *writes* the story. Their job is simply to push the limits as far as "ethical standards" allow in drawing eyes to the paper and thereby bumping up circulation and revenue.

In my case, according to what was reported in the online paper in Ann Arbor, I was stone drunk and had behaved in a bizarre way. No arrest or police report was available, since, technically, one didn't exist, so they couldn't run mug shots. Thus, the photo editors' solution to bolster the story was to pore through the stock photos taken of me in mid-sentence or with eyes in mid-blink, or both if possible. My weight had fluctuated over the past several years, so the papers naturally ran the pictures of me at my fattest.

In my prideful logic, I thought I could at least correct the weight issue. The photos of me with my eyes at half mast, or mouth contorted in speech, simply looked ridiculous, even though I almost certainly hadn't been drinking in any of the photos they ran. It was embarrassing to me because I was focused entirely on my own appearance—how the world was now seeing me. I actually thought that people cared enough to notice these things, and it bothered me terribly.

I lost about fifty pounds in the span of just four months. I checked the papers, the Web, and Wikipedia all the time. I longed for the court case to wind up and also for me to emerge triumphant with a win of some other sort. I worked desperately to get business deals done.

While all this played out, some very important developments were occurring in my life, and at the time I didn't stop to account for them, or even appreciate what was happening. The changes seemed random and awkward, though at the same time, powerful and clear. I remember each moment of these small progressions in my life.

What escaped me at first was that the people I thought I could count on had begun treating me differently. Things changed in my friendships, family, and business life. With my political friends, it was a continuation of the shifting and rearranging of relationships that had begun overnight after the GOP lost the majority in the Michigan House of Representatives, while I was Speaker. Political relationships are the most fluid and evanescent things I have experienced in my life. By the time I had uttered the words "the GOP will not keep its majority in the Michigan House of Representatives" to an Associated Press reporter, the race was on, and many of the very people I considered friends were lining up to run me out of town.

I hadn't drunk much alcohol in the two years from 2004 to 2006, and for very good reasons: I valued the trust my colleagues had placed in me in making me the youngest statewide GOP leader in the country; and in equal measure, I was scared to death of letting the public see the side of me that drank.

The month before being elected House Speaker, I turned 34 and moved into a new home twice the size of our 1,900-square-foot Colonial that I largely built and contracted myself. I hadn't bothered to sell the other house yet and was spending the reserves I had built up in business at an enormous pace. When Stacey agreed to my running for state representative two years earlier, she had done so largely on the assumption that I would be able to do the political job and my insurance business work and that I would no longer be drinking.

When I was elected Speaker, I was using alcohol to control my stress and anxiety and to help me sleep. The pressure of the events surrounding me seemed overwhelming even though I had created every one of them. Stacey, along with friends, family, and colleagues, didn't really register that I was drinking at all. In 2002, I had pledged to Stacey that I would quit drinking after she noticed that I was intoxicated by midafternoon on a day when I was supposed to go to an evening party with her. It was my first pledge to anyone, ever, to stop drinking, and I actually thought it would help me.

Two weeks later, I needed to drink to get through a piece of time or a patch of work that bothered me. I drank only a half pint of booze, and it seemed the perfect answer. This measure and application became a formula that I rationalized as a manageable solution. I never believed that for the next five years, each time the first sip passed my lips, I would be off to the races faster than ever before. It happened every time, and still I didn't get it.

To those caught in its snares, alcohol is a cunning, baffling deceiver. The drug always allowed me to use successfully for a duration of days or weeks, until I was fully ensnared, before cranking its destructive engine up to full throttle and bulldozing its way throughout my life.

By the time every challenger had conceded to me the race for Speaker, I was chemically addicted to alcohol again. Chemical addiction fans the flames of other physical, emotional, mental, and behavioral addiction issues. Medical science seems to treat chemical addiction just fine for those of us who need to withdraw from a drug, but doctors can't help with the underlying problem of addiction. That is, medicine can help us *get* clean, but it can't help us *stay* clean. The truth is, every time someone falls off the wagon and begins using drugs or alcohol again, they are sober when they start. So the solution is to be found somewhere other than in medicine.

The night I was to be voted Speaker, we had a full-session day, and I found the effects of my maintenance doses of alcohol wearing off—just before what was sure to be a two-hour meeting. I had to make the excuse that I needed to make a call home, just so I could get out of the meeting and drink the required dosage of vodka to settle the trembling and stop the sweating.

There had to be a bottle everywhere. Not a bottle of booze, though—a premix of some sort. For me, it was pop bottles of Diet 7-up or Squirt or Gatorade. I had half-crumpled water bottles, too, which I took great pains to make unattractive to anyone who might want to share, and which had carefully titrated doses of alcohol to fuel the engine. I kept them in my car, office, briefcase, gym bag, and basically anywhere else I might need them.

The night I was elected Speaker, it was a twenty-ounce bottle of original-flavor Gatorade, mixed about fifty-fifty with eighty-proof vodka. It was about three-quarters full.

I left the Radisson Hotel, where the meeting room was set up off state grounds for the partisan voting. The air was crisp for a mid-November evening. I opened my coat and jacket to feel the bracing air and to stop the sweat that was now gathering on my body, beginning to show through my thinning hair, and beading on my forehead.

Casually reaching into my briefcase, I took out my cell phone. I slowed my walk to keep my heart rate down so I wouldn't start sweating beyond what I could control.

I spoke a few words into the phone as I scanned the foot and car traffic around me on the dark Lansing street. It was a pleasant night, and seeing no cars or pedestrians of consequence, I raised the bottle, masking the four or five big gulps to look as if I had taken only a sip.

Within moments, I felt a different sort of heat: the burn I was looking for. After twenty-five years converting over to ethanol, my engines recognized their fuel of choice—the "fuel for life," as I called it in a poem in my youth.

After just two or three minutes, the bottle was empty and properly discarded in a trash can along the sidewalk. I was now performing the necessary ablutions with various breath mints and sprays, which would occupy me until I mounted the escalator to return to the caucus meeting.

My mind felt the new batch of fuel stream in steadily with each heartbeat, bringing my system and restless psyche back to the proper balance of sedation that I craved.

It didn't so much remove the fear as push it off the field of immediate concern. Anger and resentments were sunk for now beneath the liquid cloak that I had to reapply several times each day. With nothing from my past or future to worry about, I could return my focus to the task before me. Then, done with my work, I could return to finish the job I had started with the booze, and drink myself into a stupor and pass out, only to start all over again in the morning.

The Craig DeRoche my caucus was expecting to see arrived within minutes, refreshed, focused, upbeat, and ready to assume the mantle of statewide leadership over the eighth largest state economy and government in America.

I knew, of course, that the drinking wasn't a solution and that I would have to stop, just as I had done so many times before. Months before the night I was elected Speaker, I began planning to take a break and "figure out the drinking thing." I rationalized that with so much work to do before the election, I couldn't afford to screw it up and get distracted by the challenge of stopping drinking.

The difficulty in balancing alcohol intake and productivity in a very public life was a confusing, terrifying experience that I could not imagine a way to resolve. I was at a desperately low point and needed help but was too proud to ask. The only tools I had to employ were those that had worked so many times before. I could feel a crash coming, yet I feared making a move. My old diversions, tricks, and lies weren't working, but they were all I knew.

Amazingly, I got through the experience of being House Speaker for two years and then House minority leader for the two following years. It wasn't until 2009, nearly five years after I was elected Speaker, that I finally began to bottom out. This was the point when some close friends who had known me for most of my adult life started to question things. So did my closest political and business friends.

I had started a small software company to automate the dynamic formation of insurance-buying groups online. This business had been in my consciousness since I started working in insurance twenty years before. There was no particular reason for it to fail, though the company was clearly failing. The wheels were coming off the wagon, and I was barely making payments two months late on most bills.

Stacey was stretched to the breaking point between anger and disbelief, tortured with the reality that her husband of eleven years might not be a good candidate to keep the title or even to provide for her and the kids.

Chapter 5

Six months before my arrest for drunk driving in Saline, Stacey had arranged for something vitally important in my life. I didn't fully recognize it on the day it happened, but I am forever grateful to her for the care and love she gave me even during my downward slide.

That summer was when Stacey made plans to bring the whole family to a new church in our town. It was what some would call a "mega" church—the sort of place you might mistake for a large college building when driving by.

I didn't put up much of a fight. In fact, after we went the first time, I told Stacey I thought this church would be good for our kids. My cousins had been raised going to a church like this, and it set them on a good footing.

It wasn't just the kids we were talking about, though. Both Stacey and I knew we were talking also about our lives and our relationship.

The drama I injected into our relationship—the lies and skewed priorities—was certainly taking a toll. Stacey remained my biggest supporter and true love, and I think she was trying to intervene in the only way she thought she could: with an indirect confrontation.

Walking into the church was an experience in itself. The ceilings rose more than thirty feet in the atrium, where some five hundred people were bustling to and fro. The scene reminded me of the buzz of activity in a large indoor shopping mall the week after Thanksgiving.

It was different from the mall, though. For one thing, the kids seemed to be having a blast, pulling their parents forward instead of slowing them down. A large fountain stood off center in the atrium, and behind it, a massive staircase and modern glass elevator led to the second floor.

A walkway bordered the entire second floor, serving as a balcony and allowing anyone there to search the throng below for friends or family.

Taking in the view for the first time, both Stacey and I were amazed. The size, scale, and attention to detail were impressive. There was security just to enter the kids' area, and we needed to get tags to identify us with our own children before entering.

As we walked the hallway and looked in on the classes, we saw kids laughing and dancing. Each room had a stage and multimedia setup. In some rooms, the kids were singing karaoke, to the delight of dozens of their peers. In the babies' rooms, teenage girls and boys rocked the kids and played with those learning to crawl.

It was nothing like the church Stacey and I had experienced before, and we both loved it from the first moment.

The senior pastor of Oak Pointe Church was a wonkish guy with a dual doctorate who spoke the principles of spiritual truth about as plainly a tennis instructor talking about topspin to keep a hard-hit ball in bounds, without going off on tangents of physics, body position, and mechanical minutiae. For some reason, he made sense to me from the first words he spoke.

Over the next few months, we attended sporadically, and Oak Pointe became our home church. After I was arrested in Saline in February, it was Stacey who implored me to bring us all there as a family.

Just walking into the church on that day was difficult. After such a publicly humiliating experience, I assumed that just showing up there would be a further embarrassment to my family. Rather than the prideful delight I had felt on being recognized by some of the parishioners when we first arrived, I now felt only the wish to be invisible. I hoped to find help and answers in this church, but the prospect of being so public and visible in seeking help made me dizzy with fear.

"Search me out, Lord, and if there is a flaw in me that I can't see for myself, will you point it out to me?" was a rough paraphrase of what I heard in the sermon. It made sense, too. It didn't matter that the lesson from Job was far deeper and more consequential than my take. In my desperation, what I heard was a practical use for prayer that had never really occurred to me before. My logic, selfishly applied with a smidgen of humility, led to a heartfelt prayer along these lines. I knew I wasn't going to fix my drinking and my business problems anytime soon. I couldn't see what I was doing wrong, so I simply asked God for some help with it.

As I sat in that church auditorium with two thousand other people, this simple and powerful lesson connected with me, and I was ready to ask for some practical help. When the sermon concluded, I asked Stacey if it was okay for me to hang back and introduce myself to the pastor and see if I could schedule time for a meeting.

"Are you kidding me?" Stacey said. "That's why you're here! We'll be out here by the coffee stand until you get back."

I walked down and waited patiently as others spoke with Pastor Bob Shirock. I took in what they said and the casual way they addressed him.

"That was a really good sermon, Bob," said one as he moved on quickly.

"We really want to keep coming, but we're Catholic—is that okay?" said a young woman.

"I don't mind at all, and I won't turn you in," Bob said to the amusement of those nearby.

Bob stood in front of the stage with his microphone still attached to his clothes, which were as casual as everyone else's. He looked as though he didn't want to be anywhere else in the world, and he acted as if he had all the time in the world for each person he spoke to.

Bob somehow radiated this sense of calm even amid the chaotic transition that occurs at the end of a service for two thousand. Within a few minutes, it was my turn. Bob's casual demeanor and pleasant speech, along with my being the last one waiting for a moment of his time, gave me the confidence to proceed.

"Hi, Pastor, I'm Craig DeRoche, and I'm new here—I mean, I've been coming with my family since August and . . . well, I've had a really bad week, and your sermon kind of, well, uh . . ." I started fast, the words tumbling out, and by the end, I was struggling to put two syllables together.

"It's just that I . . ." I gasped for breath and composure.

I broke eye contact with Bob, and the tears came out of nowhere. Standing there, I fought back the urge to weep openly. I leaned forward to wipe my eyes, not moving any other part of my body.

I didn't want anyone to see me cry. *Laugh and the world laughs with you*, and all that.

Bob gently reached out his hand to my shoulder. "Look," he said, "why don't we come over here." He led me to a quiet corner where the stage and curtain met.

I used the time to gather myself. It didn't work. I was a mess.

It seemed forever before I could muster the ability to speak.

Even while I groped internally, my mind was careening off in another direction. I was surprised at just how overwhelmed I had become in mere seconds. I didn't understand the emotional onslaught that had taken me by storm, and I appreciated Bob's helping me up from it.

When I told him what had happened to me, he said he may have been aware of the story in the news but wasn't sure about any details, and that in either case, it didn't matter.

"I'm here anytime you want to talk about it," Bob said.

"I appreciate that," I said as I gathered myself.

It seemed that Bob had all the time in the world for me that day, even though by now other congregants were patiently waiting for our session to end. His authenticity mattered a great deal, and I felt truly welcome here.

As I turned to leave after our talk, I had a deep sense of ease and gratitude. I made my way out from the large stage area that ran a hundred feet across the front of the auditorium and past the thousands of seats toward the atrium. Inside, I wondered how this man could have helped someone like me when he had thousands of people here, most of them undoubtedly with problems of their own. The whole experience, from the moment I left the car till I rejoined Stacey, felt electric. It was disorienting, and at the same time, it brought me some much-needed peace.

When we left the building, Stacey asked me what happened, and I told her the truth. She said, "I know you're going through a lot, and maybe he can help you."

Stacey was trying to help me even though I was pushing her away, living dishonestly, and had caused her so much pain and humiliation.

* * *

When I met with Pastor Bob at Oak Pointe Church after my first arrest, he gave me some good advice. He made a point of calling the situation my "walk through life."

I thought it a funny way of speaking. "My walk through life"—it sounded like an old song, with none of the self-importance I had placed on events in my past. It did get me thinking, though. It seemed that Bob knew something I wanted to know, and I began trying to learn it.

Reading is easy for me, and picking up new ideas has never been a problem. Moreover, I had always wanted to know more about religion and the Bible. At any rate, it couldn't hurt. So I made reading the book of Romans a priority. I read it over and over again. I must have read it twenty times that day.

My understanding of Romans is that the book was taken from a letter that Paul, a Roman citizen, wrote to early Christians in Rome to clarify some things. I certainly had a need for clarity, so this helped. It didn't hurt that the author was once called Saul and was a tyrannical persecutor of Christians for the Roman government until Jesus confronted him directly one day. This helped me. Reading from a guy who was honest about what a bastard he had been, talking about what his new life was like, had great credibility to me at this point in my life. I appreciated the lessons.

That same Sunday, Stacey and I brought the kids to dinner at her parents' home in Lake Orion, Michigan. Stacey's brother, Ryan, and sister, Whitney, were there with their spouses, too.

Between our family and Whitney's, we had enough kids to warrant a separate "kids' table," which left the parents to dine alone at a long table in the more formal dining room.

"You need to go to AA," Stacey's mom, Marsha, said quite out of the blue.

"He doesn't need AA," said Tom, Stacey's dad. "What did that do for your brother?"

Marsha bristled. "That's not fair."

"I didn't mean to disparage him or you. I'm just saying it didn't work that well," Tom said. He chuckled, which eased the tension somewhat. "Anyway, don't drink any more of that fake beer I see you drink, Craig—it has booze in it, too."

"Well, I . . . ," I said, trying to wedge my way into the conversation about me that was taking place in front of me.

"Are you going to AA?" Whitney said. "Did the court make you go?"

"I just . . ."

"Jeez, everybody, let him talk!" Stacey said.

Every eye in the room was on me. I didn't get this much attention when I blew out the candles on my birthday cake.

There wasn't any wiggle room, and I had to answer. I needed to say something, but I couldn't imagine what to say. My family didn't talk this way. We didn't even tell each other when we were going to have surgery. This family, on the other hand, would talk about Grandpa's erectile dysfunction if they knew about it. Everything was fair game. The culture clash couldn't be clearer.

"I'm going to an AA meeting of sorts, and I do still have to go to court to—"

"See?" said Marsha. "I figured you'd be doing that, and I think it's good. It is good, don't you think?"

"I don't mind," I said. "You know I've had this problem for a long time, and I guess I thought I had it figured out. I didn't, though."

This quieted the room and stopped the cross talk momentarily. After some thought, Stacey's younger brother, Ryan, asked, "What're you doing to figure it out?"

"I can't really say for sure," I said. "I just know I have to figure it out. This is bad. I didn't have any reason to be drinking."

"You think?" Tom blurted.

"And I do it anyway. I always have. I don't want to drink anymore, and I still do it."

"Do you think it was a good idea not to stay at rehab?" Marsha said.

"I don't know. Everyone there was doing the detox substitute drugs, and I didn't see a point in it. I want answers, and I guess I'm not sure where I'm going to get them. This morning I kinda talked to our new pastor, and I have this feeling God can help me through this."

The family banter then resumed at full pitch, and I began to feel overwhelmed with emotion again. I didn't know why, since there wasn't any need to be emotional—no need I could think of, anyway. And yet, here I was again, with a lump growing in my throat, and tears welling in my eyes. I had never cried at a funeral. I had never cried even when a girl broke up with me or when I lost a fight, and today I was crying again. Sobbing so hard, I couldn't speak.

Chapter 6

Weeks later, I got the call from Peter, my lawyer.

"So the prosecutor set this up with the judge," he said. "We're going to go in there, they are going to amend the docket to arraign you, and I'll make a motion to enter a plea, which will be accepted. The case will be opened and closed at the same time."

"So no media circus?" I said.

"Nope, unless they get lucky. But these days, nobody can afford to keep court reporters on staff for their newspapers anymore, so I don't expect anything."

"So I just plead guilty."

"No. You plead what is called 'no contest.' It is the same thing as guilty, but the judge wasn't comfortable with you pleading guilty, because you weren't driving your car."

"Details, detai—"

"Shut up. This is the deal. Don't screw it up. It's what you wanted."

"I know."

"Will Stacey or anyone else be here to support you?"

"Um, I hadn't thought of that. No."

"Okay, let's go."

Peter led me through the oversize doors, which swung silently open and shut. In front of me was a dim seating section with several benches on either side, leading to a brightly lit area out front.

At the back of the room sat a pleasant sixty-something man with thinning straight white hair and round gold-rimmed bifocals. His rosy cheeks and nose contrasted with his otherwise pale complexion.

The judge was dispatching files with his hands while reading numbers and dates and accepting motions spoken by lawyers at such a pace, they seemed to blur their words. On cue, two staff members scurried to pick up and set down the files, and a woman sat hunched over a Stenograph machine, pushing the keys silently without once looking down at her hands or the long trail of white paper spilling from the top of the machine and gathering in a rippled pile on the floor.

I took the far left seat in the last bench, and Peter continued forward through the knee-high wooden door separating the accused from the lawyers and prosecutors.

Peter immediately leaned into the ear of a younger man who was half a head shorter than he, and they both let out a quiet laugh.

Peter was dressed in a dark-blue suit and power tie and looked like a million dollars. In his early sixties, he was still in great physical shape. His size and stature were enough to distinguish him even to someone ignorant of his background and résumé.

Peter was a former deputy US attorney and had been through the wars. He was what we in Detroit called "Irish Mafia" without implying any sort of criminality. Peter knew everyone who had ever been anyone, and he had cleaned up a lot of messes more public than mine—and certainly with more at stake. His task for me was but an errand, it seemed, and he pleasantly accepted the job even though I was paying him what you would pay the guy who advertises his DUI law business on billboards in the rough end of town. Outside legal circles, no one knows Peter; inside, everyone knows Peter. I sat there, grateful for his mastery and even a little amused at his demeanor and style.

"Come on, you're next," Peter whispered on his way back to my seat.

"Case number 113-10, the people versus Craig Michael DeRoche," the clerk announced.

I walked forward and settled into a spot where all the lights in the room seemed to be aimed.

"I see you and your client are here and that the prosecutor has accepted some sort of deal and is recommending that I accept it, is that right?"

"Yes, Your Honor," the prosecutor said.

"Yes, sir," Peter said.

"Mr. DeRoche, is that right?"

"Yes, sir."

"What's that, son?" the judge said.

"I'm sorry, I said 'yes, sir,'" I repeated in a louder voice.

With that, the plea was read and I accepted. The judge then ruled that although I had pleaded "no contest" and wasn't driving my car while I was arrested, there was sufficient evidence in his finding of fact that I had driven the car earlier and was most likely impaired. With this, he banged the gavel and found me guilty of impaired driving and instructed me to check in and sign up with the probation department on my way out and pay all fines and fees. I exhaled, turned, and started to leave.

Peter beamed a smile at me as we turned toward the exit, and I just put my head down and started walking. Peter grabbed my arm to stop me. I turned in surprise.

A man stood there, extending his arm to shake my hand. It was the prosecutor. The ringing in my ears started again, and my nerves rattled all the way back to the sleepless night before. The prosecutor was smiling and gave me a very warm vibration. To my surprise, his body language was open and inviting.

"It's an honor to meet you, Mr. DeRoche," he said. "You've done a lot of good for our state and seem either to have made a bad decision or to have a problem. Either way, I wish you the best in your life."

"Thank you," was all I could get out. I turned and pressed my way through the crowd and out to the lobby.

"That was nice," Peter said.

"Was it, Peter? I don't want to hear that."

"It's true. Don't beat yourself up."

"I'm not beating myself up. He shouldn't feel he needs to say that. He shouldn't say it that way if he means it."

"Why?"

"I don't know. It's just weird. It was nice, but weird. I didn't expect it."

"Look," he said, "there are plenty of people in this world gonna treat you like dirt. He doesn't have to be one of them. He has a job to do, and he did it. He's a Republican, and he thinks you're a good man who screwed up. Don't let him see you let your guard down on this. Get it right."

"This is what I needed: public humiliation. I plan to put this to good use as a motivator and move forward."

"Good. Don't drink. Don't screw this up. You don't seem to have as bad a problem as you say you have—not to me, anyway. This'll be over in six months. You understand what the judge said at the end, right? You have a ninety-two-day jail sentence that's suspended. 'Suspended' means you won't have to go to jail unless you violate probation. Simple."

"Simple. Got it. Thanks again, Peter. Thanks for keeping the press away. I don't know how I would have handled them in person, and Stacey would've killed me."

"So we're good? *You* good? Business good?"

"Not really, but I'll be okay. I have some things working that can come in now that this is behind me. We'll see. Thanks again."

Chapter 7

I opened my eyes and breathed in the fresh, cool night air.

Nearly an hour had passed. I was still near the patch of woods just off the road connecting my subdivision to Mick's. The night was still; even the crickets and nightjars were quiet. There was hardly any road traffic, and no one walking around.

I was safe, though, and my surroundings felt comforting. Mick hadn't returned, and I assumed he was home in bed, just as I wished to be.

Stacey was going to give me a rough ride. I wanted to be honest with her but couldn't figure out how I was even going to get a chance to speak. Stacey was a fire-spitting dragon when she was just *normally* mad. This would put her over the top.

I was amazed at the damage Mick had done to my body from head to toe. I gave this a moment's thought and quickly let it pass. I couldn't fix the physical side of my problems, either—not tonight, anyway.

My eyes wandered back up to the stars, so bright and clear in the cloudless black sky. As I walked, I felt a refreshing sprinkle of dew from the grass onto my brutalized feet and shins. It was all the respite I really needed. The adrenaline hadn't stop flowing since Mick yanked me out of Todd's car hours before, and this blunted the pain in my legs, arms, ribs, and head.

The thought of staying outside for the rest of the night came and went quickly. I was in bad shape and wanted to be home. I was worried about my kids and had already had about enough drama for one night. I wanted to go home, sleep, and then face the music.

My steps quickly turned from a measured stroll to a quick trot through the wet grass. The earth was silent. When I crossed the main road, there wasn't a car to be seen in either direction. In my neighborhood, less than a mile away, the lights were all out and the houses buttoned down. It was the kind of peace you never get to see during the day.

I jogged up to my front door and found it locked. Every light in my house was out, and the shades were drawn. I looked over at Michele and Todd's house. It was dark and silent, too. I walked to the garage and entered the code.

The whole time I did this, I assumed the inner garage door would be open since I knew I didn't lock it or turn on our security system before I left earlier that evening.

When the garage door reeled up, it broke the tranquil silence of the neighborhood and lit up the whole driveway. I went in and approached the garage door into the house, only to find it locked. I knocked gently on the door.

The knocks got no response. I briefly thought of breaking in through the door or a front window—two tricks I had mastered at my parents' house growing up. Just about every night when I sneaked out to meet up with friends or cause trouble in my youth, I hadn't really worked out how to get back in. Thus, it was forced learning, but a useful skill nonetheless.

Going back outside to the front windows, I quickly noticed that I had wisely installed locks that an amateur prowler like me couldn't get past. I went around to the back—no easy way in there, either.

Just then it occurred to me to check the back door to the deck. I didn't have a lot of hope for this option, because this was the door that seldom got opened and, thus, was always locked. I thought it worth a try, though, and was surprised when the handle turned easily. The door opened three inches before coming to a halt.

All my external doors have hotel locks on them three-quarters of the way up, ever since I read a story about a 2-year-old walking outside while his mom was in the shower and drowning in a small hole in the backyard that was full of water after a rainstorm. The story moved and terrified me, and a day later, the locks were in. But the reason for the locks was to keep our little ones in, not to keep people out.

This was the last obstacle between me and my bed. I had to break a small metal arm free from a thin strip of molding, and I was in. I hadn't even screwed the locks into the wall studs—just into less than half an inch of doorjamb molding. I didn't even have to think about what came next. I just did it.

My left hand thrust forward while my right hand held the handle.

The wood split lengthwise, making a terrible shriek as the dry, thin molding sprang loose from the wall. I lunged forward and caught the long strip of wood as it fell, before it could scratch the kitchen table. Satisfied with the successful grab, I set the molding aside and walked through the kitchen toward the bathroom.

"Who's there?" a stern but quivering voice called from the cat-walk hallway above the great room, near the kitchen. The house was dark except for the starlight shining through the two stories of windows in the great room. I walked toward the voice.

"Me," I said.

"Oh, my gosh, I thought you were a burglar!" my mother-in-law, Marsha, said. She peered down at me, her left hand to her chest in a theatrical faint. She held a phone in her right hand. "Where have you been? I mean, have you seen Mick? Look at you! You're bleeding. Are you okay?"

"No, Mom. It's been a long night, and I just want to go to bed."

"What on earth is going on with Mick?" she said. "He keeps coming back here."

"I don't know. I haven't seen him for a while."

"Why are you bleeding?"

"I don't want to talk about it."

"You know you're going to have to talk about it. Stacey is mad. She said you were drinking earlier."

"Do I seem drunk to you?"

"No, but you were drinking earlier."

"I'll have that fight with Stacey in the morning."

"I just don't like any of this. Why did you break in the back door?"

"Why didn't you answer the knocks?" I snipped. "Why lock the garage door?"

"I didn't hear you," Marsha replied, clearly perturbed by the question.

"We keep the garage door open. That's why I came in the back. You left the door open, by the way. I just broke the kid lock."

With this information, she relaxed her shoulders and put her hand on the rail. She was still looking down to where I stood, but now looked ready to walk away.

"Fine. Well, I'm just going to check on the kids. They stirred when you came in, and it scared me half to death. I called nine one one and hung up just in time when I saw it was you."

"I'm sorry I scared you," I said. "I really didn't mean to. I just wanted to get back home and go to bed. It's been a horrible night, and I really don't want to talk about it. I'm going to make a cup of decaf, and then I'm going to bed."

"All right, I'll check on the kids," Marsha said. She turned and headed down the hall toward my daughters' rooms.

I walked back into the kitchen and carefully placed the splintered molding on the kitchen table. The pain was setting in now. When I sat waiting for the coffee to drip, I could barely hold myself up without gasping for air. The pain in my lower ribs on both sides was crushing. As I stood up again, a lightning bolt of pain zinged through my body, and my muscles clenched. My lower back seized up, and I had to rise cautiously, catching my breath. I looked down at my legs, and so much skin was missing, they looked as if I had been dragged over a mile of bad road. Where there wasn't an open wound, I had sticky drying blood and that clearer ooze the body exudes to form scabs. My shins and the tops of my feet looked like street pizza.

I just wanted to go to bed, and I wanted Marsha to leave. And I knew that neither was going to happen soon enough for my liking.

"I just don't know why you would drink," she said, coming into the kitchen. "It doesn't make any sense."

"Yeah, I know," I said. "Listen, I just want to go to bed. You can leave. I don't want to be rude but—"

"I'd rather stay. I can sleep on the couch."

"That's ridiculous. There's no reason for you to stay on the couch. I just want to be alone and get some sleep. This has been a horrible night, and I'll deal with this tomorrow. The kids were asleep in bed before Mick came by, and everything keeps making it worse."

"I just don't feel comfortable leaving. I want to stay. What happened?"

"I'll tell you about it another day. Are you worried about Mick?" I wasn't sure why she cared what he was up to.

"Well, yeah . . . yes." She said it with emphasis. "He keeps coming back here, and I had to push him out the door last time. He's drunk and he isn't making sense or anything. He called the police on you earlier, and they came here, too."

"Yes," I said. "I figured." I recalled, when Mick and the city cop were talking by the roadside, the officer saying he would come by the house.

"Where were you when they came?" Marsha said.

"That's part of the story. Can I just tell you later?"

"No, I want to hear it and I don't want to leave. I'm worried about you, and I'm worried about the kids."

"Fine. I think you're worried that Mick and I had a fight and you don't want it to get worse. How about if I give you my gun. Then you don't have to worry about me or Mick anymore tonight. You can take it with you and I'll get it tomorrow. Would that make you feel better? If I give you the gun, there isn't any fighting you have to worry about. I'm not going to answer the door for Mick. I'm going to bed. I don't care what he's doing."

"Well . . ." She paused and looked down. I was already four steps up the stairs toward my room. "Okay, get me the gun and I'll take it with me and give it to Dad. I just want you to go to sleep, too. You should probably clean up first, though."

"I will. Lemme go get it."

"I don't understand you or Mick," she said under her breath as she followed up the stairs.

"I think he's trying to kill me," I replied, half to myself.

I stepped through the hall and into the master bedroom and opened my gun safe. I put the unloaded gun in one pocket and the clip in the other.

Square in my path to closing the deal and sending my mother-in-law home was Carley. My beautiful 9-year-old had emerged from her room at exactly the wrong time and was rubbing her eyes.

As I approached her, she pressed her head into my belly and said, "Daddy, why all this noise? I keep waking up."

"That's okay, bunny," I said. "Daddy's home now, and look Grandma was here the whole time. You just need to go back to bed."

"Will you tuck me in?"

"Of course I will."

I walked with Carley back toward her room, I didn't want Marsha to take the gun in front of her, because I had taught her about guns and she would wonder why it was out. She crawled into bed and pulled her covers up. I sat next to her on the mattress.

"Did we say our prayers before?"

"No, Daddy, I came out to say them after you put me to sleep, but you were asleep on the couch."

I winced in pain. This time it came from inside my heart, and it was devastating. How could I do this to my beautiful firstborn? For what reason did I need to drink?

Gathering myself, I said, "Well, let's say them now."

"Okay," she said. I remember her eyes beaming up at me, and her delight in this simple act of normality and routine on such a scary night for her. Her emotion lifted me, and by the time I left the room, I felt better.

Marsha took the gun and the clip, and went downstairs. She was leaving. I told her I would come down and lock up in a few minutes and that I appreciated her coming by.

Relieved, I went back into the bedroom and dug beneath my clothes in the closet till I found the fifth of vodka. It was nearly half full. I pressed it to my lips, leaned back, and opened my throat, swigging it down in four or five big mouthfuls until it was gone.

Drinking was my only option, the only thing I even considered doing at the time. It was the only solution I had for the pain. It was the only thing I could think of to blunt the fear I was enduring—of Mick, the police, and what was soon coming from Stacey. It took away the pressure of the unbearable guilt that had just hit me in Carley's room. It would help me shelve the self-righteous anger I had toward everyone I had encountered tonight and after my previous arrest. Nothing was working. Things were going to get worse, and I just needed the pressure from this unbelievable set of circumstances to go away until I could gather my thoughts.

What a silly end to the night, anyway, I mused. Whatever had made me think of giving my mother-in-law a gun? It wasn't as if I were going to shoot anyone, no matter how mad I was with Mick.

I heard a whimper and soft rustling down the hall in our baby's room. Phoebe was nearly 3 years old, but she had a habit of stirring in the night, and I knew I would have to attend to her before she broke into a full cry. I walked down the hallway and into her room, chomping on a fresh stick of spearmint gum to mask my breath. I could hear Marsha, still moving about down below.

Walking along the catwalk toward Phoebe's bedroom, I glanced down and noticed Marsha letting Mick in the front door. In the same flash, I felt rage, disgust, and overwhelm. For some odd reason, the overwhelm won out, and I spoke without even raising my voice.

"What are you doing here, Mick?" I said from the top of the stairs, looking down through the big crystal chandelier above his and Marsha's heads.

"I wanted to make sure you're all right," Mick said.

65

He gazed at me for a moment with a blank, drunken stare, then spoke again when the tension became too much.

"Look, there's police outside," he said. "They want you to come out and talk to them."

"Why would I want to talk to the police, Mick?" I said, watching Marsha's posture. She was standing tense, with one foot in front of the other. Her lips were clenched together, and she was peering at the side of Mick's downturned head.

"O-okay man, I called them again and said you had a gun in here, and they want to make sure everything is okay. They want you to come outside and talk to them. I told them I'd go in and bring you out."

"I can't think of anything to talk to them about, Mick. I'm going to bed. You need to leave. You're not welcome here," I said as plainly as if ordering a soda in a restaurant. I was past angry, tired, or confused at this point, and the booze was flowing in my blood. I was calming down and not caring about Mick so much anymore.

"I'm tellin' you, you're gonna have to come out," Mick said. "They won't leave."

Marsha started to speak. "Mick you should—"

"I got this, Mom," I interrupted. "Mick, leave. Now. Turn around and walk out. You're not welcome here. The police are not welcome here. If they want to stay out there tonight, that's fine. If they want to talk to me tomorrow, tell them to give me a call or I'll come by the office. This is the end of the conversation. Go."

"You need to go," Marsha said.

Mick quietly walked out with his head and shoulders down. Marsha shut the door behind him.

"Good night, Mom," I said, and went into Phoebe's bedroom.

Phoebe was tossing a bit but was still asleep. I picked her up, and her arms fell limp around my shoulders and her warm cheek nuzzled against mine. We started to rock gently back and forth as I hummed to her.

I heard the door downstairs. Marsha was finally leaving. Phoebe tightened her little arms, pressed a hug into my neck, and held it.

I smiled and felt better. It seemed that things would settle down after all. Sitting there, I began swaying gently and sang a lullaby.

"Hush, little baby, don't say a word,
Daddy's going to buy you a mockingbird.
And if that mockingbird won't sing,
Daddy's going to buy you a Diamond ring."

"Mr. DeRoche?"

A loud, stern voice pierced through the pleasant silence I was enjoying with Phoebe. "Mr. DeRoche, come out of the room." The voice came from outside the door and down the stairs. It was a man's voice, and it caught me quite off guard.

"Mr. DeRoche, we need to talk," the officer repeated as I left Phoebe's bedroom.

The bright light of the hallway contrasted with Phoebe's dark room. I turned and fixed my view on two uniformed police officers inside my front door. I stood about twelve feet above and twenty feet away from them, the officers to my right and Marsha to my left. I was still gently rocking Phoebe, and her head stayed nestled between my right cheek and shoulder.

I noticed Marsha's look of fear and guilt immediately. I took it in for no more than a blink before looking back at the police.

"We got a call that you have a gun in the house, and we wanted to talk to you," the officer said.

"I do have guns in the house—or did. I don't think that's against the law."

"We want you to come outside and talk about it."

"I don't want to come outside. It's been a long night, and I'm going to bed. If you want to talk to me, I'll come see you tomorrow. You have to leave *now*."

"Well, sir, your friend keeps calling us, and he said—"

"First of all, that he was my friend and that he wants you to talk to me? I don't think that's his choice. You're not welcome here. *He* isn't welcome here. I just told him that when he tried to come in. I told him he had to leave. And I'm telling you, you have to leave."

"We're not going to leave," the officer said.

There was nothing alarming or untoward about their posture or tone. I think my having a 3-year-old on my shoulder kept them in check. They had their hands resting on their hips, and one had his on his gun, but I saw cops doing this when ordering ice cream. I didn't think anything of it. He did seem emphatic with his last statement, though, and I couldn't figure out which way things were going.

"Listen, I just said you're not welcome here," I said. "You have to leave."

"We don't have to leave. Your mother-in-law let us in the house."

"She doesn't have the right to invite you in, because she doesn't have the right to be here, either. I just told her to leave fifteen minutes ago, and she said she was going to."

"That's true, he did tell me to leave," Marsha said, nodding, trying to break the tension. The officers didn't even look at her, though. I saw the look of relief return to a look of fear in her eyes and mouth. I turned my eyes quickly back to the officers.

"Well we're here now, and we aren't leaving. We have a report you were drinking and your mother-in-law said you handed her your gun."

"Do I seem as if I'd been drinking?"

"No, but come down and we can sort this out."

"I'm not coming down. You have to leave."

"We're not going to leave. Look, Craig, how long have we known you? Hell, you are one of the city's—"

"Unprofessional," I interrupted. "You don't have the right to come into my house and talk to me or anyone else that way. You are a police officer, and I am citizen. That's it. You get to do your job, not patronize me. I do know you. I know the chief, too. So what? I also know the laws—I used to work on them." Pausing, I wisely restrained myself from alluding to the fact that the officers were in violation of Michigan's Castle Doctrine at that very moment. I was afraid of how they might respond to this provocation.

Just then I heard Carley come out of her room and start walking my way, rubbing her eyes.

"Daddy, what is all the noise?" she said. "Why are there people in our house?"

"Go back in your room, honey," I said. "I'm just telling them to leave."

"But, Dad, I want you to come."

"Hold on, baby. I'll put Phoebe down and tell these folks to leave, and then I'll come in. Just go to your room. I'll be there in a minute."

"Okay, Daddy," Carley said as she went to her room.

"Now, get OUT of my house," I said calmly but clearly as I walked back into Phoebe's room.

I laid her in the bed and kissed her forehead. Then I breathed in, looked up, and left the room.

"Mr. DeRoche, I just talked to our supervisor, and we're not leaving. We're taking you in."

I looked back at Marsha's face and saw that all the color had drained out. She was frozen in place. I feared for her and what would come if I made the wrong move or pressed my rights too far. I understood what was going on, and was certain that she did not. I didn't want her to take my actions for drunkenness or aggression. At the same time, I wanted to protect my kids and my family. It had already been a four-month hell and media circus since my arrest in Saline.

In the seconds this took, Carley reemerged from her room, impatient at the time it was taking for me to send everyone away as promised and return to her bedside.

"Daddy?"

"Hold on, Carley, I'm coming." I raised my hand to stop her walking toward me.

"Mr. DeRoche, are you going to come downstairs, or do I have to come arrest you in front of your daughter?"

I walked down the three steps to the landing, where the stairway made a right angle and continued straight to where the officers stood. I was trying to get closer to Carley but also to stop her from coming any farther and seeing the officers.

"Everything's going to be fine, Carley. I just need to see these people out. Go back to your room."

Carley paused and stood near her door but wouldn't go into her room.

I turned back toward the police and said, "You have no right to be here."

"We just want to talk. If you come downstairs and talk to us away from your daughter on the front porch, we'll let you come back in and that'll be it for the night."

"You're *serious*?" I said. "You're trying to get me to come outside so you can arrest me? You think that'll work. I've told you to leave a dozen times. You don't have rights in here or out there," I said, pointing out the front window.

"You want us to do this in the house or out of the house—your call."

I paused and thought about the lose-lose situation the police were offering.

"Fine," I said. "I'm coming downstairs if you promise that's it and you'll leave. This was silly on my part. I was really just curious to see how blatantly the police would lie as part of their job.

"I promise. Just a few words and we're done," the officer said.

"Okay, then." I turned to Carley, "I'll be right up, honey."

I walked down the stairs quickly and asked what they wanted.

"Outside," the officer said.

I walked out my front door and stood on the porch. "What do you want?"

"I think I smell alcohol on your breath. Have you been drinking?"

"Yes, earlier. Why?"

"Well, your mother-in-law says you gave her your gun."

"Yes, so she would leave. It didn't even have a clip in it. So what? It's registered to me."

"Oh, I know. I checked. But, you see, you can't have possession of a weapon while you're drinking."

"I don't have possession of a weapon."

"But you did."

"Dude, you are making a serious mistake. I'm telling you, these things are harder to put back in the bottle than you think. I just went through this. If you arrest me, you can't just fix it and pretend you didn't."

Now a third officer had approached from behind the other two and interrupted the discussion. He was taller and heavier and spoke with more of that cop-style arrogance than the junior officer who was dealing with me before.

"Look we're taking you in," the big cop said. "It's a tough call, but it isn't ours to make out here in the field. It's being made from the higher-ups, and they said to bring you in."

"Who are you?" I asked.

"I'm the supervisor in the field, but the call came from higher up the chain of command, and the decision is made."

"You should call the chief," I said. "This is a mistake."

"We did. He's drunker than you are right now, I think. Look, there isn't anything I can do about it, Craig. It's not going to get solved tonight. We got to go."

With that, the larger officer turned and headed back toward the driveway. The junior officer looked at me, quite dejected, and the officer accompanying him just stood there.

"Look," the young officer said in a pleasant voice, "just walk toward the car and I'll cuff you when we get near it, so your daughter doesn't see it. Your kids'll be okay with their grandma." I could now clearly see "Officer Conner" on his badge.

"That isn't the point. If you want to drive me away or to someone else's house, I would understand, but I was being serious with the big guy. I don't think you should arrest me. I don't think you guys have any idea what happened tonight."

By this time, I was getting into the back of the car. While they got in the front seat, I noticed them both look at each other silently and caught the unmistakable frustration in their posture. I looked to the right of the car, and Mick was sitting on my sidewalk in front of the house, with his legs bent. His head was lowered just above his knees, like the position they want you take if the aircraft you're in is going to crash. He was vigorously pulling his interlaced fingers up and down through the hair on the back of his head.

When I looked over at Mick, it struck me all at once that I had mistaken a lot about tonight. He really was living out some stage drama like nothing I had ever seen in my life. Later, I would learn more about the night. As it turned out, I was just a small part of what Mick was up to. That's a story for later, though.

I looked back toward the front of the car. The officers had paused before pulling the car forward, even though nothing blocked their path.

"Don't you even want to know what happened tonight?" I said. "Did you see my legs?"

"Yes, they're scratched from when your buddy was trying to help you and you ran from him in the woods," Officer Conner said.

"Are you *kidding* me?" I answered.

"What happened then, Mr. DeRoche?"

"Dude, I am telling you, I'm not going to get into who-did-what-to-who with that guy on the sidewalk just to make for better media. If you can't figure it out, it's your problem, and I offered to tell you tomorrow. Before you pull away, though, look at him."

Officer Conner touched the brake. He had only just begun to let the car roll forward when I said to look.

"You said you're worried about my kids. What about Mick? He has a loaded gun in his house. *He's* on *my* sidewalk. *I'm* the one bleeding. He isn't. His kids are where? They're the exact same ages as mine. His wife is with mine, two hours from here. His house is a mile from here."

The officers both looked back at each other with that same frustrated look.

"Um, hey," Officer Conner said. "The call came in from the

higher-ups. Your friend is just trying to help you. We all are. We're going in now." And the car pulled away.

* * *

When I was taken into the Novi city police station, the pain and anger started to stir in me. Mick's aggressive behavior and his suggestion to hunt me down with dogs really rankled. Having gone through the humiliation and pain of my first arrest, I began to imagine how much worse this would be, to say nothing of the other aggravating factors on this crazy night. I remembered the lecture I had gotten from my lawyer about taking blood and breath tests willingly and for being so forthcoming about what I was doing. It wasn't in my nature to be shy when asked a question, and I didn't mind channeling my anger toward the officers I was dealing with.

I knew I shouldn't have drunk, and I was in for a world of trouble at home, but I was upset that my rights had been violated. I wanted to call my lawyer, my wife, the mayor, the chief—*somebody*. I'm sure I was being a jerk, though I wasn't raising my voice or using bad language. I was just trying to slow things down and not make it easy for them.

When it came time to take my mug shots, I wouldn't stop smiling. They tried to get me to look serious to take the picture, but I only replied "no" between my teeth as I kept smiling.

I deeply resented the entire process, and I was full of self-pity. At the station, the police were nothing but professional. I, on the other hand, was tired, angry, and in a lot of pain. I hadn't drunk enough for the pain to go away or for me to sleep.

It was going to be a long night.

I had learned about how long this sort of night is while in the drunk tank at the Saline police station. The officers there were nice, too. When we took mug shots, they took four and let me pick one out. At the time, though, the officers in Saline had no real intention of ticketing me—or so they said. I was freer there, too, but I did spend the night in the cell, which was amazingly uncomfortable.

Neither city lockup had beds or pillows. You just got a wool blanket or two to sleep or sit on. In Novi, the cell had only a dual-purpose urinal and drinking fountain, and four video cameras mounted near the ceiling. There was no way I would be able to use the toilet tonight under such pressure, but I could drink out of it, at least.

As I settled in and began to accept that no one would come to release me until they presumed my blood alcohol content was under .08 percent, I began to rest and think.

First, my thoughts were on Stacey, but it was too heavy a psychic load for me to carry at the time, and I quickly moved to other things. My next thought was on fixing my business and work situation, and I started doing the math to distract myself.

I had just deposited about forty-four thousand dollars into my business account a couple of days before, and things had started to pick up after I was completely washed out four months earlier. I feared the washout would happen again, but this time it would be worse. My longer-term contracts would be gone. I had protected the names of those employers from the media, and they had kept working with me. But a gun charge would be too great a risk for them, and I knew it. My income stream was going to dry up.

Worse, I had just incorporated a new entity with my former boss in the reinsurance business, and we had secured the first backers to enter the niche we both knew best: excess workers' compensation insurance. This deal was set to move forward and would provide a great living for my family. As I sat in the holding cell in Novi, I feared the worst for this deal and every other source of income I had.

I knew instinctively that this would be very hard on my partner. Jim had worked with me and seen me at my best and worst, both drunk and sober, but this arrest was something different. Trouble, courts, and claims are not good for the reinsurance business—or for any business, really—and this worried me a great deal.

I quietly resolved to do the right thing and call each of my partners and contracts first thing Monday, to discuss this before they could read about it in the press. It was now the early hours of Sunday morning, and I sat alone in a brightly lit empty holding cell, with nothing to do but wait until I could talk with Stacey and the many others I had let down.

As the night dragged on, my body began to revolt against the abuse it had suffered. My left arm was nearly completely numb. My joints had stiffened from sitting, and the scabby ooze that lacquered my legs had begun to set and dry. I had greatly underestimated the pain and damage to my ribs. Breathing and standing, or even sitting up, was increasingly difficult.

The numbness in my left arm was troubling. When I was 25 years old, I had a cardiac event that I at first dismissed as a panic attack. It turned out I was allergic to caffeine and went into an arrhythmia that did minor damage to my heart. I had gone through all the cardiac tests and knew I didn't have a congenital heart problem. And yet, this felt like the arrhythmia I had before. After doing several weeks of an "as seen on TV" workout (called "Insanity," of all things), I was in the best shape of my life, but I was worried. Was I having a heart attack? A panic attack? I simply didn't know.

I didn't want to alert the police to what was going on, because I wanted to avoid going to the hospital. An emergency room visit would just make for more news and more bills to pay. When I agreed to go the hospital in Saline, they had made sure nothing was covered, by coding their X-rays under some "crazy person" code so my insurance wouldn't cover it. When I called the doctor personally to ask why he did it, he said it was to "teach me a lesson not to get arrested." Nice guy. I figured this hospital would do the same, and I wanted to avoid that nasty side of getting arrested that people don't often talk about. Immediately upon arrest, the goal on all sides seems to be to make you indigent as quickly as possible.

I moved my head from side to side and massaged my neck, telling myself it was all in my head or that a pinched nerve was just making it feel numb. The pain in my legs and ribs kept getting worse, and

I really believed it was just a pinched nerve or bruising causing the numbness. Still, I was alarmed and wanted to do something about it. I didn't want to sleep on the cold concrete, and I was just flat-out angry.

The solution that seemed right at the time was to get up and begin doing some exercises. In my head, this made perfect sense. My first objective was to determine whether I was having another heart event, or just needed some movement and circulation in order to feel my left hand. I also figured it would keep me awake since the exercise and the pain would be more than anyone could sleep through.

I got up and started doing the calisthenic-style exercises I had drilled into my head from the past three months of Insanity workouts. The workout is sold on TV in between infomercials for the Clapper or the George Foreman Grill. I loved the work-outs, and within minutes I had full blood flow and was starting to sweat.

I removed my shirt and continued the movements: first jumping jacks, then push-ups. I was starting to move when a visibly disturbed officer walked up.

Looking out from the cell, the view is a bit different from how it's portrayed on the old TV shows like *Andy Griffith* or *Barney Miller*, with the officer sitting at a desk, and the prisoner behind a steel grate. Nowadays, the cells have Plexiglas walls and doors, so the jailers have an unobstructed view of the prisoner. The Plexiglas had holes drilled into it, as if for a terrarium or a birdcage.

The fluorescent lighting in both police stations gave off a bluish-green hue, and it stayed on in the cell and in the hallway at full blast at all times. The concrete floor is coated with the thick, shiny paint used on garage floors. For sleeping, a raised slab of concrete runs the width of the cell, from front to back.

I'm not sure why they bother to raise the sleeping area, since it's the same concrete. Probably some sort of psychological experiment to see who inists on the slab and who accepts the floor as the same thing.

Beyond the Plexiglas, there isn't anyone or anything to look at. I can't begin to imagine what it must be like for someone doing prison time in solitary confinement for weeks, months, or even years.

The absence of human life and interaction is unnerving.

The officer entered my view swiftly and came to the door. To my surprise, he opened it.

"Craig, what in the hell are you doing?"

"Working out to pass the time."

"Do you want people here to think you're crazy? It's the middle of the night!"

"Actually, that's appropriate. The name of my workout is Insanity—heard of it?"

"No, for crying out loud! I'm down here in a friendly way. I'm not going to write this up. I'm trying to do you a favor, man. You gotta listen to me, though."

I looked at him. He was entirely earnest in his words and body language. His hands were upturned, and I felt as though he was trying to express something I should hear.

"Nobody here on duty likes what happened to you. The guys are laying into the bosses on this. It's complete nonsense. We've never treated anyone like this or arrested anyone like this, let alone you. Thing is, we can't fix it tonight, so you're gonna just have to knock it off. I know you're mad, but play it straight. Everyone you're going to see or work with the rest of the night is on your side. They don't want to be doing this. It's not their job."

He looked straight at me to make sure I understood the messages he was all but whispering to me in the hall.

"Okay," I said.

I was looking straight at him, and I think my posture signaled to him that I had received his message and was accepting his suggestions. Then I winced as the muscles around my ribs contracted.

"Are you okay?" he said. "Do you want to get checked out?"

"Nah, I'm fine. Really."

"You're really carved up."

"I know. It's just scratches, though. I'll be fine."

The officer lowered his head and started to turn away slightly before readdressing me. The door to the cell was still open. I stood in the opening, and he was in the hallway.

"You may not remember this," he said, "but I met you back in 1997 during your first campaign. I talked to you all those years ago. I'm not trying to judge you, but you're, like, one of the best people this town has ever had, and you get wrapped up in stuff like this? I'm not saying you did anything wrong, because I'm not on your case. I'm only talking about the stuff I read in the papers. You should take this seriously. People love you, and this doesn't make any sense unless you have a problem. Hell, I couldn't *wait* to vote for you. I can't afford to live in Novi, but when you started representing my city, too, man, I was your biggest supporter."

He lowered his head again and turned, and I backed into the cell.

He shook his head and said, "Maybe I shouldn't have said anything . . ."

"No, you're fine," I interrupted. "I know what's wrong with me. I haven't taken it seriously, and what you said means a lot to me. I appreciate it. I really . . . I mean, I, well, appreciate it, and I think you understand what I'm saying."

He shut the door and walked away.

Chapter 8

Early in the morning, the officer who had given me the pep talk approached my cage and tapped on the Plexiglas wall. "Look, Craig," he said, "I talked with your wife. She called us again and said she doesn't want you to come home, but you're free to leave here in a few minutes once we get the paperwork ready, okay?"

"I know," I told him. "One of the other officers took me out to talk to her last night when she got back from Saugatuck. She called in then, too. I don't know that she'll want me home again after this. I'll figure out who to call."

"I'm sorry about that, man, but I meant what I said to you last night. Take this serious, and if you have a problem, deal with that first. I can't imagine this arrest will amount to that much, but your life matters. I worry about you." He looked down and away.

It was hard for him to say this, I could tell. He did care about me, and I was amazed that he cared still, thirteen years after the night he mentioned to me in the cell. I'm sure my little exercise display shocked the monitors and put him in a tough spot. I respected his tone and effort. I felt as if I had let him down. I knew that if I affected him this much, Stacey's pain and grief must be unbearable.

I thought about who to call. I didn't want to talk to my mom or dad. This was going to break their hearts all over again. My older brother, Paul, also had seen me through much and had patched over many of the stupid things I had done. I didn't want to bring him in. I wished my lawyer, Harold, had answered me or returned my call. When I was arrested in Saline, Stacey had left me sixteen voice-mail messages overnight. This time, when they gave me my cell phone back, there were no messages. I had blown it. It was Sunday morning, and I didn't know what to do.

The only thing I could think of—and it made perfect sense at the time—was to call Mick. It made sense because I figured he owed me for setting me up so bad, and I didn't want to let him off the hook. That was my thinking, anyway. I wanted to know what in the world he was thinking last night.

I called Mick, and he picked up right away.

"Stacey's home," he said, "and she's so mad she doesn't want to talk to you right now. She said she already talked to your mom and dad and asked them if you could come out there for a while. They said fine, so I agreed to pick you up and let you get your things and car and head over to your parents. I'll come get you, but I can't stay long, because I have a thing I need to do."

Vintage Mick. Whatever crazy stuff he was trying to pull last night was still going on. He was still trying to direct traffic and be the center of attention. After hearing that he was still working his way to the middle of this drama, I couldn't wait to see him. I wanted to know what on earth was motivating him. If I was going to overcome whatever he was doing, I had to figure out his angle. I had spent some time last night thinking about him, and I just couldn't make any sense of his behavior.

"Okay, Mick, I appreciate it," I said. "See you in a few."

This time, I didn't worry about getting the police report or even whether it would become public. I knew for a certainty it would be released quickly to the media and would set off another firestorm of negative articles and newscasts. I understood fully that this would be different, too. This wasn't a first offense. It was now my second, and it had happened within four months of the earlier incident. I had never been truly arrested before in my life. I say "truly" because I was a troublemaking kid who got picked up by the police several times for things like climbing on the school roof and being with some friends who lifted some things at a convenience store. But this was the full thing: the mug shots, the police report, the political talking heads who so eagerly step forward to make a name for themselves by commenting on TV about others' behavior.

Worse, this was happening in my backyard. This time, it was happening in the city where I had made my name in politics.

When I was 25 years old, the city fathers asked me to lead the process of writing the "20/20" vision statement for what the fastest-growing city in Michigan would look like twenty-five years later, in 2020. I led the process and wrote the document, and when they threw out my work, I ran for council and began building the machinery to throw them out of office. It took two years before I was the last incumbent politician in town still standing.

When I ran for state representative to represent Novi and six other cities, I didn't even draw an opponent in the Republican primary for the safe seat. I could raise more money than others and had hundreds of volunteers who could knock on ten thousand or more doors each day. No one showed up for the fight.

Two years later—and for the next four years when I was away in the role of a statewide leader as Speaker and GOP leader—my absence built deep-seated resentments. My arrogance fueled this. The aspiring politicians whom I treated poorly had been taking shots at me for years, though none would actually run against me for election.

There was some talk locally of my future candidacy for an open state senate seat. Even though I had no intention of seeking the post, the local leaders in Novi attacked me personally when speaking to each other, and their antipathy toward me at political meetings was visceral and overt. Even though I announced I had no intention of running, the mayor and members of the county commission and city council preemptively made it clear and public in e-mails and phone calls that they were supporting others "over me" for posts such as the state senate seat I wasn't even interested in. I think they wanted to show their dislike for me and my politics, and if I wasn't going to give them a race to strut their stuff in, they were going to fabricate one to get their message out.

It was a crazy time in Michigan politics, and I wasn't the only politician acting crazy. About a year before I started my public slide, another local politician, who was one of my vocal opponents, was arrested outside a local bar. It caused a big stir, as these sensational stories reliably do, and the police covered up his story the best they could, even "losing" the arrest videotape that was on file from two cruisers. I had helped one of my friends displace him in the primary that year over the objections and support of the clique in power at the city council, and this only salted the wounds.

After seeing some of the stuff come out about my arrest in Saline, where people didn't even know me, I assumed the worst. In time, I would learn that I was right.

I thanked the attending officers for their kindness and left with Mick when he arrived at the station.

As we drove from the police station toward my house, Mick nervously told me he had a "football thing" to bring his son to, so he had to drop me off and run. I told him that was fine and that I appreciated the ride. I was just taking in the summer sun and letting go of a situation I knew was hopeless. I was exhausted after not sleeping. I was in pain, and Mick hadn't even asked me about the scabs covering my legs and feet. He simply pointed out that he brought my flip-flops, and speculated that they had fallen off near his sidewalk. Yes, I had been barefoot all night, and he noticed this. He then jerked the car to the right and pulled into an empty business parking lot and stopped the car.

Mick paused, put the car in park, took in a deep breath, and slowly removed his sunglasses. He gathered himself and looked directly at me.

"What happened last night?"

"Are you kidding me?" I said.

"No, I mean, I remember some of it but not much. I know I called the cops, but I wanted to stop and get the story straight because the girls keep asking for details and I don't have them. I was off-the-charts drunk before Stacey even called me. I woke up this morning, and it seemed like something bad happened, but I couldn't remember it. I went out to my fire pit and counted. I had seventeen empty beer cans just stacked up there, not to mention what was in the house and yard. I really don't remember much."

"Well, I can't really help you, then, Mick."

"No, seriously, I want to know."

"Whatever, man. Just drive me home," I said. Inside, this helped me let go of the anger I had for Mick. He had certainly been in a very dark place last night, and it looked as though he might be in even worse shape now. Either he was manufacturing another elaborate lie, or he had genuinely blacked out. Either way, he would be of no use to me for information, help, or even friendship going forward. I decided to look passively ahead through the windshield, go through the motions of talking to him, and just survive the three-mile drive home.

"Are you mad at me? I'm pretty sure Stacey told me to call the police."

"I can't really help you out, Mick. I don't fully understand what happened last night. What I do know is, I can't fix it now. You can't fix it, either. I just have to deal with this. I have no idea what you were doing last night, and what you said helps me understand it a bit better. Just go. I appreciate the ride. Just drive."

Worthless. That was what I thought about the value in talking to Mick now. Why on earth would I want to tell him what he did? This entire process was long and public and incredibly painful, and it was starting all over again. This time was going to be worse, and I had already calculated in my head that I could be going to jail for up to three months. Talking was worthless. Mick, to me, was worthless.

When we arrived at my house, no one was there. I grabbed my stuff, loaded my car, and headed out.

I did this quickly since I really didn't want to encounter any of the neighbors. I worried about what they might say, and imagined them peering out from their windows in the upscale suburban neighborhood where I lived.

I drove out to my parents' condominium and set up a room for myself upstairs. Unfortunately, housing an errant child was clearly not in my parents' plans, and I took over an ornate guest room half used for storage at the time.

If you were to ask my brothers or me, my mom and dad and I have great, normal relationship. Stacey, on the other hand, thinks the personal space we give each other on health, financial, and personal issues is odd. I had moved out of their house when I was young, and had always earned my own money and blazed my own way. The unwritten rule in my home growing up seemed to be that if I didn't need any correction or help from my parents, I received no particular input or oversight that would interfere with my plans. This suited me perfectly, and I designed my childhood, educational, and troublemaking activities around it. I was what you might call, well, distant. There was love, for sure, and my parents were always my biggest fans and supporters, but I can't recall ever saying "I love you" to them or getting any kind of mushy-mush back. My plan was to carve a path through life and go as far and as fast as I could, and they seemed to give me the room.

Now their middle child was walking by and heading upstairs again for the first time in more than twenty years. The life that my mother had so expertly promoted as superior and extraordinary to her friends all these years had turned into a nightmare. And every one of those grandmas who were tired of hearing about me from my mom would get to read all about who I really was on the front pages, all over again.

I knew what this did to my parents, and the pain it caused, but I didn't know how to talk about it or express myself. I didn't even try. They didn't really try, either.

I was tired. I told them I needed some sleep, and went to bed.

* * *

When you consistently live your life below your own standards, waking up is the worst part of the day.

The midsummer sunlight glowed through the paper-thin blinds

in my parents' upstairs bedroom. I looked at the clock and noticed I had slept only about four hours. I wanted to sleep more and knew I needed to. But once my quick mental inventory confirmed that I had in fact done the things and experienced the events of last night, my mind was going at full tilt, and there was no chance of catching a few more winks.

I lunged upward to get out of bed, only to fall back down, gasping in pain. It took all my strength to hold back the girlish shriek that I felt inside.

It was an amazing pain that seemed to be tied to a trip wire triggered by my muscle movement. Thankfully, the moment I lay still, it left as quickly as it came. I looked up at the ceiling and caught my breath. I remembered everything about last night. I just needed to keep moving now. I rolled gently to the side of the bed and turned and fell toward the floor, landing gently on my feet, knees bent. I then carefully stood up and looked at the scabs on my legs.

I would take care not to make any sudden movements that would hurt my ribs as I lumbered down the stairs. Both my parents were in the kitchen, huddled close, talking. My mother has some hearing loss (as do I), so I figured they were kibitzing about my situation and doing their best to keep it to themselves.

"I appreciate your letting me stay here," I said.

"You can stay as long as you want," my dad replied.

My mother just looked at us both quietly.

"I better try to call Stacey. I haven't talked to her since I was at the police station and she was off-the-graph mad."

"Okay, son," my dad said.

I walked outside and called home. Stacey answered immediately. She was past mad. Being disgusted and raising her voice would have dignified the situation by throwing too much effort my way. She was flat, spent. Done.

"I don't want you around here," Stacey said. "I don't want you to come home."

"Look, I—"

"Don't start. I don't want to hear it," she said calmly. "Stay there. Go to rehab; don't go to rehab. I'm done. The kids are terrified. You are a selfish, heartless man. You can mess with me all you want, but you do this when I'm not here and you have the kids? How *dare* you!"

There was a pause because I didn't know what to say and, I think, Stacey didn't want to get herself worked up all over again. She was focused on getting the message out and moving on.

"I don't think our marriage is going to work," she said. "I'm not saying this because I'm mad. I've given you enough chances, and I can't trust that you will ever not drink. You blow it every time. I have the kids to worry about, and they are my focus. I do hope you figure out how to stop drinking, but I can't stick around for it. What you did last night was unbelievable. Mick told me you—"

"Mick . . . Honey, listen, he—"

"Don't even start. He told me everything. You're lucky he was around. I had to drive home with Mim and the other wives in the middle of the night because of you. It's not good enough for you to drink—you have to get arrested and ruin the only weekend I get to myself with my friends this year."

We paused again. I would have talked, but I was in the same position now as I had been in with the police last night. What Mick had done didn't make what I did any less pathetic or stupid. My drinking, not the arrest, was the issue. The arrest was just the finishing touches to the destruction that the drinking had wrought on our marriage, friendship, and trust.

The thing about arrests is, they always have a long tail. A *very* long tail. They aren't like breaking an arm and wearing a cast for six weeks. They burrow in and destroy everything you have at the time, and then continue to extract payment day after day, month after month, and, as I have learned, year after year.

"And what about the media? Are they going to find out about this, or can you redeem yourself and keep this one quiet?"

"Are you kidding me?" I said. "I was arrested for the sole purpose of *sending* this to the media. I'm sorry, honey—"

"Stop calling me 'honey.' I mean it! I am just so-o-o-o tired of this. I'm going to have to move out of the house. The news will be all over here."

"I think that's a good idea."

On the other end of the phone, I heard a ruffling noise and a soft, breathless whimper. "This isn't fair," she sniffled.

It completely hollowed me out inside. I felt like a monster for hurting her like this and for being powerless to respond or comfort her in any way.

"I'm going up to my parents'," she snapped through her tears.

"Okay. Can I talk to the kids?"

"Yes, but don't call back for me. I don't want to talk to you anymore."

I looked up at the beautiful blue Michigan summer sky with the sun blazing down. The day was so wonderfully fresh and beautiful. The surrounding grass was perfectly trimmed, and the flowers were brilliant in the afternoon light. I took in the beauty of the moment and wondered how I would have been spending the day if I had just been able to go to bed last night. Every moment since I spoke with Mick had been nightmarish, and the events kept piling up with a persistence unimaginable. I wasn't ready to speak to my daughters, yet I wanted to more than anything else in the world.

"Daddy?" Carley said into the phone.

"Bunny!" I sprang back, smiling as I faked a positive tone with my standard greeting for any of the girls.

"Um, are you coming home?"

"No, bunny, I'm at Grandma and Grandpa DeRoche's house and I'm going to be here for a while. You're going to go with Mom to Grandma and Grandpa Zoellner's for a couple days."

"But I want you to come home," she whimpered.

"This is for the best. Everything will . . ." I caught my tears and cracking voice before they were audible. Choking past the emotion, I swallowed and quickly said, "everything's going to be fine. You'll see. You're going to have a great time at Grandma's, and I have to work some things out here."

"I'm scared," she said. "Why did the police come to our house, and where did you go?"

"I went with them. I had to go to their station and they gave me a ticket last night. I left there when they were done giving me the ticket, and now I just have to take care of it. You don't have anything to be afraid of."

"Did they give you a ticket for having a gun in the house? That's what they said."

"You shouldn't be listening, bunny, because that's what makes you scared. Nothing bad happened last night that you need to worry about. Mr. Mick and I both weren't behaving well, and I got a ticket. Everything will be fine."

My 9-year-old then caught me with a right hook to the gut: "Is this going to be in the newspaper and on TV again?"

"What?" I gasped.

"Like last time when I saw you on the front page of the paper saying you were in trouble."

"You saw that?"

"Yes," she replied in a sheepish tone.

"It's okay that you looked at the paper, honey," I said as I gathered my thoughts. My hands were shaking. "You're not in trouble. People say all sorts of things about your dad. They always have. You know there have been thousands of times I've had things written about me, and most of it is good, but you should know that not everyone likes me and that I don't always do things that are the right thing. I don't want this to hurt your feelings, and you shouldn't have to worry about it. When I get home with you, I'll show you some other stories of when people say some nice things about me, and I'll show you some other things that people say about me that are silly or where they don't agree with me."

"When are you coming home?"

"I think it'll be a couple weeks for sure, honey. I don't know. Things will be fine, and you're going to have a great time with Mommy."

"But I want you to come home now. I don't want this to be in the papers. Why can't you just come home?"

"Honey, you'll see that this will be fine. Daddy's got to do a couple of things that are very important and that you want me to do. I have to figure some things out. I'll see you soon, and I just talked to Mommy and she said I should call you every day."

"Okay, Daddy."

"I love you."

"I love you, too."

"All right, bunny, I'll talk to you and your sisters tomorrow."

Tears rolled down my face as I hung up the phone. I couldn't imagine what had become of me. How horribly wicked I must be to have created this situation and to have to explain these things to my daughter. I was thankful my middle child and baby weren't available to talk.

Nothing was working, and everything kept getting worse. The day labored on for a few more hours, with calls to my older and younger brother and some other close friends.

All this was taking place in a progressive stream of failures, and the action wasn't letting up. It was Sunday evening, and things hadn't let up and I didn't have any tricks left to try. I was at the end of things. I tried to be patient, but I couldn't stop my mind from racing. I needed a break in the action, and I did the only thing I knew how to do: after dinner, I went upstairs and pulled the fifth of gin I had bought en route to my parents' place after leaving the police station, and I drank myself to sleep. I turned off the rushing sounds and the pressure from all the madness, using the very thing that had caused it all in the first place. I wished I had a choice, but it seemed that nothing else was available. I had no other choice that I could see.

The next day, I had to reach out to the two companies I was currently contracted to work with. I explained to each company the situation and my expectation that the media attention would be worse than that from my arrest in February. Both of them wished me well and informed me that they would be exercising their thirty-day options to cancel my contracts.

Then I had to make the hard phone call. I needed to explain to my friend, former boss, and new business partner what was going on. For this venture, I held out hope that there might be something to save.

Jim had more experience than anyone in the country in the line of reinsurance we both specialized in. He had over twenty years' experience leading the marketing for the largest player in the niche. This was the company where I first met him and where I worked under him for several years. The reinsurance field in our area of focus had consolidated to only two companies, and there was room for a third. In fact, to spread the risk, there was a very fundamental need for large employers and governments to have a third option. For the months leading up to my arrest in Novi, we had incorporated our partnership and had even begun contracting with large-niche players to back our venture. Our business plan called for a very conservative estimate of a hundred million in annual sales after ten years. Our experience and contacts led us to believe that much more than this was available and that it would be quite easy to gain momentum.

My task was to explain to Jim that although the arrest and possible jail time meant uncertainty in my marriage and in my finances in the short run, our business would be fine in the long run. I did the best I could, and Jim was very gracious. He said he wanted to think about things and really wanted me to focus on dealing with my issues and not to worry about something that could be pushed back.

This seemed reasonable enough to me at the time, especially given the shocking news I was delivering over the phone. I can only imagine the way the conversation sounded on his end.

When we ended the call, Jim asked if I was going to enter a drug or alcohol rehabilitation facility. I told him my father had asked me the same thing. I also said I had been in one before and wasn't sure it would help.

After we spoke, I pulled my car into a parking lot in my parents' subdivision. I told myself I was doing this to gather my thoughts and make some calls outside their house. But I knew myself well enough to know that I was really just finding a good place to knock down a few drinks.

I sat there drinking until I had enough to stabilize my nerves and distract myself from the unmanageable rush of emotions I was trying to squeeze back into a vault somewhere in my mind. I just needed to get free of the terror gripping me. My phone rang. The caller ID said it was a call from the president of a local hospital.

"Hey, Craig, it's John!"

"Hey, John," I said.

I had known John for years. He was one of the most competent young leaders I had ever met in any organization. John was a short guy with a bright smile, who just happened to be overseeing the construction of a new hospital in Novi, worth hundreds of millions of dollars. A big part of my job in the legislature had been to bring projects like this to my district, and we developed a good relationship.

As usual, he was bubbling over with enthusiasm. "Listen," he said, "I've been remiss on a duty I agreed to do for the upcoming governor's race, and I was wondering if I could put you on as a host for a fund-raiser I'm having at my house? You've always been the biggest draw in our area. I'm not asking you to buy the tickets. Just be listed as a host and maybe say a few words."

"Wow, John, you really kinda caught me at a bad time," I said, looking at the bottle of booze between my knees.

"Oh, I'm sorry. You want me to call you back?"

"I don't think that'll help," I said softly, and for some strange reason, I felt the urge to continue. "Listen, I'm sure you didn't call me to hear about this, but I want to tell you what happened, so at least one person out there can say they heard it from me. Got a minute?"

"Sure. It sounds bad, though. Are you okay?"

I paused and thought about my situation. I couldn't believe I was going to open up like this without planning it all out first, but I started anyway. "Not really, John. I screwed up again with alcohol and got arrested on Saturday night in Novi. I didn't do what the police said I did, but that's really beside the point. My marriage is basically gone. I'm going to have to deal with the press and new charges, and I assume I'll never be in politics or public service again, let alone help the next GOP governor candidate. What I really need to do is just focus. I've had this problem a long time, and I need to do something about it."

"My God," John said. "I had no idea. I mean, I heard about what happened before, but I just figured you were out with the boys, and the police and media were giving you a rough ride. I've never even seen you take a drink. I don't know what to say." He paused again. "I am so sorry this is happening."

"I appreciate that, but you don't need to be sorry," I said. "I've actually known I'm alcoholic since I was a little kid, and I guess I figured I would work it out some way. And, well, I didn't. I'm not asking for anything, but if you could wait until the news breaks, and then pass what I said on to the political people in the governor campaign, I'd appreciate it. Tell 'em I'm just going to duck low and tend to this business."

I listened to a few seconds of silence. Then John said, "I don't want to be to forward, but I just really feel it's important for me to say a few things right now, okay?"

"Okay." I had no idea what he was going to say or why he would say it. I felt relieved to have shared the truth of my situation, but I also felt bad for burdening him with my problems.

"I'm not saying you're an alcoholic, but you said you were, so say I take you at your word. I'm not trying to judge you here. You may not know this, but I was on the board of directors for a number of years at one of the world's leading rehabilitation hospitals, and they're right down the road. I've seen what they can do to help people like you. You need more help than you think, and you shouldn't underestimate this. You are one of the smartest, most talented people I've ever met, and you can do this, but you're going to have to learn that it isn't up to you *how* this gets fixed. You go to this place, and if you want, I'll send an e-mail to a friend in admissions and let them know you're coming."

John paused, and when I didn't reply, he said, "Either way, you should go."

"John, I've been to that place," I said. "I went there twice. I really don't know what will be different this time. I don't want you to do any special favors for me, either. Let me see if I can get in there on my own, and if I can't, I'll call for help."

"You promise?"

"I do. I will."

"Craig, the facility isn't going to fix you, but they're the best in the world for people who are ready. Maybe you weren't ready and you're ready now. It's not for me to say. I just know from experience that it doesn't work when people try to do this on their own. Maybe that's what you're learning."

"I guess humility isn't my strong suit," I said. "You know me pretty well. I mean, thanks for pointing that out, John!" I said with a laugh. "I didn't want to go there, but after listening to you and my dad and my older brother, I think it's the thing to do."

I called the facility immediately and found they would take me the next afternoon. I went home, told my parents what my plan was, and went up to bed. I fell asleep at about seven p.m. and woke up at five a.m. to find my duffel bag open on the floor. I stood up and walked out of the room and was promptly met by my mother. She had been waiting up all night for any sounds from the room. We may never have been an openly affectionate family, but I understood this unconditional love as I felt the full weight of the burden I had put on her for so many years.

"Are you okay, son?"

"Yes, Mom."

"I just heard you, and—"

"Mom, I want to tell you something," I said, my eyes welling up with tears. I gathered myself and said, "I know you went in and took the bottle of booze I had in my bag, and that's fine. I don't want to drink anymore, but I'm scared and I didn't know what to do. It's not an excuse for drinking earlier, but I'm not really sure if they'll take me into the rehab hospital if I'm sober. My plan was to drink more until I went in. I decided to go in tomorrow. The truth is, after talking to a friend on the phone, I didn't feel like drinking anymore. I know I just have to face this and not try to plan it or escape from it. I don't know if I can sleep, but you don't have to worry about me tonight, and you don't have to worry about me trying to drink anymore here. I'm sorry I hid this from you and Dad, and I'm saying this because I don't want to hide anything from you or anyone else again."

My dad had joined my mother in the hallway and stood behind her silently. My mom choked back a sob, and her eyes were glossy with tears. Her mouth trembled a little. Then, after a few seconds, her lips slowly curved up into a knowing smirk, and she reached up to wipe the tears from my cheek.

"I know it's going to be all right," she said. "Now, you should get some rest, honey."

"Okay, I'll try. I'm really glad we got to talk about this. Good night."

"Good night."

Chapter 9

My father and I sat eating breakfast at a local greasy spoon. Our discussion meandered toward and away from the events of the night I was arrested in Novi. We both agreed that there was something to gain from my going into the rehab hospital. Our conversation was practical and unemotional. I assured my dad that I had earned tens of thousands of dollars over the previous couple of weeks and thought my insurance would cover the visit. I rejected his offers of help. With my pride still stopping me from admitting I needed any help, I deflected his concerns.

Just as the waitress set a big plate of the house special in front of me, my phone rang. It took me a moment to recognize the name on the caller ID. It was the Novi police officer who had talked to me at the jail. I must have programmed the number in several years before, and it still was on my contact list. I looked at the name holding the phone over my perfectly cooked runny eggs and rye toast. It was an intimidating call for sure, and I would rather take it than risk letting it go to voice mail. I answered.

"Hi, Craig, it's Jimmy Miller with the Novi police."

"Hi, Jimmy."

"Um, this is a hard call for me to make. I'm doing it from my personal cell phone. I need to relay a message to you if that's okay."

"Sure, what's going on?"

I glanced up at my dad and noticed the intensity in his face. He knew the call was important.

"The prosecutor is going to issue an indictment for you. It's going to be for misdemeanor possession of a firearm while intoxicated. Do you understand what this is?"

"Yes," I said quietly into the phone.

"The reason I'm calling is to help where I can. There's a bunch of us guys who don't like what's going on. There isn't much we can do about it, but I do have a few tricks. I know an employee over at the court, and she said she doesn't plan on posting this until eleven twenty a.m. and that the judge has an opening for indictments right about that time. Do you know what this means?"

"I know you're trying to help, but I have to be honest: I don't quite follow."

"Um, your case is going out to the media and we can't control it. They're going to be all over it. The thing is, you can be in front of the judge at the same time as the indictment is entered, meaning you can be in and out before anyone finds out. It's not much, but it's all I can do."

"It's a lot," I told him, "and I appreciate it. You didn't have to do this, and it means a great deal to me. Please tell the other guys I appreciate their looking out for me, and I get what happened. I know it wasn't them. Thank you."

"Listen, I'm going to hang up. You didn't get this call. Eleven twenty." *Click.*

I paused and breathed in. I felt calmed by this simple yet powerful act of kindness. It truly did mean a lot to me. I was in a position where I couldn't really effectively tell anyone what had actually happened, and this was a weight far heavier than I had estimated. I hadn't been able to tell Stacey what happened. I wasn't interested in educating Mick, and frankly, it felt pretty good that some of the people who got paid to know what was happening might have actually figured it out. I smiled and spoke to my dad.

"That was the police. We have to eat quick and go to the courthouse in Novi."

"Who was that?" my dad said as I shoveled food into my mouth. "Why did they call?"

96

"It was a friend, I guess," I said with my mouth half full. "They're walking me through the court to avoid the media. I don't mean to sound coy, Dad, but this is a good thing. You'll see. When we're done, I'll go to the rehab facility and check in. It'll be good to get this out of the way."

We arrived at the court with a few minutes to spare, and my buddy Harold sent over his best litigator, Steve Vitale, to handle my side of things. I had never met him before and was immediately taken by his courtroom mastery. He settled everything into place with a couple of gestures and a couple of gruntlike acknowledgments to courtroom officials.

When they called my case, he was equally quick. He turned to me quickly while they were reading my case, and it distracted me from the process.

"You just say 'okay'—not another word. Are you a Christian?"

"Got it. Um, yes." I answered quickly, trying to keep up.

He kept talking even though the judge was looking our way while the clerk read. "You need to read a couple books. Maybe they'll help you spiritually."

"That's probably a good idea," I said, all the while wondering why a Jewish man who never talked to me about faith (Harold) would send someone who spoke so bluntly to me about Christianity.

After I said "okay" as instructed to the not-guilty plea, Steve and his prosecutor adversary went at it on setting a bond. Steve explained why I should be free to go on my own recognizance; and the prosecutor took his turn.

"Your Honor, this man is a risk to the community. He was arrested while intoxicated with a weapon—"

"Objection!"

"His mother-in-law called the police on him and—"

"Objection! She did nothing of the sort. Are you making this up?" Steve snapped, to the entertainment of everyone in earshot.

"Settle down, men," the judge inserted.

"Your Honor, the people recommend Mr. DeRoche post a thousand dollars bond, be confined to the community, and undergo mandatory psychological evaluations. He is a risk to his family and the community."

"Your Honor, this is as a ridiculous request," Steve replied. "Mr. DeRoche is very well known in this community and has a family here. We recommend his bond be on his own recognizance."

"I'm inclined to agree with counsel here, Mr. Prosecutor. This court acknowledges awareness of Mr. DeRoche's background, and I personally would like the record to reflect that I have had the opportunity to observe Mr. DeRoche in both a professional and a social capacity for nearly twenty years. I want this on the record because I want to state two things: first, it is my belief that this knowledge and experience will not bias me in any way during these proceedings; and, second, I don't know of any judge in the district or the county—perhaps the state—who would not have to make the same disclosure. The defendant is released on his own recognizance, with a requirement for drug-and-alcohol testing."

The judge's gavel cracked down, and his head lowered. He reached for the next file to his left and no longer paid any attention to the lawyers in front of him. This matter was clearly settled, and he moved on.

Steve grabbed my arm and pulled me toward the exit.

"You know," he said as we walked toward the door, "it bugs me when guys do that."

"What?"

"Pile on when people are down," he half whispered out of the corner of his mouth. "That prosecutor—I've known him for years. When his wife filed for divorce, he locked himself in his house and threatened to commit suicide if she wouldn't reconsider. He does this and has no problem calling you a psycho for having a gun locked in a safe in your house. Thank God we didn't tell him you owned golf clubs!" he added, and chuckled at his own joke.

As we entered the main staging area outside the chamber, I asked him what else I needed to do.

"Nothing. Go get better. I got this. I talked to Peter. The court in Saline is aware of your probation violation, and this will be handled when you get done with rehab. Focus on rehab. Read some books like I told you about, okay, buddy?"

"Sure. I don't know how long I'll be there. Maybe a week or two."

"You never know. It doesn't matter to me or the court. There will be time for this later. Now, get outta here."

"Thanks, Steve. Talk to you soon."

* * *

My dad took me on the short drive straight to the rehabilitation center, and I sat down. This was my third time entering the clinic for my own addictions, and the first time I was doing it sober. It was also the first time I had the nerve to have someone accompany me. I had been to the clinic several other times, including coming to support family, friends and a few of the legislators I had worked with in the capitol.

One day, I had to drive a legislator in myself. The night before, he had been arrested with a blood alcohol level above .40 (five times the legal limit in many states) and had done several things in the process that I really didn't want to see printed in the media. He showed up for work late, sweating profusely and mostly out of it. Since I was Speaker of the House, no one questioned me when I called off voting, closed session, and said I had somewhere to be.

To allow for committee votes in the morning, our session day began at one thirty p.m. At about two, he approached me and asked if we could speak in my office.

We entered what I called "the gymnasium." My personal office as speaker was bigger and grander than the one furnished for the leader in the US Congress. It is a sight to behold, with twenty-five-foot ceilings adorned with hand-painted designs and exquisite crown molding. The walls are also lavishly decorated with painted designs over the restored plaster. The room has enormous wood windows and ornate chandeliers with the Latin "*Tuebor*" (I will defend) from the Michigan State Seal, and images of an elk and a moose with full racks, leaping forward. It was a privilege to work in such a place, and I truly appreciated every moment I was there.

"What's going on, Chris?" I said to the legislator now standing in front of me.

"Mr. Speaker, I need your help. You ain't gonna like what I say, but you gotta hear me through because I didn't do anything."

"Give it to me."

"All right, so I was drinkin' again, and I shouldn't have been, but they arrested me in my *driveway*. I saw what you did to help Freddy [another legislator] when he got arrested last year, and I need your help."

"Who arrested you?"

"The county, I think. I was really drunk, but they can't just arrest someone in their driveway. Look, I know you don't drink, but you do know that."

"Chris, I've never been arrested for drunk driving. That doesn't mean I've never been drunk. You shouldn't assume anything."

"I'm not tryin' ta do your job, Craig. You tell me what I should do."

"First, why are you here? You look wiped out."

"I didn't know what to do. I was in the hospital all night, and then they processed me at the police station and let me go. I came straight here because I didn't know where else to go. I'm kinda hopin' this doesn't make it into the news, you know."

"Okay, hold here for a second. Let me go tell Jim we're going to be in here for a few minutes, all right?"

I walked across the sprawling room, which had the square footage of both floors of my first home, and out the grand wooden door with custom Michigan brass trim and handles.

"Jim."

"What's going on?"

"DUI. Bad news," I said quietly. "He isn't giving me the story. Do me a favor and call my guy at the sheriff's office and find out what happened and get us a reservation at the rehab clinic you put

100

me in last year. I know it's covered on our health plan. I'll drive him there on my way home."

"You're going to drive him. You think he's going to agree to go?"

"I have a feeling here. If it's different, we can cancel the appointment, but call the sheriff and see what happened. Get Resch over here, too. Can we be done upstairs with voting?"

"You're good on votes. I'll push everything back until tomorrow."

Jim was one of only two people in Lansing, the capital city of Michigan, who knew the truth about my own drinking problem. To everyone else, I just didn't drink, for some unstated reason. I think most attributed it to ambition rather than painful abstinence. Jim is one of the smartest and wisest people I have known personally and professionally in my life. A fraternity brother of mine from college, he had worked his way up to be both general counsel and policy director for the previous House speaker. We played our hand well. When I picked him to be my chief of staff, most of the gossipmongers in town didn't even know we knew each other. This was a convenient arrangement to help me stay current on who was working to take me down or build me up, without their understanding how I got my information. For the most part, Jim ran things the way I wanted anyway, and we never had to question each other when one of us pulled the trigger on a decision.

I shut the door and walked back over to the high-backed Michigan-blue leather chairs, where Chris still sat.

"Couple of things, Chris."

"Anything, Speak," he said, using the shortened nickname I often went by in the capitol.

"You're sweating and shaking. I don't know what-all is going on with you, but I'm going to ask you the same questions I asked Freddy last year. So I'm not trying to pick on you, okay?

"Sure."

"Did you do any harm to any other vehicles or people while you were driving?"

"No," he said emphatically.

"Did you try to use your position to get out of this when you were getting arrested?"

"No."

"Do you have a problem with booze?"

"Well, I mean I drink too much, but that's just my thing. I should tell you one other thing, though, Craig. I was on these painkillers my doctor gave me, too. I told them I musta' been acting drunk because of the painkillers. But those are prescription, see? That's not illegal. You understand."

"No, I don't," I said. "But I think I might understand something about the booze. You seem like you could use a drink right now. Your body is kind of coming down off the alcohol and doesn't like it. That happens when your body is used to having booze in it, Chris."

"How'd you know about that?"

"Someone I know and love has the same thing I think you have with booze, and he isn't perfect, but he's doing better because he got some help with it." I was describing myself but staying comfortably distant from this hypothetical guy.

The door opened, and Jim entered and waved me toward him. This distracted Chris, and he nodded for me to go.

"What you got?" I said to Jim. He was joined by Matt Resch. Matt was my communications director and helped me coin a number of phrases and slogans that made their way into the political lexicon of the day, including "live within our means" and "spend our tax dollars where people are choosing to live, work, and send their kids to school." This was politespeak for some of the more radical changes I sought to advance in Michigan.

"Dude, he hit someone's car and pulled away. They took his plates and called the police. The police were just coming by his house to follow up, and he was asleep in the car in his driveway. The car had the other car's paint chips on it. He gave the police an earful, the staff at the hospital another earful, and his blood draw was point four one." Jim rubbed his hand through his hair, "Oh, yeah, he was on Vicodin, too."

"Well, he told me about the drugs anyway," I said, getting a laugh out of Jim and Matt. "Seriously, Matt, what do you think?"

"I talked to the guy at the Sheriff's office. This is going in the news, but it'll be twenty-four or forty-eight hours. You get in front of this for the caucus you lead but, more importantly, for the institution you lead—the House of Representatives. If Chris agrees to take part in it, he can. Either way, you have to act."

"Yeah, that figures," I said. "Told you I had a feeling, Jim." I paused to gather my thoughts and handed out the instructions. "I'm the bad cop; you're worse, Matt. Jim, you play nice. Call his staff and get his stuff over here. He told me he was planning on staying a few nights in Lansing to avoid going home. I'll drive him myself."

"Got it," Matt said. "You want me to write something now?"

"Not yet. Come in and let's take care of this first."

I walked back in and sat down next to John while Jim and Matt stood in front of us.

"Chris, you're among friends here, and what I'm going to say is just to help you. Got it?"

"Sure, Craig," he said. His upper lip quivered. He wiped the sweat from his brow and looked away from Jim, to me.

"You either lied to me or don't remember what happened last night," I said. "Either way, it's bad. You dropped your name and title and gave a bunch of good people a rough ride. You hit a car and took off. Your blood was point four one." I paused and looked right at Chris. "You could drop dead from a heart attack right here in front of me right now. You can't come off a point four one without help. Your heart can give out. You're not a spring chicken anymore, Chris. This is screwed up. You took a bad situation and made it worse each step of the way. Then you come in here and put this into the institution of the House of Representatives. You shouldn't have been on the floor today. I appreciate you telling me what you know, but Jim or I should have known this before. I'm going to give you two choices, and you're going to choose one or the other before you leave this office."

He sat looking at me, still sweating, hanging on my every word.

"Chris, as your friend, I want to help you. I recommend you get in my car and I'll drive you to an alcohol rehab clinic straight from here. Your staff is bringing over your stuff. They don't know anything. Matt will issue a press release, and for the next thirty days, you go focus on getting better."

"What's the other option?" Chris said nervously.

"You leave my office, I strip you from your committees, and when this hits the press, you'll likely be expelled from the chamber."

"There has to be—"

"There isn't, Chris," Matt interrupted. "If you tell the truth, people will want you to get better. If you tell them the truth before they read about it, they'll respect you. If they hear what you did and you want to try to explain it later, you'll get eaten alive, and I guarantee, your colleagues will give the Speaker no choice but to throw you out. I'm just trying to tell you exactly what will happen. You don't have a day to think on this. You don't have hours. In fact, you're damn lucky we're in front of it now."

"You came to talk to Craig because you wanted help," said Jim. "You know we can help. That's why you're here. I just got confirmation that you're accepted to enter the clinic in an hour. Trust me, Chris, I'll make sure we help you."

"I don't doubt that, Jim. You're a good man and I know you can handle this. Matt, I really liked what you did for Freddy when he screwed up, too, and I wanted you to help. Craig, I'm just sorry . . ." At this point, he started blubbering.

"I didn't fix anything for Freddy," Matt said. "I helped him tell the truth, and that's what I'll do for you."

"Okay," Chris said.

I waved Jim and Matt out of the room so we could proceed. Later, as I was waiting on some last paperwork to be processed at the clinic, my cell phone rang. It was now about five p.m., and it was the governor. She had to ask me a question, and when we were talking, she said, "What's all the noise? Where are you?"

I said, "To tell you the truth, I'm at Brighton Hospital."

"You mean *the*?" She paused. "What would bring you there?"

"Did you hear about Chris today?" I asked.

"Yes, that's been breaking news this afternoon, I guess. But what does that have to do with anything?"

"Well, I drove him here to make sure he checked in. He needs help, and I wanted to make sure he got in here okay."

"You drove him there yourself?" she said, and I heard a little chuckle.

"Yes, I did. I guess I wanted to help."

"My goodness. You really caught me off guard there. I didn't mean to laugh. I guess, for all our talking, I don't know you very well. You are a *good* person, Craig."

"Don't jump to any conclusions, but thank you for thinking it," I said. I hung up and walked back inside to find that Chris had gone back to the secure area, so I wouldn't be able to say good-bye.

The governor's words stung a bit, though she would have no possible reason to know why. I thought about the brass coin I had in my pocket—the coin the clinic had given me for "successfully" completing its program the year before. A coin I rarely carried and kept hidden from everyone. I had it in my pocket because I thought that sharing who I was with Chris might help him. I knew that sharing the truth about myself would have helped him. I just couldn't bring myself to do it. I got close enough to carry it, but I couldn't bring it out of my pocket for someone who really needed a friend who understood. I wasn't at all the "good person" Governor Granholm thought I was. I was still filled with my own fears, dishonesty, and deluded sense of values. As I walked through the doors and headed home, I started to tear up at my own moral failure.

* * *

Years later, after my own arrest, Matt Resch reminded me of the lessons he had taught me more than once in handling bad news in the media, and I assured him I had taken it all in. When I was arrested in Saline, he called to congratulate me on employing "absolutely nothing I taught you, and doing the opposite" to deal with the media covering my own crazy arrest. I laughed with him about this and assured him I knew that if anything like it ever happened again, I would impress him with how well I followed his advice.

Unfortunately, it did happen again. The painful anxiety of waiting to get beat up in the press is an experience no one should ever get used to. I knew that the story was about to hit the news, because three hours had passed since my indictment hearing.

I sat in the same clinic admissions lobby where I had sat —twice before—all by myself. This afternoon, I was with my father and mother when I looked down at my phone. Feeling its pulsing vibration through my coat was enough to make my heart race. It was a text message from a *Detroit Free Press* senior reporter I had known for years. It said, "Craig, we need to speak asap. Seriously."

I had been out of office for three years, and there was only one reason to receive such a text. As I read the message, the nurse called for me to go back to my room. I smiled at my dad when he asked who sent the message. I said, "It's not important, Dad. I'll be fine. It was the newspapers. The story's out. Tell Mom. Make sure Stacey leaves the house. I better go now."

I turned off the phone and began to walk. My mom stood in front of me and opened up for a hug. In my ear, she said, "I love you."

I don't recall ever having heard her say it like that before. It melted me, but I kept sturdy and said, "I love you, too, Mom."

My Dad reached out his hand. I shook it, and he pulled me in for a hug.

I had no recollection of ever hugging my dad before, either.

I took both these moments with me and will hold them dear all the remaining days of my life. I am forever grateful that they both were there for me. I never thought they loved me any more or less before or after they so publicly displayed their affection for me, though I did appreciate the timing of these simple gestures.

I walked past them, down the familiar hallway toward my new quarters in the rehab clinic.

Chapter 10

It's hard to recognize the bottom of your existence while you're still living it.

Beautiful morning sunshine pierced the gloom of the sterile clinic bedroom. I had spent the night in the detox unit even though I entered the facility sober.

The process for entering a rehabilitation clinic involves a physical and medical exam with extensive attention paid to the substances the patient is currently taking and has been on. Most people like me push themselves to the point of physically breaking. Some actually die in the process of sobering up. There is no more important function of a rehabilitation facility's medical staff than the work they do when you first come in. The work they do for people who wish to stay on some prescribed drugs on their way out is an issue for another discussion.

This was my third first morning in rehab. The first two, I was coming down off alcohol, tossing and turning my way through a sweaty yet cold, uncomfortable, sleepless night.

Finding out who you drew for a roommate is much less fun and rewarding than you might imagine. It's a bit like learning that the dorm mate you drew in college has the flu, talks incessantly, won't sleep, and snores when he does. I don't judge anymore, because I'm certain I have been that person in someone else's reality. This time, I resolved to stay reserved, and my gratitude for actually being in the facility outweighed any inconvenience I might remember from past visits.

"Hey," my roommate said as he saw me get up and organize my bag.

"Did you sleep?" I said.

"Nah. Stuff they put me on helped, but I got a ways to go. Be a couple days. You?"

"Yeah. Okay, anyway. I actually came in sober this time and have a lot going on out there, so this was kind of my first rest in a couple of nights."

"I hear that. Dude, you're all torn up. You get run over or something?"

My roommate was looking at the vivid yellow and green bruising that had started to come in across my chest and ribs, and the scabs covering me from knees to toes and along my arms.

"Something like that," I said.

"I'm not tryin' to pry or anything, man. I get it. I've had some rough nights myself. You should see a doctor."

"I did, same as you. I'll be all right. A little pain may help me get it this time."

A nurse came into our room. In the detox unit, they enter your room all the time. They take your temperature and blood pressure every time you fall asleep, or so it seems. I didn't remember this happening last night, though. I was puzzled by it.

"Craig D. You have a new room, so get your stuff and let's go," she announced. "You have to talk to the counselor, too."

"All right. I'm ready. See you on the other side, my man," I said to my roommate, who clearly was going to stay in detox for a couple more days.

We walked down the long hallway, past the nurses' station. The rickety old building hadn't changed any.

The white-painted cinder-block walls and the fluorescent lights made the polished tile floor gleam. The employees who weren't teachers wore scrubs like hospital staff. The facility was, in fact, called a hospital, but it really functioned as a boarding school of sorts once the patient was off the drugs and alcohol.

Because most patients were required to take some sort of

medication for several days at a minimum, the nurses' station, located between the detox unit and the rehab unit, was a hub of activity throughout the day. Across the hall from the nurses' station were a couple of doctors' offices, used for discussions and taking weight measurements and vital signs.

Throughout the day, names were read over a loudspeaker system that reached every room of the building as well as the grounds outside. "Craig D to the nurses' station," or "Jim P to Dr. So-and-so's office."

Beyond the nurses' station (which also served as the post office) was the cafeteria, then another long hallway of rooms for the patients, or "guests," as some called us. The kitchen was vintage high school stuff. The food was surprisingly good and made from the tastiest, highest-calorie ingredients. This was for a good reason: most rehab patients can't eat very well, so the goal was to attract us to the food and help us keep it down. Just about everything had gravy on it, and there were always pies, cakes, and puddings.

I kept walking with the nurse, past the breakfast crowd. We went all the way to the end of the building, to a wheelchair-accessible room. The room was bigger than the others, and the bathroom was downright spacious, with a walk-in shower and bath area. I set my duffel bag down on the hospital-style bed and thanked the nurse.

"Listen, honey, I'm not done with you yet," she said. "You're in detox still, so you aren't missing classes yet, but there was a problem with your file and you got to go to the office. They'll call you in a bit."

Crap. I knew that checking into a rehab clinic sober created problems with insurance, but thought my history here would "qualify" me to stay. This was the first time I really wanted to be in the clinic. I needed help, and being here made me feel safe. My world had been destroyed, and I just wanted things to be quiet enough for me to think and have some days to try to get better. That's what I thought, anyway.

I had called Stacey earlier, and she told me, "Your being in rehab doesn't change anything. I think our marriage is over. I won't go get a lawyer or anything while you're there, but I don't think I'll ever trust you again, and the kids are scared to have you home. They think this will happen again."

I bristled when she brought the kids into it. "That isn't fair. How on earth are the kids scared of me? You weren't even there! I did nothing to make the kids scared. I behaved fine. Ask your mom!"

She agreed with me on my behavior in the house but then said, "Carley heard me talking on the phone, and she's telling Zoe everything. You really did it this time."

"Why aren't my debit cards working?" I asked.

"Because I took all the money out."

"Why would you do that? I can't even buy soap!"

"Because for all I knew, you were going to do the same thing. Like I said, I don't trust you anymore."

"Great. I earned the money and I need some of it. They may not even keep me here."

"Don't come home if they kick you out. You've got to figure it out for yourself. This is your mess, not mine!"

"I'll have to use a credit card," I said.

"That's on you," she said, and hung up.

When the nurse left my room, I called my cell phone to check the voice mail. In rehab, they took everything away from you except your clothes and books—and they checked the books. No cell phones or electronics were allowed. They provided a phone on a small desk between the two beds, and the patient could use a calling card to operate it. Besides these bare-bones accommodations, there were shades on the windows, and a couple of inspirational pictures you might see in a 1980s junior executive's office—the kind of picture with a caption that says "hope" or "patience" and has a glorious picture above with some catchy definition that isn't in the dictionary.

I clicked through the voice mail quickly. Reporter. *Delete*. Reporter. *Delete*. Reporter. *Delete*. Reporter. *Delete*. Paul.

Paul is my older brother. Paul was a character back then. Some would say he was just like my younger brother Kirk and me, but I would argue otherwise. Actually, we were all different in all kinds of ways. You could call us small, medium, and large. It wasn't just our weight, even though Paul weighed 150 pounds soaking wet, I was about 190 at the time, and Kirk was about 250. We all were about the same height.

Kirk's nickname in college was either "Elvis," for his large lifestyle, or "Lumpy," after the character on *Leave It to Beaver*, because everyone's mom or girlfriend thought he was just the sweetest person they had ever met.

Paul never had much in the way of nicknames, because he was always such a straight arrow. He always kept every aspect of his life on the rails. Of course, I knew him better than that. He was out there most nights running the town, drinking, hotwiring the golf carts, and jumping off the thirty-foot diving tower with me and the others. He would also blow it out partying and causing trouble, but looking back, I suspect he may have planned even that. His life now was a measured success in everything he tried. Paul had money not just because what he made each year but because he was disciplined in how he used and invested it. These were alien concepts to me.

Paul and I were quite close because he was only a year and a half older than me and because school-year timing put us only one grade apart. In college, I caught up with him because I graduated in three years and he took four. We both had degrees in finance. There's a reason for that, too. It happened simply because I looked up to Paul and wanted to mimic the aspects of his life that I had always viewed as successful. I learned in adult life that a college degree doesn't necessarily buy you this. At the university, though, it seemed the thing to do.

I can't say that any of the three brothers was actually smarter than any other, but I will say that Paul had to work harder at school and that everything he learned he used for growth and deliberate application. My skills, on the other hand, enabled me to get a finance degree while drunk, do it in three years, and be named Outstanding Student Leader at the university. The week I graduated, though, I bounced a check for my cap and gown and had to look up how to figure out the payments on a car I was looking to buy. I retain only what I think I need, and most things I was learning didn't interest me at the time. Kirk had the broadest intellect and could recite from history, geography, and literature far beyond anything he could have been exposed to in school. In fact, getting him to go to school was the hard part.

Three brothers—same cloth, different cuts.

Paul's input always mattered to me. My dad never corrected me much, but he didn't need to—I had Paul. He knew what I was up to, because he was in on a lot of it. He always backed me, and I had done my fair share of letting him down. The good thing about my brothers was, we let each other have it when something was amiss. It started with the boxing gloves almost every night and progressed to a pretty direct verbal equivalent as we grew older.

"Whatever kind of Hollywood hideout scam you're trying to pull by checking into rehab isn't going to help you," the voice mail from Paul said. "Your story's on every channel and in every newspaper. Rehab didn't help you before. Your whole world is blowing up, and I can't do a damn thing about it. I heard you lost all your income over this and are facing time in jail. Stacey's talking to Jill and saying she thinks you're going to end up getting divorced. Stacey and Jill also think it's a good idea to have her and your girls come out for my annual party on the lake for Fourth of July this weekend. I suppose they want to do this so the girls can all badmouth you. I don't want to be around it and I won't stand for it, and I said so to Jill. So whatever you're doing to hide from the media and spin your latest screw-up, you need to just do it. You need to fix it, and you need to get it fixed by this weekend so I don't have to put up with your drama at my house without you here." The voice mail ended.

My political calculator started whirring, as usual, but this time it really never got past a weak sputter. I was out of moves. Every angle I had in life was cut off. I had no money. My family was going away. I couldn't really ask for help, because Paul was through with me, Kirk was in Afghanistan fighting the war, and my parents had been retired for thirteen years. My name and reputation in insurance, politics, and business had been the only thing that separated me from any other start up or entry-level salesperson, and that reputation was now worse than mud. I was heading to the hospital offices right now to get kicked out for lack of insurance. Without money, with my arrest record, and with Stacey so bitter toward me, I probably couldn't be the dad I wanted to be. I also wondered what I had been smoking to think a few days in rehab would fix what I had been trying to fix since I was 10 years old. I felt stupid for even *thinking* about solutions. I didn't know what to do. I was numb.

I walked downstairs and outside to the smoking area, to wait for them to call me to the office. Sunshine and a bright blue sky met me as I opened the door. I walked slowly past the scores of people chatting in small groups near the picnic tables. I wasn't even listening to what anyone said anymore, and just zoned in on my own conscience. I walked to the back of the smokers and other patients and sat on a waist-high brick retaining wall that faced back toward the building. The sun felt warm on my face, and I felt the air gently waft over me. I closed my eyes. There wasn't a thought in my mind. I was done.

The enormity of all I had lost, the love I had known and forgotten, and the pain of all my failures hit me all at once. Where it really counted, I had failed at every single turn for so many years. So many nights I had told myself that things would be different, and they never were. Everything just got worse. I could take over the world and accomplish anything I set out to do, and I was nothing but a failure and a slave who had lost everything. I was hollowed out, and I was broken.

I don't fully know why I did what I did next, but it changed my life. It was the barest whisper that I heard through deafening pain and loss.

God, I don't know how to do this anymore. I have been trying for twenty-nine years, and I give up. Everything I thought was good is gone, and I don't care about it anymore. I just want this to go away. If you can help me, I will do whatever you want.

113

I sat there, perfectly still and a little surprised at how this came out in my thoughts and how thorough it was. I had captured everything in my thoughts in the moment I said "it" in "I don't care about it anymore." I meant it completely. "It" was everything else in the world. I was completely lost, and I wanted the torment gone.

I opened my eyes.

"Goo-ood morning, guests. We hope you've had a splendid start to your day and are ready for class, because they are starting now. We need everyone in the chapel. You have five minutes. Everyone in your seats and ready for class in five minutes, please."

I felt better. A weight had lifted when I gave up trying. At that moment, I didn't really have any self-pity left, either. That would have required me to be holding on to something, and I had finally opened my grip and let it all go.

As I walked into the building to go to class, a man in a business suit asked me, "Are you Craig D.?"

I paused and stepped out of the foot traffic headed to class. I sized him up. People didn't wear suits in rehab, and I knew he was different in some way.

"Yes, I am."

"Oh, good! I've been looking for you, but I didn't want to call you over the speaker. Can we talk?"

"Sure," I said, stopping where I was.

"No, I mean, can we talk upstairs?"

Now I get it, I thought. *This is the discharge.*

* * *

The hospital administrator led me to my room, which meant for sure that I was being asked to pack up and leave.

The man introduced himself pleasantly enough as "Simon." As we walked, he filled in what would have been an awkward silence, but the small talk felt so genuine I almost forgot where we were going and why. I didn't have time to think of what would come next, and was just relieved at having expressed my heart to God. I walked peacefully alongside and kept up my end of the conversation.

At last, we turned and entered the room, and Simon shut the door behind him.

"I know who you are."

I paused for a moment, then grabbed the name tag affixed to a lanyard around my neck.

"Right, I'm Craig D."

With a tone reinforcing the awkwardness of the moment, he said, "No. I mean, I know who you are."

I looked him in the eye again. I knew what he meant, but the whole thing just surprised me and seemed irrelevant to the situation.

"Oh, that. Well, I don't like throwing my name around anyway, and under these circumstances, well—"

"Please, I'm not trying to embarrass you. Just the opposite. Well, anyway, different. What I, um, mean is, well, I was driving in to work this morning and I was listening to the Frank Beckmann show on WJR, and they were talking about you."

I lowered my head. Frank Beckmann was a friend and he had hundreds of thousands of listeners each morning.

"Listen, don't worry about what they say," Simon went on. "It doesn't matter, and that is not what I wanted to talk to you about."

"Okay," I said.

"I am the hospital's administrator for patients and finance. I don't work with patients, but when I was listening to the show, I just had this overwhelming feeling from I don't know where that you might be here. I drove in and looked in my computer and saw that you were. I also saw that they were getting ready to discharge you, and I went through your file. I looked at your file from 2005 and the one from earlier this year, too. I think you need help, and I think we are the ones who can give it to you. I asked for a team meeting with the administrators, counselors, and your doctor, and we took a second look, and we all agreed that you should stay here."

Tears were welling in my eyes, and a lump formed in my throat. I hadn't asked for this and was quite clear that I didn't deserve any special treatment. And yet, here was a light piercing through the darkness I had endured for days.

"Most people don't know this or care to learn about it, because we treat everyone in the public as part of our mission, but this hospital is owned by a Christian organization. And our mission is to serve God and to help His children when they are sick and living away from Him. Insurance isn't the issue today and isn't a concern to us. I have seen you lead and do amazing things for this state, even for the health-care system, and help a lot of people. You can't fix your situation on your own, and it's time you let others help you."

My gaze had wandered downward as my emotions overcame me. Tears were flowing more freely than I could recall since my youngest childhood memories. My throat ached, and the air seemed to leave my lungs all at once. I couldn't speak or control my body anymore as it shook and I cried without a sound. It was all I could do to take in short gasps of air. Simon was relentless, though. He continued speaking.

"I know what you're going to say, too. You're going to tell me that you need to leave and deal with the media that you need to try to save your marriage and look after your kids, or that you can't afford the time away from your business. But I want to tell you what I believe and what the others who work here believe: God has a bigger plan for you than this, but you aren't going to be any good to Him or anyone else if you don't stay here and deal with your drinking first. I hope you will accept our offer to stay here as our guest for the next thirty days. We have a world-class program, and we can deal with media. They respect us, and we have closed our perimeter to them. You're safe here now. Stay and get better."

I had been crying breathlessly like a small child the entire time that he spoke. I couldn't have uttered a word if I had to, and I was glad I had listened.

I looked up at Simon while he concluded speaking, and something amazing happened. Behind his head, I could see brief sentences stating everything I had done wrong in my life. I could see them all as if they were real. I actually *read* them. The words were in white handwriting, as though they were text on a blackboard. They appeared flat, as though fixed to a transparent surface, and moved with my eyes from left to right. The reading was quite unnecessary, though, because my brain could process all the words and accept them in an instant. It was a supernatural occurrence, and one that I couldn't have imagined before and had never heard of in my life. Later, I would hear of someone else whom God spoke to in this fashion, but that's for later in this story.

The words didn't surprise me at all. I owned each of them. Many of the misdeeds, lies, thefts, and indiscretions had fled my memory altogether through my years of active addiction. The delusion that I had let cover over these memories was removed at once, and I felt better for knowing the truth as it was revealed. It was *my* truth, and I felt safe. I also knew at once that God was, in fact, quite real and was present with me in the room.

"That isn't what I was going to say," I said after holding in my first breath successfully. I was still looking at the words behind Simon's head.

"What, then, were you going to say?"

I wiped my hand across my eyes and nose to clear the tears. "I just said a prayer—maybe the first real prayer in my whole life—like, two minutes ago, asking for help. I couldn't have imagined any of this, but as far as I'm concerned, God Himself sent you here to do this for me, and I will do whatever you say."

I said nothing of the rest of what I was seeing, and continued to take it in.

"Good, then," he said. "It's settled. You let me know if you need anything, but don't worry about finances or the other things. Relax and try to take in what we can teach you."

"Simon, I really don't know what to say about this," I said. "Thank you. This means more to me than anything. I really appreciate this."

"No problem. I know what I'm doing, and it's for the good, trust me."

"I do, and I won't need anything special. Just the chance you are helping me with is all."

"Good. You can plug into class whenever you're ready. I'm off to the business office."

The door closed behind Simon. As he left, my lips broke into the biggest smile I had ever felt, and the hurricane of activity inside me stopped whirling and fizzled out. The peace I felt was inexplicable because I had just been fully reminded of a surprisingly long list of misdeeds in my life. It was peace, though, and for that moment it was an entirely unrecognizable state of being. I had a new sense of certainty. Not much had changed in the world, and yet, my entire world view was upended and a new discovery set in its place, all in an instant.

I gathered my things and went to class.

Chapter 11

After kindergarten, there is nothing new about the dynamics of any peer-group assembly in this world, except the reason why we happen to be in the room.

All the subsequent grades of education mimic our earliest interactions as people. Groups of co-workers share the politics, and in politics, the roles of who will lead the group, or who the cool people, the pretty people, and the nerds are seem to scale out roughly as they do in high school. Not much changes, it seems. This is true for addiction rehabilitation clinics and legislative caucus rooms and every corporate culture I have ever seen. Sure, you are a leader in one group, a nerd in another, and sometimes even one of the cool kids. But the rhythm is the same.

The funny thing about addiction is the strong belief that *my* struggle with addiction is unique. We hold fast to the belief that our circumstances have never happened before in the history of the world. I suffered from this as much as anyone. When I say "funny," I say it as a survivor of addiction. For those of us who end up understanding this paradoxical and ridiculously inflated sense of self-importance, it is actually quite funny to look back at the tragic episodes it took to break the spell that addiction had on us. Clearly understanding my place as a complete peer of all the others in the class was the first gift I received. Today, I could see myself quite clearly in each person here. Before, I would have sworn that my circumstances and life experiences entitled me to different consideration. The new understanding was wondrously refreshing, even as the first sessions in this enlightened viewpoint were thoroughly humbling. No matter how bad a day one of my peers was having, I could remember being there myself. I felt particularly grateful for my new gift, and entirely unsure how to express that gratitude to others. It seemed best just to listen, for once, and start learning from the most basic of instructions.

When I got back to my room, I got to meet Glenn, my new roommate.

"Hello-o-o, Craig, my name's Glenn," he said in a low tone, holding on unnaturally long to certain words in his speech.

"Hi, Glenn."

"Do you snore, Craig?"

"Actually, the answer is yes, Glenn. I snore horribly, but the good news is, I have a breathing machine, so you won't hear a thing."

He looked at me through his thick, yellowish glasses. His shoulders were hunched over his wire-thin frame, and he raised a wrinkled arm to adjust his view before speaking. He hadn't understood a word I said.

"Um-m, well, then. At least, I am glad I got an adult roommate in here instead of one of these kids who are running round doing drugs and chasing girls. I don't understand them a'tall."

"So you're just an alcohol guy, too, eh?" I said.

"Why? Are you into drugs? Everybody takes drugs now. I just drink beer. I know'd I had a problem for some time, but I just drink beer. Maybe a'more than beer, and sometimes I black out and do things I shouldn't do, but it's just beer. You understand, right?"

"Well, I just do alcohol myself, too. I tried a lot of drugs when I was really young, but I had this crazy trick God put on me when He made me. I can drink a fifth of booze and carry on without people really noticing, but I'm not strong enough to take aspirin, decongestants, or even caffeine."

"Oh, caffeine. They don't even let me have my coffee in here. I have a meeting with the staff to talk about this," Glenn declared as though he ran the place. "I am seventy-seven years old and was in the Army, and I don't need to be told what to do about everything. I am not one of these kids."

I looked at his shirt and hat and noticed that both memorialized his service to the country in the Korean War era. I thanked him for his service, as my brother Kirk had taught me to do. He appreciated this and then jumped into an extensive review of what MacArthur had done right and wrong, moving on to what was going on in the current wars, and even catching me up to speed on which of the flowers on the grounds I could pick and eat if I didn't like the cafeteria food.

Glenn was the quite the conversationalist. As time went by, I became adept at sliding in and out of the room at just the right intervals to keep the lectures to a reasonable limit. When it came to addiction, Glenn wasn't any different from me, but it was clear he was in the clinic for his wife and daughter. He didn't buy into any of the feed they were pushing on him to stopping drinking, improve relationships, or any of that sort of thing. I felt bad for him and found myself looking after him more and more as the two weeks we spent together went by.

I wasn't in the room all that much, and Glenn didn't want to talk about much that had happened in the past thirty years, so I found that I spent most of my time trying to participate in class and socializing with others outside. The gorgeous summer days floated past, one after another, and from a weather standpoint it was as if the clinic had been magically transported to Hawaii or Shangri-la. Every day was just about eighty degrees, with seldom a wisp of cloud in the sky. The intense blue skies and balmy sun were healing in their own way.

This time around, my time in and out of the clinic buildings was something quite special. Just walking through the halls of thickly painted concrete walls and seeing the different cultures, struggles, and animated conversations was something I truly began to appreciate.

I found my mind wandering back over my previous visit, years before, and the relationships I had made. There is something special about the motley collection of people assembled in a rehab clinic. The shared desperation and brokenness creates an energy of its own—surprisingly, not a negative energy but a hopeful one. The intimate nature of the discussions, sharing, and general behavior is extraordinary. Some of the time, people let this intimacy lead them toward a romantic type of attraction. The joke from the staff and recovered visitors was always "Don't break those two up, or they'll spread the infection to the rest of the people trying to get better." I can honestly say I felt bad for the people using their time in the clinic to behave the same as they did on the outside. It's far worse than just a waste of time or money. It's a waste of an important slice of life, an opportunity. And for many, it can be the last lifeline that ever gets tossed their way.

About a month after I left the clinic in 2005, I got word that one of the people I knew there had died. His name was Hank.

* * *

I got the call from a friend, Jesse, who had run his company of three hundred employees into the dirt and was running from the IRS and just about everyone else when he landed in the clinic. His downhill slide had started innocently enough.

"Cocaine was always my problem," he told me. "I gave it up when I was about twenty-two, cold turkey. Then, thirty years later, I'm sitting on this beach, just crazy successful and having a great time with my wife, and this dude stops and, out of the blue, asks if we want to buy an eight ball. I thought I would be good and could handle it, but that was, like, three years ago, and I'm losing everything."

He told me the turning point was when his company's controller confronted him after he stole checks out of her filing cabinet and cashed them to buy coke. Awash with guilt and embarrassment, he didn't know what to do. He didn't even have a high school degree and had built a large business from nothing. Then he lost it all. He was a great guy, and I loved talking with him.

"What's up, Jesse?" I said into my cell phone.

"Oh, I'm good, man. I mean, things are bad and all, but I'm trying to step up and sort it out. My wife is still with me. She's an angel. I was calling you about Hank, though. Did you hear?"

"No, what's up?"

"Ah, man, he went and killed himself."

"What do you mean, 'killed himself'? Did he—"

"*Shot*, Craig. He shot himself, like, two days ago. He went down and checked into a motel in Detroit and drank most of two cases of beer, and they said he put a shotgun in his mouth and pulled the trigger with his foot. What a friggin' mess. Can you *believe* it?"

"Uh, no." I paused. "Well, he told me a couple of things and, well, I guess I didn't think he was being literal or anything. That sucks. It's awful. You still good, though?"

"Yeah, man. I mean, I ain't gonna get high over this. Hell, it'd keep me sober if I was gonna get high today, y'know?"

"I do. Listen, I'll catch you later. Thanks for calling."

I hung up and played back in my head the last conversation I had with Hank. At the clinic, we would play volleyball together most nights because neither of us was coordinated enough to make even a simple lay-up shot in basketball. Hank stood about six five and weighed about 280, all of it muscle. He had huge tattoos and wore his machine workers' union jacket and clothes everywhere. A real biker blue-collar guy with a great heart.

About a month before Jesse called me with the news, Hank and I were in the rehab clinic, playing two-on-two volleyball as teammates. In one game, he set the ball up for me to spike, and my five-feet-ten inches barely got it down for the point.

"Nice close, D," Hank said.

"You want to go over this again, big guy?" I said. "I set the ball; you spike it. I set; you spike. Me small and chubby; you tall and strong. Remember?"

We were both laughing straight through the talk.

"You're small and chubby, true. That's *why* I send it to you. You try to get it like you're still in high school. It's hilarious!"

"Ha, ha. You want to lose, tough guy? Keep it up, and these guys'll be talking trash all night."

Turning toward our two opponents on the other side of the net, we stopped talking to focus on the serve.

Smack. The overhand serve went straight to Hank. He jumped and smashed it down and off the floor before it could even reach our side of the net. The game was over.

We turned and gave each other a high five and walked off the court. (With so many people there, even winners had to rotate out of the game.)

Hank wiped the sweat from his brow with his T-shirt and said, "Hey, Craig, what are you gonna do when you get out of here?"

"Serious?"

"Kind of, yeah."

"Go back to work, Hank. I gotta go back to work. I should be there now. You?"

"This is it for me. This is my last chance."

"With the wife or the job?"

"Neither. My old lady can take it. My kids think I'm a loser, though. My job is good, too. Union protects me," he said as we walked over to the weight room. "I mean, I'm done. I can't take this anymore. I've tried everything. If I can't stay sober when I get out of here . . ." He opened the door to the weight room and looked me in the eyes. "If I can't stay sober when I get out of here this time, I'm going to blow my head off and get out of everyone's way. This is a terrible curse, and that'll end it."

"I had a friend do that once," I said. "*Once*, Hank, if you catch my drift. Why don't you come up with a better plan and we can hash it out?"

"I just need something that tells me this is it. This is serious. I need that pressure so rehab works this time."

"Fine if it's for pressure, I guess," I said. "Just don't think it's a real option."

"It *is* a real option, Craig, but I'm not gonna need it, because it's gonna work this time." He smiled as he picked up a dumbbell and started curling it. I smiled back. I thought he was just being dramatic. I had no idea he was serious.

The last time I saw him, he was checking out and brimming with excitement and smiles. His big, muscular arms were pulling everyone into his chest, and he looked like a man on his way forward. I was sorry to hear about what happened to him and too many others over the past five years.

My experience with Hank and dozens of others had been a dour but useful education on the real consequences of addiction. Living with addiction is painful; dying from it looked far worse. My mind clicked through the memories of another four or five people I had known or shared a room with on my previous two visits to rehab. I felt a pang of worry now for each of them. Glenn had captured my concern almost immediately. He was older and not really interested in changing his life. I wondered how his triumph or defeat might play out. I wasn't judging him at all. After all, I was back in the same rehab again for a third time—not exactly a success story.

Everything in the rehab hospital was the same as before. The general descriptions of the people were the same, too, though they each had their own vibrant personal stories of adventure, success, failure, tragedy—and, for far too many, horrifying stories of victimization, neglect, and abuse.

Every single person I have ever met in a rehabilitation clinic is someone I would like to help in some way. Being a parent, I look at it as I would if I came across another's child who was scared, hurt, broken, and in a heap of trouble. My goal would always be to help them out. If the kid were mine, though, I might be too mad and scared to do anything more than yell or punish first. When you aren't the one whose heart they broke or whose wallet they stole from, it's different. You just see the pain. I'm sure others saw the pain in me, too, although, being proud, I tried not to show it much.

* * *

"Hey, man, I recognize you," Henry said. He was organizing some weights as he closed up the gym for the night. Henry was a recognizable face for me. He was the athletic and activities director for the clinic, as he had been when I met him five years earlier.

Henry turned his small but muscular frame my way after finishing the stack. I was still lying down on a bench. I gasped at the pain that clenched in my ribs when I tried to sit up. I rolled off the bench and tried to shrug it off the best I could.

"You're pretty banged up," Henry said. "What's the other guy look like?"

"He's fine. I was just trying to get away."

"Did you get away?"

"Yeah, but not from the police."

"That sucks. When were you here before?"

"Two thousand five."

"Oh, yeah. Your brother came through here, too." He smiled. "You're the politician dude that brought that other politician in here, too. Damn, you went back out?"

"Yes. I would drink a few weekends or trips each year since 05. I thought I had things under control, and, well . . . ."

"Yes, sir! I know that well, brother. Good you're here," he said in his raspy voice. Henry hadn't aged much in five years. He already had graying hair before, and his bodybuilder frame was as rippled as ever. "You know, I used to be a fighter. I've seen that wince before. Anyone look at your ribs?"

"Nah, I'm good," I said, trying to look normal despite the gripping pain in my side.

"Lemme see 'em."

"Okay," I said, lifting my shirt.

Henry looked over the swirl of yellow, orange, and green bruising. "Ow-wee, yes sir, and that ain't done hurtin', either. It's just comin' in. Can't do nothin' about that except ride it out."

"Yeah, I figured. That's why I haven't brought it up to the docs."

"Hard talkin' about the stuff we do that makes us look that stupid, ain't it?"

"Yes, that, too."

"You doin' okay, though? Things working out?"

"Nah, I blew it all out this time. Wife. Business. Money. Life."

"How's your brother doin'?"

"I'm not sure. I'm going to call him tonight. I think he's sober."

"Good. Good that you blew it out, too. Hard for you hotshots to get it. Hell, it was hard for me to get it, and I had nothing. Man, I came here straight out of Jackson Prison, you know. I used to run the yard there. Bad life. I'm glad I got it, though. This is all a gift. My son never had to pick up any of this stuff."

"That's good to hear. I hope the same for my kids."

Henry looked me up and down. I could see pity in his eyes. He was a hard man who had lived a hard life, yet he had compassion for me. He knew I was a hotshot, and he was the hardest man in the place. Even the young, arrogant unbreakables coming through the clinic were no match for him.

"It's like I said, I used to run the yard. Know what that means?" he said. "That means I was the enforcer for the prison, and I had to work my way there. I did a lot of bad stuff to earn that respect. I killed two guys. One of 'em—man, this guy was a bad seed. He terrorized everyone. No one was safe. He was stabbin' and fightin' and conspiring to hurt everyone for everything. One day, he made a run at me, and I held him just like this . . . ."

He put his arm around my neck and grabbed his other shoulder. His other arm pressed against the top of my head. He lifted a bit, and I instinctively rose to my toes.

"Feel that?" he said. "That was just where he was, and the guards came out to me and knew what I was doin', and they gave me the time to do it. One just nodded."

Henry relaxed his hold and let go of me. He said, "I whispered in his ear just before I did it. 'You're gonna die, brother. How's that feel?' And then I just went *click* and dropped him and walked over to the guard. I said, 'What'd you want?' And he said he was trying to break up the fight. He looked back, and the guy's eyes were open; he was dead. 'Fight's over,' I said, and that was it. See, I did some things like that, and I regret them. I needed to do something to stop that guy, but I didn't have to kill him. But you know, what really bugs me are the things I *didn't* do. There was this guy and he was a white dude—probably stole from his work or something and didn't have no place in the prison like people that live there. I heard some noise one day in the bathroom, and I walk around the corner and this Aryan Nation dude puts his forearm across my chest and says, 'This ain't with you, A-rab. We got no problem with you. We respect you. Keep walkin.' I could see them, about five of them raping this guy. You know, I could have stopped it. I coulda' beat all five of those racist pricks into the ground—and did on other days—but that day I walked away.

"This is the thing with addiction, Craig. Guys like you and me don't know how to reconcile stuff like that, either good or bad. We think about the past and future and stuff we don't control. You got to accept what you did, good or bad, and if it's bad and you can't fix it, you got to forgive yourself. Maybe, in some way, what I'm doing now can help that dude I walked past. I dunno, but I can't take back that day. The reason why I fought others and killed that guy, I can't change, and it might have been part of a better plan than mine. I did it, though, and I paid my debt and don't live that way no more. I don't know for sure why I'm tellin' you this, but it seems like you need to know this stuff if you're gonna help other people and if you're gonna stay sober."

I walked back toward the weight bench. "Nah, Henry, I appreciate this," I said. "I get what you're saying, and I have a bunch of stuff to unwind. In fact, one of the gifts God gave me was to understand and know what I'd been doing wrong—a whole bunch of stuff I had either blocked out or drunk away, or was just delusional about. It's come back into my memory since I got here, and I know I have to work through it."

"And you want to accept that what's done is done. Even the hard stuff. Got it?"

"Got it," I said, with a big smile on my face. As funky a pep talk as that was, it made me feel better.

"Now, get out of here. You playin' softball tonight? You're pretty good for a guy who can't even sit up straight yet!"

"Thanks, Henry. I'll be out there. We'll see if I can swing a bat tonight."

Henry was the guy I did come back for after my visit to the rehab clinic in 2005. Just after I left, I bought some art supplies and dropped them off. I appreciated Henry's dedication and service and wanted to support his work. Here was a man with no material wealth, who worked countless hours. The money he made could barely support him living off site, and still he bought the art supplies for others out of his own pocket.

While I was in the clinic back then, they didn't have anything functional for art other than the smattering of new stuff that Henry brought in. We were left to use this hodgepodge of broken and uncleaned brushes, pastels, and whatever paper we could find. During my first stay, I learned that the clinic had a great many talented guests, which really didn't surprise me. Back then and already this summer, I was spending my time in the art room when the other activities and classes were done for the night.

It took me a while, but I got what Henry was saying when he told me the story about prison. You can't fix or paper over the past by buying a few things and dropping them off. You have to do the thing that is a lot harder. The choice isn't hard because it is complicated—it's actually the simplest thing in the world to do. The right choice is generally the simplest, and at the same time, it can be overwhelmingly difficult. I don't think Henry intended to deliver such a high-minded lecture. (We didn't even talk about my gesture five years earlier.) But God uses us all, whether we know it or not, for his own plan. Hearing Henry's story changed a lot of things in me all at once.

I went back upstairs to my room. Walking past the busybodies conversing in every corner, I was still thinking about what Henry had said. I passed by the cafeteria, where the sober and clean addicts picked at pudding and slices of pie during the snack hour. My spirits were high, and I noticed I was smiling again. I had been smiling nearly every moment of every day, and I wasn't even quite sure why. It wasn't because my life had gotten any better. My marriage, finances, and legal situation were all still on thin ice. There was just something there in that string of weathered fifty-year-old single-story buildings that formed a rehab clinic. There was something magical in the air and in that collection of physically broken, spiritually tattered people sharing and savoring the shards of hope. And it pulsed through every interaction.

It had now been nearly two weeks since I entered the rehab clinic, and the phone messages had died away. I had accumulated a fairly long list of contacts I needed to make in the time we had for calls each evening. One of them was my younger brother, Kirk.

I had held back on calling Kirk for a couple of days after getting his voice mail. I didn't call, because I wasn't ready to hear his take on things. He and I were the same in many ways and different in many more. One thing we did share was our addiction to alcohol. Kirk could do drugs, too, although he wasn't as active in those pursuits as in his drinking. Over the years, we both had given each other advice from our different vantage points, though neither of us had a clue. I knew it was his turn to talk down to me, and I tried to avoid it.

I sat at the little desk in my room and dialed Kirk's cell phone. "Hey, man."

"What's up, Kirk?"

"Sorry I'm not there."

"You kidding? You're better off in Tennessee. Heck, you'd be better off back in Afghanistan, considering what the media wrote up here. I did a number on the ol' DeRoche name in town."

"Oh, it made the papers in Tennessee, too!"

"Idiot."

"Nah, I just wanted you to know I feel for what you're going through. I mean, I've been there. You know that. Dad said you were staying for thirty days. I think this is a really good thing. You know, I was in there for twenty-eight days the last time, and it makes a big difference. Are you paying attention this time?"

"I got to," I said. "I'm out of room. Things are pretty bad."

"You don't need to buy into all that crap they try to put you through, though. I just needed the time and space, and I kinda figured it out my own way. I've been sober now since I was there—off alcohol, anyway."

I was in no position to point out the concern I had for my brother, but it was always there. Commenting on it right then would have been ridiculous, though.

Kirk had been sober for more than three years, though he had gone through periods of heavy prescription drug use, only taking them at prescribed levels. He was diligent about this. His physicians at the Veterans' Administration Hospitals prescribed them to deal with injuries and PTSD. To Kirk, and other veterans and patients, this made sense. But the family worried because the drugs altered the way he spoke and wiped him out mentally and physically. It was the first thing on my mind, and thankfully, he brought it up.

"There is one thing I should've taken your advice on when I was there," Kirk said.

"*My* advice? It must be really good, because I'm back in rehab."

"Ha, ha! Seriously, though," Kirk started, then cleared his throat. "When I checked in you were there with me. It was after you'd been in there when you were Speaker. You told me to watch out for the doctors and that they would try to put me on other drugs. You said not to take 'em. Well, I did, and I'm still on 'em. I want off, but the doctor's don't agree, I guess, they are helping me with pain and anxiety from the war. I figure I'll get around to dealing with it. But for now, things are good here and I don't want to drink, so you should know you can do it, too. I thought you *were* doing it. What the hell happened?"

Kirk wouldn't need a play-by-play to understand the score. I knew this and just gave him the key points. "I was only drinking here and there. I probably just drank about ten days this year, but I'm pretty bad now when I do drink. Look at the percentages: I got arrested two of those times!"

"Ha! Nice work. What about Stacey and the kids? You got money?"

"Bad. And no," I answered. "I mean, I came in here with a decent chunk, but I'm losing it as we speak. I don't have any contracts running when I leave, either. I have a big insurance deal going with my former boss at the reinsurance company, and that's what's left. We'll see. As far as the marriage goes, I went to see the counselor with Stacey today, and things aren't so good."

"What'd she say?"

"That she wanted a divorce but didn't want to put the kids through any more immediate shocks, so she wanted to live together for the next six months."

"Ouch. You think she means it?"

"Pretty sure. There was one interesting thing that happened in the conversation, though, and it surprised me. The counselor, who's been sober for, like, twenty-eight years, knows knuckleheads like me. She looked right at Stacey at one point because Stacey was just so resentful and venomously mad. She said, 'Look, honey, I'm not talkin' to him; I'm talkin' to *you*. Block him out right now. You got something in your life you need to do, whether you like it or not. You need to do it for your own good. I want you to listen. Either you work this out with this guy and find your peace with him, or you're gonna take it to your next relationship and destroy that one, too. Only the new guy didn't do anything—it'll be you. You can't just write off your kids' daddy and think you can get away with being angry with him forever. You'll destroy your own happiness. Hear me?'"

"You're kidding me! Nice lady!" Kirk crowed into the phone. I think he and Paul were both very concerned about my marriage and were looking for any bit of good news.

"Well, Stacey's a client, too, I guess. It was kind of surreal to hear it, but it makes a lot of sense. I'm thinking, where on earth did this old lady with Coke-bottle glasses get her Confucius moves?"

"*Zap*. She leveled you."

I said, "If it works for Stacey, I'll be happy. I took a lot out of her, and she has every reason to be as mad as she is. I don't know that I would put up with it if she had done what I did." I was up from the desk now, pacing and chewing my fingernails while I talked.

"So you're gonna do it this time. You need to find something to do to fill your days. That's what I do: try to stay busy."

"Man, I tried that. I spent the first year in the basement, painting oil portraits till three in the morning to fill in the space. I can't fill it in, though. My brain doesn't shut off."

"I hear that. It's my problem, too."

"But this time, things are different already," I said. "I've never been more peaceful in my whole life. It's like I got a whole new perspective on things all at once. It's hard to describe, but I lost everything and I gave up, and now I'm not worried about a single thing. The police even referred Stacey and me to Child Services with the arrest. Still, I think things are going to be fine."

"They *what*?" Kirk said.

"They sent out Child Services."

Right after saying I thought things would be fine, I got emotional thinking about what was happening back home. I paused, and there was silence on the phone. Kirk was waiting for me to talk.

"You know, the ones that take away the kids? How's that? This prosecutor is all in, too. I can't tell the truth about that night, because my lawyers say to keep quiet, and I'm facing ninety days in the clink for my DUI, and now they're going to say I'm a bad parent. This really hit Stacey hard. Talk about resentment!"

"So why do you think things are going to be fine?"

"Because I gave up. If the twelve steps they teach here are worth anything, I went all in at the giving-up part. Looking back on what happened, I didn't even mean to. It wasn't a plan. I was just done. Right away, everything started changing. So I'm just following what's worked for others, I guess. No plan and no need for a plan. I got nothing to angle for. There isn't anything left of value for me to position myself for. I just don't want to be who I was anymore."

"So are you going to go to, like, meetings and stuff when you get out?"

"I don't know. Not really thinking about it. For now, I'm just working on a couple of things, and they're magic. I focus on honesty, acceptance, and living only in the moment. Just these three things took away a whole bunch of bad. They really are antidotes for the anxiety, too."

"Well, they can't hurt you, anyway."

"Look, man, I gotta run," I said. "Stacey and the kids are coming in to the kids' class tomorrow, and I want to have all my stuff done, because I'll be there instead of in my own sessions."

"Good luck."

I hung up and thought about my last sentence. Both Carley and Zoe were coming to a class to learn about addiction. It felt like the right thing to do, and at the same time, I was concerned about it. I couldn't imagine what I would face. The kids had been coming in with Stacey for Saturday visits, and I talked to them on the phone each night before bed. They cried and complained about why I was gone, and it broke my heart each time. I would talk the best I could and mask my tears and breathless gasps and listen to their precious words as they touched my heart.

Now we were going to talk about things together—the whole family there except Phoebe, aged 3. What on earth could I say? How was Stacey going to handle it?

I really had made a mess of things.

Chapter 12

"Daddy!" Carley and Zoe screamed on their way through the door.

"Bunnies!" I called back to them.

They ran to me, and I picked them each up and swung them around in a circle while hugging and kissing them. I took in their beautiful blue eyes and sun-bleached, blond hair as they gazed at me. Their exuberance was contagious. I knelt down to their eye level to take it all in.

"Are you going to be with us all day?" Carley said.

"You betcha!" I said. "Actually, Mom and Dad will be in our meetings for a little while, but then we'll all be together. It's going to be very cool. You get to paint and other things, too!"

This was the first time in weeks the girls would get to see their parents together, talking about things. The circumstances and my time away had had a significant effect on both of them. They expressed it different ways, and it was clear to me in every sense.

Carley felt as though she needed to protect and defend me. She had the posture and manner of speaking of a trained defense lawyer. She wouldn't open up or acknowledge anything that bothered her. During our previous visits, when Zoe would ask questions about why I was in the clinic and why the police came, Carley would snap to my defense and say I hadn't done anything wrong and that she didn't like the police. I couldn't imagine where this might come from. I knew for sure it wasn't her mother's influence. I guess some of it is just built in from birth. I didn't like what she was doing, and

135

explained it away by telling her everything was fine and that she had misunderstood. I told her it might have been scary, but it was just adults having conversations, and everything was fine. I made it clear that while the night was scary and my being gone was hard, I needed to do it to get better and to make sure I never drank again. This gave her hope, and she reacted to it with smiles and happy expressions, but she would return over and over again to her frustration over what she had seen.

Zoe, on the other hand, expressed herself visually. She always brought me paintings and drawings. She was my little artist. She was also my flamboyant, show-stopper child. Her clothes seldom matched and were emblazoned with every color, stripe, and accessory she could assemble. Her drawings mirrored this love of a broad palette, and I always looked forward to her bright, colorful expressions. Since she had been visiting me, her drawings had changed. She presented me drawings in black and red crayon. The paintings were equally bleak. They were hard to look through even when she was nuzzling into my side and explaining them to me. I asked her once why they weren't colorful anymore, and she simply said, "I don't know, Daddy."

After exchanging hugs and kisses with Carley and Zoe, it was time to head out to class. We walked through the sunny atrium and welcome lobby, toward the door. There, we met with the kids' counselors, who took Zoe and Carley off to their class. Stacey and I looked at each other.

"Well, here we go," Stacey said, cocking an eyebrow.

"Thanks for coming and doing all this," I said as we walked toward the conference room where our meeting was to begin.

Inside the room, we sat in humble, postwar-era chairs around a long conference table. The room was small and left little room, and the chairs nearly touched the walls. There were no windows, though the room was brightly lit.

In the parents' meeting, Stacey seemed surprised by the candor of the other couples and the situations they found themselves in. I'm quite certain she had sized up the fix I created, and saw it as the worst possible situation she could imagine on earth. Hearing about the devastation addiction had wrought in the marriages, finances, and hopes of the others seemed to reach her. She leaned forward in the conversations, as if she had forgotten I was even there.

After the parents concluded our meeting and discussion about life and parenting in recovery from addiction, we joined the kids in their classroom. The show was about to begin.

The kids were still running around and wrapping up after their snack break. The room looked like a big, bright, sunlit schoolroom. The little plastic children's chairs were assembled in a circle around the room, and the parents and kids took their places.

"Okay, parents, we have something special to show you all, and you're just in time!" Larry, the kids' class instructor, said. He could have done well in any elementary school or church, or even as a tour guide at the zoo. His genuine enthusiasm was infectious, whipping the kids' energy up every time he spoke.

"We've been doing something very special today, haven't we, kids?"

"Yes!" Their high-pitched yell filled the room.

"Now, hold on, kids. I have to explain where we are to the parents, okay?

"Yes, Larry!" they cried.

"Folks, your kids and I have been working on a project. We had a stack of rocks with words painted on them. The words were things like 'fear,' 'guilt,' 'anger,' 'resentment,' 'jealousy,' and 'shame.' We took the time to explain to each other what each word meant, and then we gave examples of where we each had felt these feelings in our own lives."

The kids and spouses were all hanging on his every syllable, and to me it sounded like the same hocus-pocus I kept learning about in class—the stuff everyone talked about that didn't seem related to my drinking at all. I honestly never understood why the twelve-step programs and counselors and group sessions all talked about these things. After all, my drinking problem was a *drinking* problem, pure and simple. I really just wanted to learn how to fix my problem and move on. Larry seemed to be a guy who took this New Age stuff and made it fun for kids.

"All right, kids, settle down," Larry said. They were all shouting what they were afraid of or what they were angry with, so their parents could hear.

"Parents, you can see the burlap sacks the kids have next to them. When we started today, all the sacks were empty. The kids were carrying them around the class, and no one complained or really noticed the sack at all. Once we identified a fear or something we were angry about or jealous of, we put the rock with those words on it in the bag."

The room was now silent with anticipation of where Larry was going with this. He paused and took in the silence.

"Ready?" Larry said.

"Ye-e-es!" the kids replied.

"Okay, now you can pick up your bags and walk around the room!"

The kids seemed puzzled by this. I think, with all Larry's gestures and grandiose expressions, they were expecting a different trick out of him. They paused, looked down, and picked up their sacks. Most couldn't even hoist the gathered tops of the burlap over their shoulders and quickly gave up. One boy made a show of successfully carrying his bag like a miniature Santa, but his cheeks and huffy-puffy breathing gave him away.

"Okay, great. That's enough, that's enough. Set them down and listen to me, okay? Set them down," Larry continued until order was restored.

I leaned forward to listen. Larry's theatrics had a point, it seemed, and I was now interested in hearing him out.

"Wowie, oh, man! Can you believe how heavy that was?"

"Aaah!" the kids moaned.

"What was in the bags, kids? That's right, your fear, anger, resentment, guilt, and other problems, right?"

"Yes!"

"And they are pretty heavy to carry around, too, right?"

"Yes!"

"Does anyone want to keep carrying those around?"

"No!"

"What if you had to carry them all day every day?"

"Boo! No way!" they shouted.

"Well, let me tell you something—and it's important you listen to this," Larry said as he sat down. The room calmed. "Your parents who have been addicted to drugs or alcohol have been carrying around a bag full of rocks. They've been carrying around these problems the same as you, only they never learned how to take them out of the bag. They never wanted to have the rocks in the first place, but everyone gets the same feelings. *Everyone* gets them. Nobody *wants* to carry the rocks around. Your parents don't want to carry them any more than you do. Since the problems—the rocks—cause pain, your parents tried a drug or alcohol, and you know what this did?"

The room was silent. I was stunned.

"The alcohol took it away. At first, it made them forget about how bad carrying the rocks felt, and they could be happy. But with drugs or alcohol, this doesn't really help you, because the rocks *stay in the bag*. And pretty soon, you need more and more drugs or drinks, and then not even the drugs or drinks help you forget about the rocks you're carrying—in fact, the drinks and drugs make the bag heavier!"

The kids looked up to him as if he were a magician pulling live doves out of his hat. He may as well as said, "Voila!" I couldn't believe the simple, beautiful truth of what I was hearing. Suddenly, twenty-nine pretty good but frustratingly encumbered years of my life made sense to me, and this clarity was coming out of a guy who could have been one of the Wiggles kids' TV characters.

"So your parents have been lugging their way through life . . . ." Larry got up, swung a full bag of rocks over his shoulder, and staggered across the room. "They've been carrying around this bag of rocks, and they've been in a lot of pain. They want to be better to you and to your family, but it's hard. And they thought drinking would help, but did it?"

"No!" the chorus of kids' voices cried.

"Wouldn't it be great if your parents knew how to take the rocks out of their bag?"

"Yes!"

"I agree!" Larry exclaimed. "And that is what they are here to do. No one has to carry around the rocks, and if you learn this, you never will have to, ever in your whole life. "We are here . . ." Larry began to lift the rocks, one by one, out of the bag and set them on a table. ". . . to take out the rocks and to teach your parents how to take these problems—*all* of them—one at a time and let them go. God will take them all away if you just learn how to ask, and this will work for each of them and everyone else you know. See, your parents aren't different from other people. They're just the same. We all have the same problems; it's just how we deal with them that makes us different. Your parents didn't know how to deal with them like other people, and they made a choice to use drugs or alcohol. Do you think that was a good choice?"

"No!"

"But it's okay now, because you know what? They made the best choice of all. They made the choice to *fix* this. Your parents love you and they know drugs and alcohol don't work, and they want to know how to make the right choices. This is what they learn when they're in the grown-up classes. Isn't that great?"

"Yes!"

The kids screamed and applauded, and I choked back tears. Of all the unlikely ways to learn something in this world, the simple, functional problems of my everyday life were summed up and explained to me in a kids' class.

* * *

I was born the day Janis Joplin died. This intrigued me when I walked past her *Greatest Hits* anthology compact disc display in a retail store that used her birth and death dates for cover art.

Something about seeing my birth date written out caught my eye. I thought to myself at the time that whatever demon took her down must have leaped from her right into me. When I saw this, it was probably ten years before my arrest.

Self-pity is part of the deal, I guess. It comes along in the same package with self-righteousness, self-centeredness, selfishness, and any other form of living for self-will that lures people into pain, resentment, fear, and, inevitably, failure. The living for self, being driven by self-will to seek self-made solutions, was my thing, though. Fancying myself a dab hand at this method, I pursued it right into the cauldron of burning wreckage from each blistering failure. Then I would get right back up and do it again.

The progression would sometimes take only days from rise to dramatic fall. Sometimes, it would take long years of joyless toil, managing booze on a daily basis before something finally fell apart.

The hard thing about changing had always been the endless stream of jumping-off points from the real path to peace, freedom, and happiness. Looking back on the decades I spent fighting the battle my own way, the seed of truth planted in me on various occasions was sometimes snatched away because I didn't understand it. Or I abandoned it at the first sign of trouble. Sometimes, I disregarded the seed and wrote it off as unnecessary because my life was otherwise good by the material standards of the world.

This time, though, things were taking root. God loved me enough to take away any material distraction or wealth. My family was all but gone, my finances ruined, my ability to earn an income shot, and I faced jail time. No form of trouble could add to the hill of hurt I had acquired. Any new problem stones thrown on the pile would only cause others to fall off. I was at my bottom beneath this crushing weight. When I no longer fought anyone or anything, things changed. The seed planted in my heart landed in deep, rich soil where it could grow unrestrained by emotions or circumstance. Most of all, God had quite visibly and unmistakably shown Himself to me. Nothing in this world could ever shake me from the clear understanding of what had happened. Yes, God had given me the gift of understanding all that had passed unnoticed during all those years.

* * *

After the kids' class finished, I went into the lobby of the newer wing in the rehab clinic, where I now had a room. This section of the unit was called "partial." There wasn't anything "halfway" about the place, though. It just meant that the patients in this area of the hospital had a couple of hours' more time to themselves each day.

In the original building, the day was scheduled down to the minute, from six a.m. until lights-out, with only minor breaks. The new building presented itself in a much brighter light. Gone were the old-style cinder-block walls with narrow slat windows just beneath the 1950s-style drop ceiling. In their place were much newer-looking cinder-block walls with floor-to-ceiling windows every couple of feet. Outside were flowers and beautiful landscaping. Everything about the place was fresh, new, and peaceful. It looked like the image I would have had of a psych ward in a high-end hospital. I laughed to myself when struck by the fact that it was indeed a psych ward of sorts, in a high-end hospital.

Gathering my thoughts, I returned to my room and collected my homework and some questionnaires I had filled out. Today, I was to meet a new counselor, and I wanted to be prepared. I felt at peace after what had happened in the kids' class earlier. So much had changed in me. A puzzle had been solved. Normally, this would have led to my coming up with ingenious ideas about the simple truth I had learned. In my life, I had spent a great deal of time and energy trying to solve my own problems and, when the opportunity arose, others' as well. It didn't matter that the other person might not want my help. I fancied myself a helpful person, and I would pore over the things that didn't seem right in my life or someone else's. I would search for fixes and try to help where I could. Many times, people saw this as me being smart and helpful. I'm sure that just as many times, people thought me cocky, self-righteous, and high-minded (to put it nicely). Because of my position and success, people listened, and some were probably astute enough to sift the good ideas from the blather. But this time, I remember not needing to know anything else beyond *this one solution*. It helped solve an important problem. For twenty-nine years, I hadn't even known what the problem was, and now I had learned of the problem and its solution in the same instant.

As I sat in the sunlit waiting area for my appointment with the counselor, I said a small prayer. It went something like this:

"God, thank you for all you've done in my life, and thank you for what you showed me earlier today. I know that you have better plans for me, and in time, things will work out the way you want. Please, Lord, help me. Show me how you want me to repair the damage I have done to my marriage and family, my job, and my ability to earn a living."

While I prayed the last sentence, I was thinking. I know that when Jesus and the Bible referred to your "heart," they didn't mean the blood-pumping muscle in your chest. It seems to me that what the Bible is talking about is your thoughts or, more specifically, your innermost subconscious thoughts. At the moment I was saying this prayer, my thoughts weren't all that subconscious, though. I was running them in plain view, right next to words I spoke in my mind.

I was thinking about how I would fix my political career. It was a crazy notion, I knew. I had told myself and accepted that I was done and needed to move on. I had let go of everything—even the thoughts of keeping my house and marriage—and had made great progress as a result. All of a sudden, though, in my head I was thinking about what I could fix! I was truly incorrigible to the very end. And I felt it even as I let my selfish subconscious roll, free and undisciplined, alongside my prayer.

"Who said I did these things so you could run for governor?"

"What?" I said in my mind.

I snapped to attention. A shock wave went up my spine, and I could feel the surge of adrenaline. The hair rose on my neck and arms. *What the heck just happened?* I looked left and right and tried to keep my composure.

"Who just said that?" I thought in my head to buy myself time.

But I knew who had said it. It was clear and almost audible. Even more, when I heard the word "these," I understood what "these" were, and saw the image of several of "these things" in my mind's eye. It was as though my brain was being run externally and I was being shown a path. It was unlike any path I had imagined, though. This path didn't show me anything about where I was going. It just showed me, in a shocking and humbling way, where I came from and why. It happened all at once.

My eyes were open, and I was composed, and inside I was turned completely upside-down and picked back up in the same instant. I was at once utterly disoriented and at peace. The only lingering confusion was driven by my wanting to know more. I would receive no more instructions, though. The message had been delivered, and I had received it. It was clear. I didn't fully understand it, though I was able to let go of all my silly ambitious, prideful notions immediately. I gave an audible laugh. Then the door opened, and my new counselor called me in.

"Mr. DeRoche, nice to meet you," she said.

"It's good to be here," I said. I was sitting upright and smiling with a certain sense of giddy delight at the thoughts streaming through my head.

"You certainly seem to be happy to be here."

"Oh, it's just, I had this cool thing happen just now and I'm feeling better about some things."

"Anything you need to share?" she said as she sat down while gesturing for me to do the same. I sat in a metal office chair. She sat behind a fake-wood desk of the kind they sell at a discount office-supply superstore. Her leather office chair looked well worn but comfortable.

"Not really, no. Nothing bad. All good."

"Okay, let's get started, then. I've spent some time with your file and read it all the way through. It's quite a story,"

"What do you mean?"

"I'm not trying to embarrass you, Craig. Can I ask you a question?"

"Sure."

"Why are you here?"

The question took me by surprise. This older woman with dull red hair, wrinkles, and a warm, inviting smile looked straight at me over her reading glasses and waited for a response. I had told a lot of stories in my past, including to counselors, but I knew that my report had been updated. I was in the hospital for the third time and had been honest about who I was and what I was facing, and I had accurately described my drinking career.

It took me a moment, but I began. "Well, I guess I just, um . . . well, I destroyed everything in my life outside of here and couldn't even stay here without help. And I've been trying to figure this out for twenty-nine years, and I just want it gone. I realized I couldn't fix it, and I gave up trying to do it my way, and I've been trying to learn about what works for real."

She never took her eyes off me while I spoke. It was hard for me to speak this directly and succinctly to someone else about who I really was and what I really wanted in my heart. Something in me was different, though. I spoke the words softly, but I felt great inside as I said them. It was a new experience for me, and a new sensation altogether.

She looked back into her notes and smirked, then looked up at me and said, "It's just not what I'm used to seeing, that's all."

"*What* isn't?" I said.

"People like you," she said, and paused. She focused on my eyes again. "It's just that you are highly functional. In fact, you are *really* highly functional. I don't think I've ever seen anything like it." Her words ended with a little laugh.

"I'm not sure I—"

"Oh, heavens, look at you. I am not putting you down."

"I didn't think that. I just don't—"

"Don't explain yourself. Let me explain now," she said.

I sat back in my seat as she continued. "I've been doing this for twenty-eight years now. I see everyone come through here: business leaders, rock stars, and all sorts of other accomplished people. It comes with being one of the leading facilities for addiction in the world. I'm just amazed that you seem to *get* it. I can't imagine what happened to you, but it's a blessing to see it. I wasn't sure it was possible. People like you almost never get it. You always try to do things your own way. Many can even stay sober, but they don't get the gift, because they can't let go. Do you know what I'm talking about?"

"Um, I'm not sure about other people, and I'm not really sure how it happened to me if we're talking about the same type of thing. I'm just happy now. Even though everything is still a mess, I haven't ever felt like this."

She giggled. It was a funny experience. I giggled back, and I wasn't sure why, but I was in great spirits, and her humor was contagious.

"I'm in recovery myself. I wasn't able to do much of anything when I was out there using, though. I wasn't functional for much of anything. I never had any success or things to hold on to, and so it was easier for me. People like you believe you can succeed on your own, no matter what you have destroyed. You always try to fix it up with your skill and talent and what you have left. If I could bottle up what happened to you and give it to others, I would. I simply don't know how to do it, though, as a counselor. I just have to let my Higher Power do it."

I looked at her a little sheepishly. "So where am I? You say I'm highly functional, and all that. I don't want to be too down on myself, but I really don't have the ambition or desire I had before I came in here. At least, it's different now."

"Exactly my point." She leaned forward and raised her hand above the desk to make her point. "Stop moving. Let things happen. Pray for the answers and solutions. Have you read the third-step prayer?"

"Yes."

"Keep reading it. You'll have some work to do, and you're going to find that you are never really out of the woods. The good news is, that doesn't make you weird. No one else is ever perfect, either— or even close. They cut themselves off from good because they don't understand the humility of that particular prayer or they think the prayer is only for alcoholics. Don't try to fix your situation. Keep speaking honestly and start asking for help when you need it. I can see that you have humility, and you should make sure you keep it. I'm guessing you weren't like that before."

"Far from it," I said with a smile.

We both giggled again, and she rose from her chair and extended her hand.

"It's a pleasure to meet you and see what God can do."

"Thanks," I said. "He's doing a lot today."

Chapter 13

It was my last day in rehab, the first day after a twenty-eight-day cycle. I figured I had already attended the full curriculum, and so I came armed with my journal and other odds and ends to finish.

It was a beautiful, sunny Michigan day—not a cloud in the sky, and about eighty degrees outside. Another perfect day. Every day had been perfect, it seemed. The entire month had no more than a couple of hours of rain.

My rhythm was well set by this point: wake up at six thirty a.m., eat a healthy breakfast, attend classes, work out in the gym for at least an hour, and read everything I could get my hands on. I felt good and was in the best shape I had been in since my days as a student athlete. Even the massive gouges on my shins and feet where starting to resemble normal scabs. My feet had a beautiful white strip of skin across them where the straps of my flip-flops covered them each day. By this sign alone, I knew I had caught up on my peace and rest.

Being here for a month made me different from most of the other guests. Only a few of us stayed for a month. With changes in insurance policies, and with people driven by their belief that they could figure out their own solutions, it seemed that most left after five to seven days. I had the privilege of getting to know some terrific people who had been through some terrible times. The way the classes and activities worked, you got to interact with most of the ninety-seven people who were there as patients on any given day. I spoke with hundreds of people like me, and I truly valued my time with each of them.

Today, I had to get ready for the real world, though. I had only one ear on class as I sped through my duties and arranged my affairs. Nothing on the outside had improved. I was welcome to move home, but Stacey was still unsure whether our marriage would survive six months. And she made it clear I could forget about trying anything to avoid that outcome. I was to be a roommate and a comfort for the kids and nothing more. I needed to answer for myself in two courts and was certain to get jail time. The media were waiting for me, too. The papers and TV stations ran stories with every change in my case, right down to the smallest item, including date changes for hearings. Not much money was left in our accounts, and no new dollars had come in since the money I earned the month before my arrest. I was in a world of hurt and had to face it head-on.

Sitting in class that afternoon, we were asked to do an exercise on death. The instructor said he could choose birth, divorce, or some other life event, but he wanted to make a point. He chose death. He said the death of others we know and love can affect us, and many who suffer in addiction never look back at what this means.

Blather, blather, I thought. What on earth could it mean to me? My first experience with death came in 1989, when my great-grandmother died at 102. We were happy for her at the funeral. Both my mother's parents had lived long and good lives, too. My father's dad had lived into his eighties, which was young for my family, but he had smoked for more than fifty of those years. It just didn't seem as though this topic was a big concern to me.

I went back to writing in my journal. I wanted to capture the thoughts I had upon leaving and document some of my fears and remaining anger and resentments. I was really quite at peace despite the oversize to-do list I had waiting for me when I got home. I sat there, scribbling away on my notes and mostly tuning out the chatter of class, when I was struck with a thought out of the blue: *Jeff.*

What? I asked myself inside my head. *Why Jeff?*

Hmmm. I must have flashed on him for some reason. What was it, though?

I allowed myself to relax and think about Jeff. I hadn't thought about him for at least a couple of years. The nightmares that lasted for several years following his death were gone. It wasn't as though I had bad dreams every night, but they had stayed steady at three or four a year since he died at age 23.

It was the afternoon of December 20, 1993. I had graduated from college in 1991 and was working my second professional job, for an insurance company, as a workers' compensation claims adjuster for large companies and governments that self-insured their exposure. I managed a team and was fascinated by the dozen or so companies I managed risk for. Many of the executives would compliment me on my abilities and talent and ask why someone like me didn't handle their account. "That's where the money is," they would say.

My brother Paul and I had bought a residential maid service and were trying on our entrepreneurial hat. The business was flat, and we merely broke even on $125,000 in sales. It wasn't much fun, and we both had professional jobs. Owning the business taught us nothing other than that absentee ownership was unsustainable at such a small level. We were stuck, though. We had bought the business on a note that had about $25,000 to pay down, so we committed to run it through. In our spare time, we did have success buying houses with very little down payment. We would buy the houses, move into them, and then rent them out. It was helpful to be young, single, and flexible enough to move quickly. One such move took only two weeks from start to finish: buying the house, occupying it, and then moving out for a paying tenant.

There were little secrets, tips, and techniques for every angle of the businesses we pursued, and the rental business was the most straightforward. For years, I had been buying and selling cars and motorcycles. I had even worked out an insurance policy. Before buying something that I thought I could sell for a profit, I would place an ad for it in the local paper. If I got more than twenty phone calls in the first two days, I knew it would sell at that price. Knowing this, I would then go buy the vehicle or, in the example of the house, arrange financing with payments less than I could expect in rent, and move forward. It was simple and repeatable.

Everything in my life that has ever worked has been simple and repeatable. Nothing complex has ever paid enough to be worth my labor or investment. I knew this at an early age, and yet, I continued to be attracted to the complicated and laborious failures. Case in point: the maid service.

I was working on yet another angle to prop up the housekeeping business and make it pay, when I got the call.

"Hey, Mike," I said. "What's up?"

"It's Jeff," Mike said, sniveling and gasping into the phone.

"What?"

"I've been trying to call . . . to call you all day, and . . . ." Mike wasn't getting the words out. "He's dead."

"Mike, I . . . What the . . . !"

"I can't believe it, either, but it's true. Last night."

"But how? Did he get in an accident?"

"No, Craig. He killed himself. In his own garage. I . . . I just don't understand it."

I could almost understand it, in my own perverse way. I loved Jeff. He, Mike, Paul, and I had caused so much trouble together and shared so many adventures that I intuitively felt his pain. After we all left home for college, Mike had been close with Jeff. They were roommates at Ferris State University while Paul and I moved our circus to Central Michigan University. We saw each other enough because the two schools were only an hour apart, but things had changed. And now things were changing again.

When Jeff died, Paul and I had been out of school for a couple of years, and Mike was graduating. Something in me just felt some burden that Jeff was carrying, and I never stopped to think about things. For the longest time, I couldn't even bring myself to cry. It didn't seem real then. And it still didn't seem real when I reviewed what happened in my mind during the exercise in alcoholic class nearly two decades later.

The days after Jeff's death are burned in my memory. Everyone I grew up with came home and assembled for the funeral. Each day, we were together around the clock. We mourned, caught up on each other's lives, and at night we even smiled and drank. I remember thinking one night, when my friends had stopped drinking, because they had been drinking for a week straight and we weren't on spring break anymore, that I no longer could turn it off. Not even for a day. I couldn't turn it off on spring break back in 1988, either, when Jeff, Mike, and I went to Daytona Beach, Florida, for ten days with ten guys in two cars.

These were my closest friends at the time, and all ten of us shared a hotel room. We had ten guys and ten days, so we decided that each day one of us would buy ten cases of beer and some booze so we all weren't having to do math and shell out money all the time. It worked well, especially for me. I never really did turn it off after that week and a half.

It was Christmas night, six days after Jeff's death and two days after his burial. The friends from high school had gathered for one last party after our family visits and Christmas festivities. We all were loose now, and the party was loud and fun. Friends were shooting pool, playing cards, and living it up. We were finally moving forward a bit.

I remember my friend Tim, who had also been on the spring break trip, coming by and telling me he was leaving at about eleven p.m. He was out of school, had a long-term girlfriend, and had become an avid snowmobiler.

"Why so early?" I asked.

"I have to go snowmobiling and want to be on the road first thing in the morning."

"Stay, you daisy!" I said.

"Nah, I want to go. I'm serious. I've had enough of this. I'm going up north and gonna blow off some steam. You stay and party—daisy!"

"All right, see ya, man," I said. "Drive safe."

"I'm not drunk. I knew I was driving."

"*Ciao.*"

"'Bye."

I got a call the next night. Tim was dead. A car had hit him while he was crossing the road on his snowmobile.

Tim had gone ahead of the pack to mind the traffic for the rest of the crew he was riding with. Apparently, his snowmobile had come off the steep incline and flopped right down on the road, which had no shoulder. The trucker that hit him didn't have a chance. Tim didn't have a chance. It was a moment, an eyeblink, and he was gone.

Tim looked peaceful, almost restful, in his coffin. That was what I took away from the viewing. I didn't have anything to say, and I couldn't feel any of it. I was grasping for something and didn't know what it was. It didn't hurt, and I didn't cry. I felt emotionally paralyzed. I was disconnected from the events and from what I saw in my friends' reactions.

On the inside, though, my anxiety grew until it felt as if it would break through my skin or shoot out of my ears. It wouldn't stop. It never did stop. But when I drank, it slowed down. And when it was slowed down, I could manage it—or so I thought.

I made it through about three more weeks of work before asking Walter Fueller, my boss's boss and the president of the insurance company, for a meeting. He had taken a liking to me and took time to mentor and guide me through some tossing and turning in my job. He often mentioned that he expected "bigger things" of me in my future. I wasn't quite sure what I was going to say, and surprised myself with what came out.

We were sitting in his big office, surrounded by wall plaques and bookshelves. He lounged back in his oversize chair as though he was about to put his feet up on the desk. He rested his hands on his belly.

"What's up, Craig? You wanted to talk?"

"I can't do this anymore." I just blurted it out.

He straightened up in his chair and leaned forward. "You mean you aren't happy with your team, or your job in general?"

He was surprised and confused by what I was saying, but he helped me along.

"You know I lost a couple of close friends two weeks ago, right?"

"Yes. I don't mean to be disrespectful, but that news traveled fast around here. What a horrible circumstance for them and their families, and also for you and all your friends. Are you okay?"

"Yes, but when I say I can't do this anymore, I mean I can't work here anymore. I have a very specific thing I need to do and have been afraid to do it. I realize how short life is, and, well, I think I just need to get after it."

"So you intend to quit? Where are you going to go? If I thought I could match a salary or change your title or work here, I'd do it in a heartbeat, but I don't think that's what we're talking about. Do you have another job?"

"No, I don't have another job, and no, I don't know exactly what I'll do next. I just wanted to share this with you and maybe get some advice. I know this is backward—"

"Ha!" he said with a smile. "Look, I think the whole world is out there for you. Can I give you my thought?"

"Sure," I said.

"Go and sell these accounts for a living. The companies love you. Make the real money. The work is nothing once you get going. If you want, I'll help refer you into one of our agencies looking for a young producer of new clients."

"Thanks," I said. "I will take you up on that."

I left the meeting with my job and permission to shop around. I thought it was a pretty cool offer—maybe even too cool. I never did take him up on his offer to help. I was too determined to blaze my own trail. I was gone from there within a month and never looked back.

I was off to the races. When Jeff died, it was like the starter's gun going off to begin the race of my life. I started running and never looked back. And since that moment, it had been seventeen years of blissful highs and torturous bottoms, and never a thought given to the race itself or when I started it.

Sitting in my last class in rehab, I was broke, getting divorced, facing jail time and a media circus; and my career, reputation, and ability to get new clients were gone.

I felt peaceful and grateful for the death exercise in this class. When I thought about how I intended to tune out the lecturer, I was even more grateful that I could make use of the time and think through such a pivotal time in my life, even though it had occurred seventeen years earlier.

I could miss Jeff and Tim and value my life and be grateful for it. And I didn't have to get back on the treadmill if I didn't want to. Even if I got back on, I didn't have to run off willy-nilly again. I could wait and make sure that what I did was of use to myself and my family. That was the notion I had sitting in that classroom. And that thought made me feel better about where I was and what the future might hold.

Every moment of my life since these events was colored by what happened to Jeff and Tim, but I had refused to admit it or face my own fears. It was time for me to look inward and accept what had happened. When they died, the starting gun had fired, and I was off and running to avoid their fate. I wanted to live and didn't know how. I was afraid to let my dreams go unrealized and decided to take bold and decisive action. What was the purpose of my life? I was trying to figure it out on my own. Sitting there in my last class on my third visit to rehab, something dawned on me. If I couldn't reconcile the past in a healthy way, I would always need something to relieve my stress, fear, pain, and anxiety.

I can't say I wrote much for the rest of the hour, but the teacher's choice of topic was key to my making the connection.

When class was over, I got up, packed up, and moved out of my room in the rehab hospital.

While my paperwork was being processed, the staff gathered those of us leaving on that day outside for a send-off. They called it a "coining ceremony." At the small gathering, the staff gave me a brass coin for completing the one-month program and asked me to speak.

I said, "I consider alcoholism to be a blessing, because without it, I wouldn't have lost everything. And without losing everything, I wouldn't have surrendered and found this new peace and happiness. I was far too selfish and prideful to learn this on my own or in my other two stays here. I am blessed, and I wish I could bottle up what I feel, and give it to each of you. Remember, we're the lucky ones, too, because we're here. A lot of other people are out there dying today who didn't get here. Worse, there are a lot of eighty-year-olds out there who are going to die as angry, fearful jerks, who never had a chance to change their lives, because their character flaws didn't force the issue to a head or get them arrested. I'm glad my world collapsed and I got arrested. Now, wish me luck in court!"

My little speech met with laughter and applause.

I said my good-byes, exchanged phone numbers and plans with some new friends, and headed home.

Chapter 14

Harold, my attorney, put his hand on the back of the bench. "You sit here."

We entered the darkened section of the municipal courtroom, where the guests, the defendants, and their lawyers sat. The room was empty except for the two of us.

"I didn't see any media out there, but you never know," Harold said. "People in the court and police tip off the media for money, so the judges can't control it. I'm going to find out what's happening. I want you to be in and out here. I want to find out if the prosecutor will cut a deal so you move past this. There won't be anything today except scheduling of your trial in a couple of months. No big deal. You won't have to say a word. Sit still and don't talk to anyone."

"I can handle it," I said.

Harold strode past the tables for the defense and prosecution and went out the big door where the judge enters and leaves.

I was sitting there, feeling nervous but hopeful since the room was empty. I'd been home a couple of days, and Stacey hadn't been mean, hostile, or even rude to me. We didn't talk about anything, but she sure wasn't coming at me the way I thought she would.

My thoughts wandered to my problems. First, I had to deal with this court case. Second, I had to deal with my court case and probation violation in Saline. That would probably get me three months in jail. I had to deal with my marriage and the kids. I needed to find something to do to earn money. I had to deal with the media.

I had about fifty calls to return, many concerning friendships lost or gained.

First things first, Craig. You can deal only with this now. Don't worry about the other things. You can't fix them today. I felt better thinking this way and returned my focus to the matter before me.

I heard some clatter in the background as a man and a woman entered. They sat immediately to my right, and I nodded to them as they set up their camera gear. They both nodded back and carried on with their conversation.

"Any idea if he's actually going to be here today?" the man with the camera said. It was a big one, with a huge lens.

"No, but they said he would be," said the woman with the notepad in her hand. "That's the best I can do."

"Well, I've been out here twice, and it's a long drive and a waste of time. We should have plenty of pictures of him already."

"The news editor said we needed one of him today. He wanted it here for effect. I don't follow politics, but this guy's sort of a lion in the Republican Party, I guess. He's done some big things, and we get to cover him going down."

I grimaced but tried not to show any reaction.

"Sounds like a loser if you ask me," the cameraman said. "Was he trying to kill someone or not? I mean, they make it into a big deal, and if he was running around trying to shoot his kids, then it should *be* a big deal."

"I talked to his friend, Mick. He said he saved Craig's life. He was trying to be the hero. This Mick guy's a piece of work. Not the kind of friend you want to have. I don't know what this Craig was doing, because Mick didn't see anything, but the editor says this is news."

"I don't think it is. It doesn't sound like he did anything, and everyone's making a big brouhaha about it anyway, and then he's going to call his rich Republican friends and he's going to get off. I don't know him, and I already don't like him."

I kept looking forward. It was obvious they weren't playing with me. They simply didn't recognize me. Funny, but all those pictures the newspapers ran of me when I was fifty pounds heavier and had a full head of hair were good for something after all!

Harold reentered the courtroom, followed by the clerks and the judge.

"All rise!"

We all stood.

"The clerk will read."

"Yes, Your Honor. The first case is that of People versus Craig DeRoche."

"Will the defendant and counsel come forward. Mr. Prosecutor, I see you're here."

I stood and glanced at the reporter and photographer as I walked by. They stared openmouthed.

"I'm going to schedule this trial for two months from now. Does that give sufficient time to both sides?"

"It does, Your Honor," the prosecutor said.

"Yes, sir," Harold replied.

"And, Mr. DeRoche, I understand you are going to stand mute today, but I'm going to explain some things to you. I have known you for some time, and I know your brother. I know you're a good man, but I see that you have what appears to be a problem with alcohol. By record of where you have been for the past month, I recognize that you are working on this, and I applaud your effort. I do not, however, trust that this has fixed anything. You will stay out on bail awaiting trial on your own personal recognizance, but as a condition of this privilege, you will test for drugs and alcohol daily between six and nine a.m. If you fail to test or fail a test, your personal bond will be revoked and you will go to jail. You are not to travel outside the county, either. Do you understand this? Nod if you do."

I nodded.

The judge banged his gavel, and we were dismissed for the day.

The whole time I stood at the defendant's podium, the cameraman snapped away. The judge let him walk around the court and into the jury box so he could have a clear shot at me. This frustrated me. It seemed entirely unfair to do this to someone accused of a crime, but I let it go. The media were beyond my control, and I knew as much.

* * *

At home Stacey was in the kitchen, sorting through the mail on our island countertop. She looked me up and down, noticed that I was wearing a suit even though I didn't have a job.

"You're going to have to watch out for the newspapers again tomorrow to make sure Carley doesn't see the headlines," I said.

"Why would you be in the paper again?" she said.

"Because I was just in court, and the reporter was there with a cameraman."

"Great. You get out of rehab for what, two days, and go right back to wrecking our lives. Thanks. Great work. I'm glad the kids' friends are too young to read the paper. Why were you in court, anyway? Is it done?" Stacey was angry for good reason. I hadn't told her about the ongoing court dates, because she said she didn't want to know about them. They were my problem, not hers. Still, she expected this to be fixed at some point, and when I brought up the reporters, it was clear that it wasn't happening.

"No, and it isn't going to be done for a while this time."

"Why? Why can't you just go plead guilty like before?"

"Because it's a gun crime. I know you don't want to hear this, but I—"

"You're right. I don't want to hear it," she said, tears streaming down her cheeks. She turned and walked from the room. I could see her sobbing in the next room.

When the pressure of the day started in on me, I found peace in remembering I could focus only on what was in front of me for each day. I knew I couldn't fix the days and months to come. I found peace in this, but I underestimated what that burden looked like to others.

Stacey was rightfully distraught about everything, and not just what happened in court on one case. The whole circumstance was a nightmare for her, and it was clear she wanted to escape it, end it, or just make it all go away if she could. And here I was, still the problem, giving her more bad news.

My mind started whirring again, just as it always had before. I started to process the angles and run through the likely outcomes in my head. Instantly, I felt the surge of resentment and anger toward Mick, the police, and the legal system. My thoughts wandered from angry thoughts of vindication toward what I would need to do in Saline to avoid jail, and from there I found myself angling for what I would do to earn a living.

Just one pressure point touched in the morning, and I was off to the races again. I got myself so worked up in mere moments, the dissonance was stunning to me. I noticed my anger and fear and pulled back from it.

If my mind was a calculator running formulas to solve problems, I had gained an external view of the formula—and its flaws—for the first time in my life. It occurred to me that when I was faced with a problem, my instinctive response was to run all the angles toward the best possible solution and then to put forth all my effort and skill toward creating the solution I desired.

All at once, I recognized the structural flaws of this approach.

I didn't control the people, places, and circumstances outside myself, so the formulas were never valid to begin with. Thus, I was wasting nearly all my time and energy. All I was creating with this effort on daily problems was a life of servitude to the problems, fuel for anxiety and grief, and the perpetuation of my anger and fear.

I was startled to learn that I was running around spending my whole life thinking that my efforts could make the dice roll a seven every time, instead of accepting that the dice would land wherever they did and my job was just to make the best of it.

This was a powerful discovery and a liberating concept. For the moment, my peace had returned.

With this new nugget of knowledge, my thoughts turned from pain and misery toward awe and inspiration. Could life really be this free?

As I learned in that moment (and relearned many times since), the answer is clearly yes. But remembering it after wearing in a pattern of behavior for thirty-nine years was a pretty steep order. I literally couldn't stop my mind from returning to the painful realization of what was in front of me. Worse, the first thing I had to accept was that I couldn't comfort Stacey, explain things to her, or even carry on a civil conversation yet. I just had to accept the circumstances for what they were, and plug in when I had the chance.

I didn't control my marriage. I wasn't lord of my career. I didn't run the courts, prosecutors, or police. I couldn't control what other people thought or did.

There was a lot coming at me, and all of it "bad." I couldn't see the least glimmer of hope for any money, love, happiness, or peace. Materially, I was broke. Publicly, I was an embarrassment. In marriage, I was a failure. I evoked resentment in many. In my own kids, I stirred fear. And amid all this, I felt better—indescribably better, in fact. I had received a gift that could not be tarnished by this incoming barrage of explosions and destruction. I could accept things for what they were, and this gave me peace, happiness, love, and hope in a way I hadn't known was possible. I saw things differently, and it felt wonderful. I knew that there was an answer to the problems, a release for others' pain, and a pathway and purpose for me. But I also knew I was no longer the architect or author of the solutions. I had let go and found this wonderful new life that I hadn't even known existed, and I was committed to staying in it with all I was. The answers were here, not in my old ways and methods.

I committed to follow the path of discovery and learned quickly that the choice does not go uncontested.

Chapter 15

I have come to believe that both light and dark are in this world. Good and evil. Both are everywhere and pervade every life, circumstance, and experience. I also believe that not a moment, thought, word, or gesture—not one square inch of the battlefield— is ever conceded. The enemy doesn't willingly give up a thing, ever. The good news is, the dark always loses if we follow the light.

Life on earth, in modern America, isn't exactly set up for following the light, though. This is something I know firsthand. How I always chose to fix things was by doing it my own way. I had come to realize that this strategy didn't work. And yet, in every area of my life, trying to fix things my own way was what I knew. It was comfortable to me. I had made decisions about how to solve a problem the first time I encountered it—when I ran out of money, got caught in a lie, or needed some relief—and I hadn't deviated much since I was a little kid.

I reflected internally and reminded myself: *Don't do it your way, Craig. Let go of your anger over what has been done with the money you had and all the money you earned in the past twelve years.* My resentment toward Stacey was real, eclipsed only by the fear that I wouldn't be able to fix it this time.

"Where did all the money go?" Stacey said. She was leaving our home office, just next to the front entryway. I assumed she had just gone online and checked our bank balances. She and I stood face-to-face in the hallway.

"Let's just do the best we can with what we have," I said.

"We don't have much left, though."

"Well we had a lot—"

"Don't you go blaming me for these money problems," she snapped. "You're the one who can't get his act straight, and I had to be here as a single parent while you were off in a nice rehab hospital. You didn't have to put up with the kids each day. They were scared to death. I had to keep them occupied. Screw you if you think I spent too much money."

"I—"

"No. Don't. You made this mess. Fix it!" she said as she stormed out of the room. The conversation was over, and I had learned a lesson.

In Alcoholics Anonymous, they teach a vitally important principle: "Focus exclusively on your side of the street."

If you have been living in addiction, you will begin to notice how messy and unkempt this "street"—your path through life—looks. At the same time, you begin to notice the messiness of others' paths. Commenting on this, or even *thinking* about the other person's path—does some powerfully bad things to you. It distracts you from cleaning up your own messes. It fuels the core problems, such as resentment, anger, and fear, that made life messy in the first place. It promotes self-righteousness, pride, and self-centeredness in general. In short, it's the worst thing you can do. And it was the first thing I did with Stacey.

Thank God she didn't even let me finish my sentence.

I retreated to my home office to begin taking a couple of inventories. The first was a financial inventory. The second was the inventory of problems I needed to respond to and clean up. And finally, I needed to begin that dreaded inventory of what I had done wrong in my life—the last one being the big one. Thankfully, God himself had given me a preview of it. I liked his list. It was very detailed and included some surprisingly small items, along with some whoppers I was well aware of.

I began with the finances because this was what Stacey and I had argued about. Finances had always been a big problem for me. This is ironic in someone who graduated from college with honors and a finance degree. In school, they can teach you to be good at math. But they can't teach you to be good at *applying* the math to your own decisions. Whether I earned three thousand or three hundred thousand in a year, it seemed I never had enough money to last a week. This fueled fear and resentment each day. Rather than deal with the problem, I thought I could run from it by drinking and focusing on always getting more money. How wrong could I be?

Since I was self-employed and had bought myself bad insurance, I had about $17,000 in medical bills due. We had a car payment, a boat payment, plus a mountain of unsecured debt I had arranged to prop up the business. The house was upside down, like most of Michigan and the country at the time, and this gave me a negative net worth.

The mortgages and other bills hadn't been paid since I left a month earlier, so between business and personal expenses, I had tens of thousands that needed to be paid immediately.

I began the process of organizing and digesting this, and again I committed to myself that I would do only what I could each day. The hill was too steep to climb, and the thought of it terrified me. Just a few weeks earlier, this kind of pressure would have sent me straight to the liquor store.

The second list was shorter than the money list but far harder to begin. I had partners in a failing business, who needed some answers. I had washed out any chance of our business surviving. On another business front, which was extremely promising and really taking off, I had received a devastating call.

"Craig, I want to thank you for calling me about the arrest and what's going on out your way. I hate to do this after all we've been through, but I talked it over with Barb. Man, I wish I wasn't doing this on your voice mail. Anyway, with the arrest and what they're saying you did in the papers, I need to exit our partnership. I'm going my own way. I hope you understand. We had a great opportunity, and I know it would have worked, but I can't wait for you to go through the court system to get started. If there's ever anything I can do for you, I will. You know that. I'm not mad at you. I feel sorry for you and wish I could help, but I just can't do this."

Jim McKinney left me this voice mail while I was in rehab. He is a great man and a good friend. He himself had overcome a great many challenges, including cancer. When he was diagnosed, he left the company we both worked for, and became semi-retired. He was still young, in his fifties, and had a successful career with over twenty years leading the sales for the largest carrier in our niche business.

Jim and I had joined forces to reenter that business with a new company. Our plan was simple. We both had relationships that we could approach without encumbrance. Both Jim's and my non-compete clauses had expired years before. We incorporated our effort, had already secured an exclusive relationship with one leading national insurance market, and were in talks with others. We would grow our business by $10 million in premiums a year to over $100 million in ten years. This would give us about $20 million in annual revenue by that time.

It was a realistic plan. Jim had been responsible for growing one company from $20 million to over $300 million in revenue. And I had put together deals that would grow us at $10 million per year.

The timing was perfect, and everything was falling into place, and then it was gone. The arrest had done this. I understood Jim's perspective, and I felt not a whit of anger or resentment toward him. The arrest had done it, and the damage was complete the moment I was booked at Novi PD.

I simply needed to let it go, act professionally, and contact Jim. I made this call first. The arrest had screwed Jim as much as it had me, and I felt sorry for him.

He was gracious and made a simple exit from our fifty-fifty ownership of the corporation we had formed. I agreed to pay for the legal and accounting to make it work. As time went on and Jim succeeded with sales that closely tracked what we had imagined, I was glad to see that our plan was, in fact, viable. I still feel a sense of remorse, though, since my arrest made him lose the opportunity and leverage I had provided as his partner. Thus, Jim decided to go to work for another firm and raise their sales and profitability instead of owning the operation himself.

My partners in the insurance software venture were understanding as well. Each had surprising insights into what I had been going through—and surprising empathy. All understood that our venture had languished before and was now likely dead. I promised to keep the company open on the off chance that our developed products could be of use to a buyer, but otherwise cut off all involvement.

The direct contracts I had held for professional service were expiring. All the companies exercised their thirty-day cancellation notices, which, thankfully, meant my operations were funded for another month. I had spoken with everyone personally before entering the rehab hospital, but called again. The bridges weren't burned, but they were gone all the same. There would be no future opportunities with any of those former clients.

This brought me back to the bills and the personal inventory. I chose to use our remaining money to pay the bills that were at risk of affecting our credit or going to a collections agency. This made a sizable dent in our cash position, but we had entered survival mode, and I prayed it was just for the time being.

I began to note down everything in my personal inventory of things I had done wrong, and soon realized that it was far more than I could have imagined at the start. Listing the things I had done was easy. But identifying *why* I had done them, and my true role in them, was painful and wonderful at the same time. I was discovering utterly new territories in life, which hold the greatest value to me now. I hadn't even an inkling of understanding before. I had unearthed an existence that was always present, though untapped, within me. This exercise took a lot of arduous work over several weeks, and I couldn't have done it without the help of the wisest men I have ever met— a man I was about to meet quite inadvertently.

* * *

While in rehab, I had asked a man name Bruce to help me once I got out. I met him my first Friday night there. We were in the hospital dining hall for the evening recovery meetings. There was no food, but the tables made for a good lecture hall, too. Bruce came back each Friday to help teach us the solutions that had worked, and continued to work, in his life. He had been sober over twenty-two years at the time and still made it a point to give chunks of his time to others.

Throughout my life both personally and professionally, I have observed that nearly everyone who taught or made themselves available to others by seeking out the opportunity to speak had an angle. This isn't something to be cynical about—purely an observation.

With Bruce, it was something different entirely. He was simply walking people through who he was, what he had done, what happened to him, and how his life looked today. What he didn't have in dramatic oratory, he more than made up for in the truth he spoke.

His story was entirely different from mine in scenery, circumstances, and external influences. And at the same time, it was clear that I was just like him.

My willingness to accept that I couldn't figure out my problems on my own was at a lifetime high. I would literally do anything to change my situation. I was prepared to go to any length, and this made breaking my lifelong aversion to asking for help an easy hurdle to clear.

As the other patients left the dining hall, I walked up to Bruce. He was near the empty buffet stand, finishing a conversation.

"Um, I really appreciated what you had to say today," I said, groping for words. "And, well, I'm going to be here for a month, and I was wondering if there were any other times you would be around. I'm in a whole pack of trouble. Kinda like you were back in the eighties but, of course, different in details. I was hoping I could get some advice."

"Huh," he said, smiling. "So it isn't getting any better out there for people like us when we decide to drink, eh?"

"Not in my case, anyway."

Bruce laughed in a disarming and comforting way. "What'd ya do, anyway, to get in here? Why are you stopping now?"

"Well, I really blew it. In fact, you might have heard what I did. It was in the papers. I'm the former government official who was arrested last weekend. They say I was drunk with a gun and—"

"Oh, you're that guy? I read about you." He gave another disarming chuckle.

"Yeah, well, I blew everything up and I don't know where to go with this, but I don't want to live this way anymore."

"Good. Without that, you can't change a bloody thing. Why are you asking me about these things?"

"Well, I liked what you said, and you seem a lot like me," I said. Then I paused. I thought for a moment about what I was really asking for, because I didn't just want advice. I wanted something else. "Well, you seem to have this great life now and it was really busted up before, and my point is, I want someday to have a better life. Better than this and better than it was even before."

"You're already getting it," he said. "Here's the trick— and why I'm here, really. I couldn't figure out for myself how to do the right thing to change. I had to find others who had made the change already. I looked for the people whose life was attractive to me, and learned to imitate them. They helped me, too. See, I still can't figure things out good for myself sometimes, and I have people I can get help from. At the same time, my experience can help others. I can't help myself, but I can help others. Remember that. It's how you grow. You don't have anything to give today, but you will, and the more you give, the more you get. Sure, I'll talk to you. I'll be back next Friday."

He did come back the next Friday, and we talked some more. My pretensions about seeking scholarly advice, reading books, and talking to physicians and psychiatrists were gone. It appeared that the wisest person I'd met on the subjects I was dealing with had begun his journey with a wild life of criminal prosecutions and tragically stupid errors, and without even a high school diploma.

In the twenty years since, he had graduated from high school and college and had a great job in the auto industry. It was quite a story, and he didn't take a single short cut in telling it.

When I left the rehab hospital, I asked him to be what, in addiction circles, is known as a *sponsor*. A sponsor is someone who has had a spiritual awakening as a result of the steps he or she took. Sponsors have learned that only in helping others will their own growth continue. At the time, I didn't understand the importance of spiritual growth, and despite the overwhelming spiritual experiences I had been blessed with, I wasn't really sure what role spirituality would play for me in my new life.

So Bruce checked in on me and others each week and shared stories. He never talked about what we should do for ourselves—only about what worked and didn't work for him, all the while being completely transparent about who he was inside. This was the important part. When he shared his thoughts about drinking, they mirrored mine. When he talked about what he did to live differently, it made perfect sense, but I would never have thought of it on my own. Most of it was counterintuitive, anyway: Give to others and you start getting more. Surrender the problem and it is solved for you; fight it and it never gets fixed. Be honest and people won't lie to you or be angry with you, even if they don't like the truth you share. Recognize that you are no better than others, and you will be held in higher esteem. Don't give other people advice unless you can explain how the advice worked in your own life.

I liked what Bruce had, and I wanted it. I saw it in the others who came in with Bruce to help out, too. Plenty of people who worked there had it, too. The employees were a bit more constrained in sharing, because they worked in a professional capacity in a medical environment, but in many ways it was evident. Pretty soon, I could distinguish who had been set free and who was still fighting life; who was there to give, and who was there just for the job. Everyone had good intentions; not everyone had received the gift.

One fellow pulled me aside when we were going through "The Serenity Prayer," written by Reinhold Neibuhr:

God, grant me the serenity
to accept the things I cannot change;
courage to change the things I can;
and wisdom to know the difference.

Living one day at a time;
enjoying one moment at a time;
accepting hardships as the pathway to peace;
taking, as He did, this sinful world
as it is, not as I would have it;
trusting that He will make all things right
if I surrender to His will;
that I may be reasonably happy in this life
and supremely happy with Him
forever and ever in the next.
Amen.

The first paragraph is what is usually read or prayed aloud in addiction recovery circles. I have grown to appreciate every word, but at the time, I didn't fully understand even the beginning. The fellow who came up next to me before we read it must have picked this up in me.

"You know what that means, don't ya?"

"What *what* means?" I said.

"The prayer we just said." He smiled warmly.

"Well, just what it says, I suppose."

"You know, what helped me when I was new like you was how another guy explained it to me. He said to remember it means, 'God, grant me the serenity to accept that I can't change other people, places, things, or situations; courage to change the things I can (which is myself); and the wisdom to remember which is which.'"

In retrospect, this little pearl of wisdom helped me understand how far I had to strip myself down, how simple and basic I had to become, before I could proceed with living in a new way. His comment helped me immeasurably to understand my role in things, and it has given me a great deal of serenity over the years since.

When I left the rehabilitation facility after thirty days, I called Bruce and asked him if he would be my sponsor. It was a big deal to me. I thought about it for days. I think I had an easier time asking a girl out in junior high school than I did asking for help.

"Hey, Bruce," I said, "I really appreciate your helping me out in the hospital, and I just wanted to let you know I was out and going to meetings like you said. And, well, I know you're really busy and helping a bunch of guys—in fact, I met a few who came with you to help new guys like me. And, well, I just thought I would ask anyway in case you had room for one more. It's okay if you don't, but I wanted to ask because you make a lot of sense to me."

He let me finish my ramble completely.

"That's all right. I want to help. I am really busy, but you seem pretty willing, and I know your life is upside down. If you really want me to help you, though, I would want you to follow some suggestions I give you. If you don't follow the suggestions, it's hard to stay sober. I have seen this a bunch over the past twenty years. What do you think?"

"Of course. I . . . I wouldn't really know what to do anyway without some guidance . . . besides read and go to meetings."

"That's a good start, but the answer comes from somewhere else. I'd suggest you do the steps, and as far as meetings go, I have one for you that would be perfect."

"Oh, yeah? Which one?"

"It's called the Dignitary Sympathy Group, and it meets Monday nights at seven thirty sharp. It's a little different from what you have experienced, but it'll probably help you a great deal."

"Great. I'll see you Monday, then."

I hung up the phone, satisfied that I had some real coaching in my corner. I felt as comfortable as ever talking with Bruce. I went home and talked to Stacey about it. She said it was a good thing I had a sponsor, and asked what the name of the group meant. I replied that I didn't know, but speculated that it might be a group of professionals or something. I told her I had heard of separate groups for lawyers, judges, and police, and this may be something like it.

The next Monday, when I arrived at the group, I was surprised completely. I walked into the lower level of a grand church in a small town just west of where I lived. Inside was a grouping of long folding tables, assembled in a big circle. There was room for about fifty people to sit in chairs around the room. The gathering had assembled and settled in as Bruce said, at seven thirty sharp. It was all men in the room, and they ranged widely in height, weight, and ethnicity. Their style of dress was also diverse, from military camouflage to mechanic's coveralls, to tailored business suits.

"My name is Mike, and I am alcoholic."

"Hi Mi—" I was the only one in the room to answer, and I stopped myself short.

He continued, "This week, to stay sober, I prayed in the morning every day, at night every day, I went to five meetings, I read two pages out of the book—four days, I think—and called sponsors six days. I didn't call on Tuesday."

This was different, I thought. No greetings or banter?

"Is anyone new to this meeting today?" Mike said.

I raised my hand, and so did another guy.

"Well this is what we call the Dignitary Sympathy Group, and it's a little different from the other meetings you might have gone to. We're a break-off group from the original group that started about forty years ago up in Lansing. There was a bunch of people working in the capitol that thought the name was funny. You should know, there ain't no dignitaries here and you won't get much sympathy, but there is a lot of sobriety. People here got twenty, thirty, forty years sober. They follow a simple plan, and it works. Every day, we have five things we do, and you just heard me report them for myself. We are what's called an accountability group. Before you speak, you need to report whether or not you did your 'Five Basics,' and then you can share what's going on. There isn't an order, and we don't go around the room. You speak when you feel you need to. Oh, and one other thing: we give feedback here. So if someone else hears what you're saying and starts giving you feedback, it's your turn to be quiet and listen. The rule is no feedback on feedback. If you spend the time thinking up an answer for what the feedback is, you probably aren't really listening to the advice being given anyway. If you think the person is giving you bad feedback, you can come back next week and talk about it. As for me, I get mad at feedback all the time because I'm a selfish, prideful son of a bitch. Once I let it sink in, though, I usually accept that it's something I oughta work on instead of defend myself from. I give other people the right to be wrong even though it usually turns out they were right and I was wrong. Got it?"

He wasn't even making eye contact with the new guy or me; he was just stating the ground rules. The meeting began. I was glad I didn't have to speak, because I was as nervous as I'd ever been, working through thoughts about what I would say if I did speak or got called on.

Shortly into the meeting, the anxiety grew a bit. A guy was explaining how something his wife did really angered him, and he gave quite a compelling case for anger on his part.

"What's your wife's name?" someone said, interrupting him.

"Glenda, why?"

"Well, I found in my life that when I describe my wife, Debbie, as 'my wife' or 'the wife,' I dehumanize her, and my anger starts right there. Also, what she did would make a lot of guys mad, and I guess that's fine for a lot of guys, except for me anger is a big problem because I don't deal with it in a healthy way. See, for me I learned I can't control what my wife or other people do, but while they're acting the way they are, I can look for what I contributed to it, even if it's a small thing, and focus on working on that. The miracle is, I did that for a while, and my wife stayed angry for literally years because I did selfish things for, like, twelve years before I got sober. But in the end, she started appreciating me in a way she never did. We still fight, but we get along better than ever. I can't fix my wife or the situation or make her change or accept the new me when I snap my fingers, but I can live different, and things get better—a lot better."

I was listening to this conversation in awe. It was surprising to hear these selfless, humble, genuine pearls of wisdom earned on the battlefield of life, expressed by people who didn't share the first thing with my upbringing, lifestyle, or experience. And yet, here they were, dissecting each others' stories and pointing each other on pathways to freedom. When it came to life, the toothless guy without a place to live was as wise as the pediatrician. A college student knew more about balance than most grandparents I knew. The guys who didn't accept God weren't run over by those who recognized Him as their Savior. A guy who was sober but still selling drugs got to talk through his growth in sobriety and the incongruity of his choices. He wanted a life of permanent freedom and needed not judgment but help getting there. Guys were talking about literally everything and receiving stern feedback that was mostly without judgment. The sharpest feedback always came from someone who had acted in a similar manner and got a bad result, not from someone who had an opinion on where the person's behavior was going to lead.

The examples were attention getters too: "You see, when I chose to drive without a license, I ended up having to go without a license for five more years. I just got it back. You have a chance to avoid that, so I suggest you learn to ask for help and stop driving. There's fifty guys here. Just ask for a ride."

Others described penalties ranging from divorce, estrangement from their children, returns to prison, loss of a job, and just about every consequence imaginable to make their point. I learned in time that the people sharing their own pain and progress were living what members of Alcoholics Anonymous call the "Ninth Step Promises." They read:

If we are painstaking about this phase of our development, we will be amazed before we are halfway through. We are going to know a new freedom and a new happiness. We will not regret the past nor wish to shut the door on it. We will comprehend the word serenity and we will know peace. **No matter how far down the scale we have gone, we will see how our experience can benefit others.** *That feeling of uselessness and self-pity will disappear. We will lose interest in selfish things and gain interest in our fellows. Self-seeking will slip away. Our whole attitude and outlook upon life will change. Fear of people and of economic insecurity will leave us. We will intuitively know how to handle situations which used to baffle us. We will suddenly realize that God is doing for us what we could not do for ourselves.*

Are these extravagant promises? We think not. They are being fulfilled among us—sometimes quickly, sometimes slowly. They will always materialize if we work for them.
(*The Big Book*, 83–84)

I had heard the promises read before and had read them myself. But I never truly understood what they would look like or how, someday, they would apply to a wretch like me. I felt my faith growing that I could live this way in the future, though I honestly didn't yet know how I would ever feel this way or be of use to others as I saw it being lived out. I knew for sure that I heard God speak clearly in my head weeks before: "Who said I did these things so you could run for governor?"

I knew what God meant by "these." That was a custom list straight out of Craig's list of material wants and needs for earthly praise with prideful achievement.

Would the promises come true for me? Why did God do "these" things, then? I was left to wonder, listen, and wait.

Chapter 16

Going to jail was now about to be a reality in my life. Even with all my poor choices, I had never thought that jail would ever be a possibility. When the news reports or politicians talk about people who need to be in jail, they always make their words seem as if they were talking about someone entirely different from themselves. "Those people" is how they phrase it. Not you, not me. Other people.

Today, I joined the ranks of "those people." At least, in my head I did. I knew what I was facing when I sat down at the desk in my home office and called my attorney, Peter, on the phone. I was out of the rehab hospital now and needed to deal with the probation violation for my arrest and conviction in Saline four months earlier.

Peter picked up. "Well, I'd wear clean clothes," he said. "You could go straight to jail. Look, you made the judge look bad. You came into his court, pled no contest and accepted his punishment, and said you'd abide by his rules. And then you didn't."

I had nothing to say.

"I don't want you to go to jail, and I haven't figured out what the judge wants to do. I'm telling you what *I* would be inclined to do if I were judge on this. You bring a flock of media trucks with you, and that puts a lot of pressure on judges and prosecutors to play the tough guy."

"Like I want the media there. I'm not trying to be a pain."

"But you *are* a pain, my friend. A real pain. But I love you and think you're doing the right thing. I'll let them all know this. Hell, you're like a different person, really. I don't know what they did to you in the hospital, but you talk different now."

I sighed and took a deep breath. "Peter, they know I violated my probation. I didn't lie to the probation officer when she called me. She said she was reading about me in the news, and asked if I had anything to say. She says I'm a pain, too. She says the media call her and want to get her notes through the Freedom of Information Act. I didn't know what to say, so I apologized."

Peter said, "The judge and the probation officer have got experience dealing with jerks and alcoholics, and believe me, you stand out as different. They both appreciate your responsiveness to their requests, and we're just going to have to go see them for the violation motion they filed. It has to be done, but I don't think they will act on it and send you to jail, because you haven't been found guilty of anything in Novi."

I couldn't get the thought of this out of my head. When I returned from rehab, I was living with this great sense of peace, but the thought of going back in front of the judge so soon got my wheels turning. I knew that stewing on the problem wasn't healthy, so when I went to the Dignitary Sympathy meeting, I decided to try my hand at sharing a real problem with the group.

I explained the whole situation of facing a probation violation on a ninety-two-day suspended sentence and began to explain what I thought I was facing in a couple of days at the "show cause" hearing.

"I think I heard enough," Tom said.

Tom was one of the guys at the meeting with more than two decades of sobriety. He was sitting at the end of the assembled long tables, with his arms resting across his ample belly. His hands neatly touched and allowed his fingers enough of a platform to pivot and gesture from the mound of his protruding middle. Tom was a dedicated servant who would help anyone in need. His manner of providing the help was startling, though.

"You're talkin' like a selfish prick," Tom continued. "What're you, the king of the court or somethin'? You gonna sit there and figure out in your head how to make a wreckage of your future like that and 'spect me to sit here and listen?"

"Well, I—"

"Shut up, please. I'm talking now," Tom continued in a nasal monotone.

I shut up and listened.

"Why don't you try somethin' new for yourself? Maybe the truth wouldn't hurt you. Think the judge looks forward to people tryin' to run an angle or explain themselves? Hell, I can't take it. You screwed up. Work the program here, and there's a pretty good chance you won't screw up again. Just do the basics. Tell the truth. Nothing else worked for me, anyway. I was just like you, 'cept I screwed up more than once before I figgered it out. You got a chance to do it right this time. Just sayin'."

I took his critique and kept quiet. After Tom had finished with his feedback, someone else started sharing, and the conversation moved on.

Inside, I was boiling over. I kept my composure, though, and didn't lower my head or move my body much in any way. I didn't want to let on to the others that I had been cut up pretty well by the comments. I'm sure they knew, but my pride was hurt and I wanted to shore it up.

Still bristling over this, I left the meeting with Bruce.

"You may not like what Tom said, but you ought to think about it," Bruce said with his customary mild manner.

"I will," I said. "It's not that big a deal. Sure, I didn't think I was as far off as he said, but you know I'll think on it."

"Good boy," Bruce replied with a snicker in his voice.

Thinking about it wasn't going to be my problem. I thought about it a lot. It was a very disruptive issue in my thoughts, and I knew that dealing with the thoughts was vastly more important than the court appearance itself. The thoughts were always what screwed me up, and the actions wouldn't be there without the thoughts.

After about a day and half of brooding and pondering, something funny happened. All at once, what Tom had said to me made sense. I'm not sure why, but it did. I knew, more than anything, that I didn't want to run away from who I was anymore. I knew that lying was a death sentence for me and my progress. When I had backed off even a little on the truth after the Saline arrest, I was back to full-on lying within a day.

The comment about "making a wreckage of my future" was helpful, too. I hadn't been in the courtroom yet and had no idea what was going to happen. I could fully accept that whatever was going to happen was out of my control, too, so I resolved to bring my focus back to the here and now.

By the time the court day arrived a couple of days later, I had almost completely relaxed on the subject. In fact, I may have been a little *too* relaxed.

When Peter and I gathered in the front lobby of the courtroom, he pulled me aside by the shoulder. My file was under his other arm. Peter was all business. He still looked like a million bucks, but his face revealed genuine concern. I had really screwed up the case he did such a good job of closing. He had even arranged for me to be sentenced outside of the view of the media. I hadn't given him a leg to stand on, and I knew this. Peter was a former deputy US attorney, and wearing his old hat, he would likely have torn up a deal on a deferred jail sentence like this in no time flat.

"All I want you to do is be quiet. You don't have to say a thing since your charges in Novi are still pending. There is no evidence yet you were drinking that day, and we have time until that is found to be a fact in court. The time will give you a chance to demonstrate you've turned a corner. Sure, this case will now go on indefinitely with the other one, but you won't have to go to jail."

"Indefinitely?" I asked.

"Well, if they can't settle the violation until the other court case is heard, they'll probably sentence you on the violation when the other court reaches its verdict."

"But I didn't do anything illegal in the other court. I did something illegal here, and I violated my probation here. I didn't do anything to affect Novi."

"Take that up with Harold," Peter said. "I'm only your lawyer for here." He was frustrated now. I was doing it again. I didn't want to do it, but I was pressing again.

"But, Peter, I'd rather—"

"DeRoche!" shouted the clerk.

"Look, Craig, we gotta go in. Just follow my lead."

I was overcome with disappointment upon hearing that it would now be several months before I could even admit to violating probation. I didn't want to wait. I knew I had done wrong, and figured I would rather just own up to it and start moving forward.

A wave of powerful emotion surged through me, and it made me feel good, relaxed, and confident. The sudden rush continued as I walked toward the stand. I said a quick prayer as I approached the podium and asked God to guide me through this and follow His will instead of my own plans.

All at once, I was at peace, and I started to listen to the exchange between lawyers and the judge.

After the formalities of why we were in the court, the purpose of the hearing, and the concerns raised about me in the media, it was the judge's turn to speak.

"Mr. DeRoche, before we go any further in this hearing, I need to advise you that you have rights. You are protected by the Fifth Amendment to the US Constitution, against incriminating yourself. You have rights that will be protected here and, I presume, rights that will be protected in Novi. You have not had a chance to present your facts in that trial, and you are under no obligation to present them here at this ti—"

"That's okay," I said. I actually interrupted the judge. "I have something I want to say, and I understand my rights, but I waive them."

I looked over at Peter as I began speaking. I had blindsided him. He went ashen, then purplish, with the stress I was inflicting on him.

I turned and looked back at the front of the room and saw I had placed the judge in a similar situation. His face was now pale and motionless.

In fact, no one in the court was moving or speaking. Time seemed to stand still, and I had everyone's complete attention. I felt sure now of what I needed to do.

I said, "I didn't do anything like they said I did in the newspapers in Novi, so I'm not concerned with incriminating myself. What I did do, though, was drink alcohol on that day. I wanted to say that here and now. I wanted to tell you the truth. I violated my probation and I disrespected your authority and this court. I lied to you about the magnitude of my problem, but frankly, Your Honor, I was lying to myself that day, too. You see, I have a real problem with alcohol, and I always thought I could handle it myself, and the truth is, I can't. That is where I have been the past month. I have to live my life differently. And I know that whatever the punishment you give me today, however long it may be for, the truth is that what I have to deal with will last me a lifetime. So respectfully, I am willing to accept whatever punishment you feel is fair for drinking and violating the probation you gave me."

I stopped talking. The silence continued. Peter shuffled a little bit with his papers but decided not to speak. He was breathing again, at least.

The judge took a bit longer to compose himself. His first motion was to shift forward in his oversized black-leather executive chair. He, too, opted to shuffle some papers while gathering his thoughts.

The judge cleared his throat and lifted his right hand up and set his reading glasses back up higher on the bridge of his nose.

"Um, well, I want to," he began as he continued to shuffle the papers. Then he let them go and looked me in the eye.

"I want to tell you that in one way, I am very pleased with your appearance today. I'm quite certain I have never had anyone lay the truth out so completely as you have here. I want you to know, sir, that I believe what you said. I believe you are coming to understand the magnitude of your real problem, and I believe from your actions that you do have a problem. I also know from experience that spending ninety-two days in jail does very little, if any, good for the type of problem you have."

The judge now adjusted his posture. He seemed to be finding his stride.

"It seems that these turns of events have got your attention, but I intend to keep it. You have said you're in this for the long haul, and I applaud you for understanding it. While you are in it with me, though—for the rest of your probation—you will test for drugs and alcohol daily. Trust but verify, as they say. You have broken my trust, and now you will verify each day. Understood?"

"Yes!" Peter interrupted. He was wresting control back from me and took the first shot he had to reassert who was actually supposed to be speaking.

"Further, you will now see your probation officer more often, report your alcoholic recovery activities, and fulfill a number of other requirements to give this court confidence in your progress. Do you understand?"

"Yes," Peter replied. I nodded.

"Does the prosecutor object to this?"

I turned to my right as all eyes fell on the prosecutor. There was a great deal of tension in the moments the prosecutor took to evaluate what he had just heard and seen play out.

"No, Your Honor, the prosecution does not object."

"Then this show-cause hearing is closed." The judge banged his gavel. He then continued as I turned to leave the room with Peter.

"Mr. DeRoche."

I turned to face him again, a few feet back from the stand.

"Get this wrong once—drink or do drugs once—and you get ninety-two days. Understood? There are no other chances or excuses."

"Yes, Your Honor," I said.

Peter and I turned and left the courtroom. He then ushered me outside by gripping my elbow fiercely and pulling me along.

As soon as the exterior glass door shut behind us and I could feel the sun and late summer air, Peter pulled my elbow down and stopped in his tracks.

"What the heck was that!"

He was back to having a hard time breathing. He raised his hand and turned the back of it to his forehead the way a woman might do when making a histrionic fainting gesture. But I don't think Peter was faking it. This manly, worldly man actually needed to raise his hand like that.

"I have never seen anything like that in my whole career. Are you freaking kidding me! You just . . . man . . . wow! You are some kind of complete idiot or the smartest guy I have ever seen. I can't get over that. The judge didn't even know what to do. That kind of worked for you, by the way!" he said as his attitude lightened. When he spoke of the judge, he even smiled and socked me playfully on the shoulder.

I actually think Peter had a good time at the hearing and, at the same time, was convinced that he never wanted another client to try that move for any reason, ever.

I said, "I just wanted to tell the truth, Peter. It was important to me. It wasn't a trick. I meant what I said. I get it now. I'm in this now—all in. I got to get it right. The court isn't that big a deal compared to what I'm up against. I've lost everything, and I know I'll never get any of it back if I'm not sober. I really have only one thing I'm up against. I get that right, and everything else will be fine."

He smiled and said, "That was truly amazing, my friend! Now, try a stunt like that again, and I'll put you out of both of our misery!"

We both laughed and walked.

When we got to our cars, he said, "Whatever happened to you is a very good thing. I don't know what it was, but it is something to see. You're going to be fine."

I smiled as I pulled away. I thought about Tom, the old man at the Dignitary Sympathy group who had made me so mad with what turned out to be some pretty important advice.

The truth set me free. I was free, even if only from this one burden. A huge weight was lifted from me all at once, and it came by doing the exact opposite of what I had done for so many years before. I smiled to myself in the sweetness of the moment. I am still smiling now, years later as I write this.

Chapter 17

So I wasn't going to the county jail, but I had created a cage of my own.

It was now a couple of days after my successful hearing in Saline. I hadn't even bothered to tell Stacey what I faced that day. She caught me before I could escape to the home office and shut the doors. We stood in the hallway, facing each other.

"You need to get a job," she said. "I've been telling you this. Paul said the same thing, and my parents think so, too. You need to get over yourself and these grandiose schemes. You screwed up, and you're not going to get a great job, but you should take anything. We're almost out of money."

I seethed with anger at hearing Stacey say these words in that stern voice. It was as if she had again assumed the role of mothering me and condescended to tell me what we should do. I rapidly thought through how many indiscriminate and completely useless purchases she had made and continued to make. *You buy something for twenty bucks fifty times a month, and it's a thousand dollars, honey!*

I stayed silent, though, and collected myself. While others thought I just rolled with the punches, she knew the truth about my paper-thin skin.

Hearing her say this hurt for sure. The truth, on the other hand, was worse. I took a moment to collect myself and responded.

"I have tried to find a job."

"Really, where?" She was angry that I responded at all. Angrier that I seemed to have a ready response. The fact that my lips were moving and I hadn't yet offered an excuse must have tripped her internal lie detector.

"Well, it didn't go too well, but I applied for two."

She could tell I wasn't lying, and I suppose my mannerisms contorted toward the pathetic as I explained the humiliating reception I had received.

"What happened? I didn't even know?" she said. I hadn't explained this to her, because we still weren't really talking. I had tried to answer a question about what happened the night I was arrested, and this led to her shutting me off in disgust. The truth about that night was coming out. She had envisioned that I was 100 percent the culprit and should be damned for my actions. I had reaffirmed that I was, in fact, the culprit for 100 percent of what I had done, and should pay the consequences. But there were other details we should be concerned with. Because the messy details coming out about Mick and the behavior of the police didn't make me sound like the raving sot she envisioned, she would lash me back into my rightful place. I was properly guilty of other crimes in our relationship, and she didn't want any daylight shining through on the crowning achievement of my stupidity.

"Well, I didn't want to tell you, but I have been trying to look for work. I know how bad it is. I've been paying the bills, and I know exactly how upside down we are. I honestly don't know what to do. I can't go back into insurance. Politics is gone forever, and, well, I haven't done anything else in my professional career. I don't have the money to start a business, and it would take months to get it going."

"So why are you telling me this? What type of job were you trying to get?"

"Well, I applied for one at a hospital system that needed a lower-level, government-affairs person. I called my friends there first, and I could tell they were hesitant, but they encouraged me to try. I know all the executives there, too, and had worked with them on their issues for years. I did a résumé and sent it in and, well . . . they sent me a rejection letter. I didn't even get a phone call telling me I was passed over. I figure this is how a lot of people will treat it."

"So what! Stop trying to count on people from politics who weren't really your friends anyway. Just try to find *anything*."

"If you'd let me finish . . . You'd be surprised at how many people have reached out to help, but there aren't any jobs. *Nobody* has a job, if you haven't noticed. Michigan has the worst economy since the Great Depression." I was working up the courage to continue. The next part of the story was hard for *me* to hear. I could only imagine what Stacey would think.

"So I went to this job Website called the Ladders, which is for job listings that are more than a hundred thousand a year. I figure with my résumé and the fact that I have earned a lot more than that in the past ten years, I'd look around. They had this promotion running where I could get a résumé and placement coach session for free, so I signed up."

"And?"

"Let me finish!"

"Why? You already told me you didn't get a job. That's the story, isn't it?"

"Kind of, but worse. The lady on the phone, my counselor, said my résumé was incredibly strong—probably the most impressive string of accomplishments she had ever seen—but it was poorly written and seemed as if I was almost holding back. She said employers look for people who are ambitious and strong, and my wording was passive and weak."

"I can edit and fix that for you, too," Stacey said. A trained journalist, she had worked in public relations before we had the girls.

"I know, but that wasn't her point. She said she Googled my name and that every employer Googles names nowadays, and that what comes up for me is page after page about my arrests. She said—and these are her words—'they make you sound like you were a barricaded gunman.' She told me that with what the papers say about me, I couldn't get a job working at McDonald's or on the docks at Sam's Club."

At the end, I was talking in a monotone to the floor. I couldn't look up at Stacey, but I wanted to. The fact was, I didn't know what to do.

I stopped talking. I heard her sigh. Then, she turned and started walking away.

"We're screwed," she said as she turned the corner.

Yep, honey. We're screwed. I turned and walked into the office and shut the doors.

Every day, my mind raced and I called in on the deals I was chasing. The entire economy in America had been flipped over in late 2008, and a lot of banks and properties were mired in the mucky remains of the once great Motor City. I had done some deals helping local businesses and banks settle their problems and was owed a lot of money. The problem was, none of the debts were collectible. I was chasing after rainbows and knew it.

I had only reluctantly been led to the proper level of humility. My efforts to press forward doing it my own way crashed completely, and this brought me humility. Pride, for me, was a persistent encumbrance on progress.

The earnest words of the résumé coach rang in my ears, and I heard every word. My brain instantly distanced itself from the reality, though. It came as an indigestible shock. This was yet another hill too steep for me to climb on my own. My years owning and running Web-based businesses convinced me that there was no fighting the Internet. Once something showed up on the Web, it was true. What this complete stranger had observed while trying to help me would be easy enough for everyone else to assume, too. I didn't panic or act, though, because there was nothing for me to do.

It felt good for me to tell Stacey. I wasn't looking for sympathy, though I was probably hoping she might understand that I was, in fact, being punished for my actions. I felt sorry for her and the punishments unfairly laid at her feet by me. She was publicly embarrassed beyond any measure that a wife could be expected to tolerate. She stood to lose a marriage, a house, and the happy home of her dreams for our kids, and this ate away at her. She would lament the way friends talked to her and what people said about her behind her back or even within earshot. She was embarrassed to go shopping or take the kids out in public. Now she had heard from me the blunt truth that the humiliation was worse than expected. It was based on the hysterical images painted by a drunken neighbor and my creative political opponents in city hall, and it would stick.

Stacey was speechless. I don't know whether she felt disgust or pity for me—probably a measure of both. She simply turned and walked away, and I shut myself into my home office again, trying to figure things out.

Days later, we had round two of our discussions about money when she noticed I had continued to pay the bills. Her desperation was obvious, as was her disdain for my presence in a decision-making role within the family.

"I think you're crazy to keep paying the mortgage," she said. "Everyone is losing their house. There have been four more foreclosures in our subdivision already this year. You have no prospect of earning any money, and you're spending what little we have left on a house we won't be able to keep. We ought to consider doing what others have done and accept that we're going to lose it."

She had a basis for what she was saying. I was washed out, with no prospects for earning money. The summer had withered away into fall, and the weather was changing.

Stacey and I had small dust-up arguments over spending on back-to-school and other necessities, but we both were guarding the remaining dollars well. Paying the mortgage and car payments were the biggest hits. I knew this and, at the same time, remained convinced that something would come through.

I was stuck in a routine of haunting old business partners and real estate deals for money that wasn't available and transactions that would never occur. It was a routine. I got up in the morning, made my list, and then set about making fruitless calls.

Nothing was working, and Stacey knew it. Her fear was bubbling to the surface, and she found the strength to address this with me, her semiestranged husband who was paying the bills with the last of our reserves.

"I just don't think it's going to work," she said. "You should accept it. With everything else that's happened, this shouldn't even be that embarrassing. We have responsibilities to the kids and so many people we owe. How am I going to pay for their school stuff? What are we going to do for food? Do you even have a plan?"

She was crying and trying to speak at the same time. We were standing in the kitchen of our house—a beautiful, sunlit room with cherrywood floors and cabinets. As she spoke, her back hunched over and her shoulders quivered. The sight of this drained whatever strength and durability I had left in me.

I started to cry as well.

"I never wanted any of this," I said, "and all I'm supposed to say is 'sorry.' I can't tell you I can fix it, when I can't. I don't know what's next, and I'm as scared as you. My whole life, I could do anything and get whatever I wanted, and the truth was, it was killing me. Now I'm trying to do things differently and nothing is working. I just—"

"And the girls' dance classes. Tuition is due. And preschool needs tuition. Are the kids not going to do dance? Is Phoebe going to go without preschool?" Stacey sobbed the words. Her quivers had now progressed to sobbing and trying to catch a breath in between words.

She got through her words and left me standing there in the big, empty kitchen. She had said what she needed to say. She retreated upstairs, broken and sobbing, and I stood there collecting my thoughts.

I had never let another person down like this at any time in my entire life. I didn't even think I could inflict this much pain on another human being if I tried. Without saying it, Stacey made it clear to me that I had dashed all her hopes and dreams of a marriage, parenting, and life. All this, and I didn't even have a soothing lie to tell her as I had so many times before.

It was clear to me that behind her anger and recriminations toward me over my drinking and failings through the years, there had really been just her fear. I never realized this before. She was afraid that the man she committed her life to in marriage was going to let her down. And had he ever let her down! I had dazzled her with the magic in the heady days of money, private jets, travel, and social status, only to show her the straw I had built our dreams of.

The straw house was now set ablaze, and I didn't know what to do or say.

Hearing Stacey's anguished sobs destroyed something in me. It was a healthy demolition, though. Seeing the embodiment of my failures and their toll on my beautiful, loving wife helped me understand fully who I was, and I didn't want to be that person ever again.

* * *

Weeks went by as the cash reserves dwindled and my prospects for employment or cash from business deals dimmed. All the while, the tension between Stacey and me grew.

My determination to continue paying the bills was intractable, and I kept at it. I kept everything just ahead of being turned off or sent to collections.

Our arguments grew worse, and Stacey had more or less settled into a strategy of getting in her shots at me as fiercely as she could and then moving on before I could reply. She wasn't interested in my reply, anyway. She wanted to remind me of the pain I was causing her, and the magnitude of the failure.

The credit card that I had paid off just before entering rehab was now maxed out. I had reset all our bills and payment plans to reduce any expense possible. I was thrashing about, looking for anything I could in the way of relief or revenue.

"What about a loan? Do you think your parents could help?" Stacey asked.

"No, and I can't really ask. My dad's been on a fixed income for thirteen years, and I know from Paul he doesn't really have any room."

"My parents don't either. With my dad laid off, they can barely keep up."

"I'm not mad you're asking. I just don't think there is anyone to loan us money."

"What about your brothers?"

"Kirk? Are you kidding me? He's talking about going back over to Afghanistan for his fifth tour because he can't find work in Michigan, and his third kid is on the way. He'll be gone for a year."

I paused and thought. Paul would have the money. I was sure of it. Paul was the successful, rigidly disciplined one of us three brothers. He always had money because he planned to have money for everything. He actually followed all the advice we both learned when we got our finance degrees from Central Michigan University all those years ago. He followed it to a T and was a huge success as a stockbroker and financial planner.

On the other hand, Paul was a former business partner and roommate of mine after college. He had always supported me and my crazy ideas. In fact, he plugged himself in more times than I could count, playing the straight man in my wild schemes whether he profited from it or not.

I am quite certain that being the oldest of three brothers is a challenge. For Paul, it must have been a particular challenge because both Kirk and I blazed such reckless trails through life, in stark contrast to his slow and steady snowballing of success.

I thought for a moment about what asking for a loan from Paul would look like, and quickly found myself with another debt to pay that was more than monetary.

The fact was, I already owed Paul six thousand dollars. He had loaned it to me the year before, and I could have paid it back a couple of times but chose not to. I had taken advantage of our casual, brotherly exchanges on matters like this and had been plainly selfish without even having it consciously register in my head.

I cringed at the awareness of what I had done.

"No. I don't think I should ask Paul for money. The fact is, I owe him six thousand already. I could have paid him back before and didn't. I don't think it's fair to even ask."

"So, then, we're screwed? Great," Stacey said as she walked away from me. The conversation was again over without a real ending. I felt an anxious pain in my gut and had started to leave the room myself when I heard her yell from the top of the stairs, "You tell the girls about dance!"

"What about dance?" Carley yelled from across the house in the living room. The living room was actually the toy room, and calling it a toy room merely means this was where the kids generally piled their toys from wall to wall. This allowed us one space in the house to push their stuff back into.

Now Carley was headed up the stairs, too. She wanted to talk to her mom about her dance class, which was the focus of talk with her and the other girls in the neighborhood. Between our two closest neighbor families and ours, we had eight girls under the age of 10, and dance was their activity of choice after school. It was now September, and back-to-school was upon us. Tuition was due. Actually, as I thought about it, tuition was past due. And I remembered that Katie of Katie's School of Dance was both delightful with the kids and diligent when it came to money matters. No money, no dance. I simply didn't have a solution.

I forgot completely about the specter of an unpaid mortgage next month, or not having a couple of hundred dollars for food next week. I didn't even care so much that I didn't have the cash for gas to drive my car and had resorted to staying home and using the phone to meet people. The real pinch was when I couldn't make the two-hundred-fifty-dollar down payment on the girls' dance tuition, knowing full well this would exclude them from the first and most important social circle they had encountered in life—and an activity they truly loved at the time.

When I was young and my parents came into the room or corralled me to talk about something, be it money, sex, or some other educational or family-decision topic, I actually started speculating on what went into the pretalk. Hearing my parents explain something that had always been a mystery was a fascinating experience. The way they talked and looked at me was different, and I knew that those were important times to listen.

I never did figure out what they did, and I have never read any tips on how to handle this sort of ramp-up in a pinch. I figure, if there were tips to be given, they probably didn't apply to a situation where one of the parents was bitterly angry at the other. Or maybe this very thing was what led to the special tone and posture of the talks to begin with.

All I knew at the time was that it made me queasy. My senses were on high alert, and my stomach felt sick in the same instant. A thousand first words seemed to rush past me before I simply settled on "Carley, let's go talk in your room."

"Okay, Dad," she said with resignation.

I could tell that Carley already knew the score and was counting on me to explain it to her. I still didn't know what to say—only that I had to start talking.

"Honey, you know things are tough here, right? Dad has had trouble earning money like he used to, and, well, the truth is, I just don't have money for dance right now. I think everything's going to be fine, but I don't know when. I hope you can understand this."

"I know, but when is it going to be like it was?" she said with tears welling past her eyelids and spilling down her cheeks. Looking at her beautiful, sad, blue eyes and long, summer-sun bleached hair, I saw what it looked like to have my own child keep her faith in me at the same time as express her utter heartbreak over what was happening.

She continued. "All my friends have started dance, and that's all they talk about and do. I want to go with them. Do you think it's only going to be a couple of weeks?"

"God, I wish I knew, honey. I'm so sorry I let you down," I said as the tears started down my cheeks as well. "I need you to do me a favor, okay? I want you to understand that you, your mommy, and your sisters are the most important things in my life. Sometimes, things happen that we don't want, but we have to live through them and know that things will get better. I just can't tell you when. We still have this house, and we're all together and healthy and have a lot to be happy about."

"I know," she said. She was no longer looking at me and had turned her head down toward her bed. "Mom says we may not get to keep the house."

"Hmm-m. Then we'd have to get another one, and that could be fun, right? You don't have to think *everything* is bad. I know things are going to be better than fine, and better than anything we can imagine today. Lots of people move, and lots of people's families aren't even together, and even with some of your friends their family has health issues. We can be happy wherever we are, and I know you and your friends will be happy together, too. I want you to dance, and if I can get the money, I'll do whatever I can to get you there. You know that, right?" I said, with a smile and a hug.

"I know, Dad. I'm happy for the other things. I just wish I could dance."

"And I wish you could, too, and I think there may just be a chance you will. We'll see together, right?"

"Okay," she said, and she smiled.

The beautiful thing about Carley is, she can pour herself out into a discussion no matter what's on her mind. And no matter how upset she may be, she still listens for the answers she can accept. The love she expressed to me during this discussion was unconditional, and it was one of the most important and incredibly difficult conversations I had ever had.

As I left her in her room and shut the door, I thought, *What kind of a monster does this to his kids? How did I let it run this far?*

When I returned downstairs, Stacey asked me what had happened, and I told her that Carley understood. I think Stacey understood how difficult the discussion was, so she didn't really follow up at all with any questions, concerns, or orders for me to follow. I think she knew that the reality of the damage I had done to the family was doing just fine in speaking for itself.

* * *

Over the next couple of days, things went from bad to worse as our cash situation spiraled downward beyond any possibility of repair that I could imagine. Our credit cards had been maxed out—thank goodness, at a low level of debt. My credit score would not allow for any new extensions of credit. The bills owed to medical providers stood at more than $20,000, and most of the other bills had aged more than 30 days. The unnecessary bills from computer services, subscriptions, and cable TV had progressed to being shut off. The cash balance in our account was negative, and we had a couple of hundred dollars left in cash, including every quarter, dime, nickel, and penny in the house. Every instrument of value was converted—even the change from the kids' piggy banks. I had made the mortgage and the car payment just before they fell to sixty days late. I recounted all this to my beautiful wife, who was managing her grief, humiliation, resentment, and fear.

Stacey was doing better than most could hope to do, but one evening, her fear and anger overcame her all at once. It was a couple of weeks after my conversation with her and Carley about taking the girls out of dance class.

It was a Thursday, and it was already dark outside. Stacey had spent the evening pacing back and forth through the house, slamming things around, while I sat on the couch and pretended to ignore the tension. This continued until about eleven p.m.

I kept running thoughts through my head over and over again. I had two meetings scheduled for the next day. I needed to get to them because both were with leaders of large companies and interests in Michigan. I needed to drive about forty miles to do it, and I felt that this was my top priority, though I couldn't say why.

My thoughts bounced back and forth. What would I say? I hadn't told them I was coming to ask for help, a job, a loan, or anything. I simply told them I wanted to touch base. My honest purpose was to stay visible and let people know that despite the wreckage I had caused, my life internally was getting better. At some point, it would be important for people to know I was getting better and not worse, but was this really a top priority *now*?

I allowed my thoughts to venture into the future. I recognized that we had no access or options left for cash except for the buckets of returnable aluminum soda cans in the garage. How pathetic is that? I had never counted on Michigan's ten-cent returnables for money even in college, and here I was, wondering how much gas that would buy for my ten-year-old Cadillac DHS. Would it get me to tomorrow's meetings? What if they wanted to have lunch?

The Cadillac! It hit me all at once. I owned it outright. It must be worth five thousand dollars, and that would buy some groceries and keep us current on the mortgage for another month. *Time.* That was what I needed, and selling the car would buy me a couple of weeks. I decided to sell the car.

Relieved at the breathing room I had found, I stood up from the couch and walked over to our love seat sofa. I knelt down and began to pray, "God, I want to ask for forgiveness because I—"

"What are you doing?" Stacey snapped. She was standing directly behind me. I was kneeling on the carpet and had my elbows on the armrest of the sofa.

I looked over my shoulder and said, "Praying."

"What good does that do? We have no money. How is prayer going to fix *that*? Are you going to pray for a million dollars? Is God going to give *that* to you?"

"I'm—"

"Don't tell me what you're going to do or how it's all going to be fine. It's not going to be fine. What are you doing tomorrow about this? How are we going to eat? Why don't you get over yourself and get a job? I mean *any* job, not just some big-shot job. You're not a big shot anymore. You screwed up. Deal with it. Send your résumé out."

"I'm meeting with two people tomorrow."

"Are they job interviews?"

"No, but listen! I know you're mad, and I want you to understand something. I have been trying to get a job. I do have a résumé. In fact, I sent it out to be professionally reviewed and I got help, but there's a problem."

"What problem?"

"You heard me tell you about this before: what's on the Internet. The person doing the review of my résumé doesn't know me from Adam and said she couldn't help me with what they wrote. And you know what? I have to deal with that, and I don't know how to do it. It hurts every day, and I know I'm the one who created the mess, and I can't fix it and I have to break our little kids' hearts because I'm a failure. I understand it. I get it! I'm on my knees for a reason. I don't know what else to do, and God has removed my desire to drink and spoken directly to me, and there isn't anything I can believe in that has ever worked in my life the way God has, so I'm going to pray. It's all I have."

"Well, go on and pray, then, but for the record, I want you to know I have lost faith in you and I have lost faith that God will help us. Goodnight."

She walked past me, and I could see her shoulders literally vibrate with anger and fear. She banged each step heavily and slammed the bedroom door and left me on my knees in the big, dark, and now silent great room.

I caught my breath and rested my hands back on the armrest.

"God, this is all my fault. I prayed to you saying I couldn't fix my drinking and that I would follow you anywhere, and you took away my desire to drink. I thank you for this. I am so selfish, though. Look at what I've done. I have ruined Stacey's faith in you. I have tried to fix my finances in my own way, and I've failed again. Forgive me for this. I don't deserve to have you fix anything for me. I am willing to let this marriage fail, Lord. I am willing to lose this house, Lord. I don't need the things I have. I can sell my car and give the money to Stacey. I know, Lord, if there is a plan for my kids to understand the damage I have done, I will be able to explain it to them someday. I give up. I am tired of trying to fix this every day and chasing after business deals and wild schemes. I'll do it your way. Just guide me. Relieve me of the bondage of self, that I might better do your will. Take away these difficulties that I might bear witness to those I would help see your power, your grace, your love, and your way of life. May I do your will in all that I say and think and do tomorrow, Lord. Thank you for the blessings in my life. Thank you for saving me. I didn't deserve it, and you have given me the greatest gift I could ever have imagined. I praise you for it. Thank you. Amen."

I knew in my heart I was completely powerless over my situation in marriage, finances, career, and, now, even basic sustenance. I imagined Stacey moving back home to her parents and our house going to the bank. I was okay with the notion of this and had complete faith it would all be for the best. I went upstairs. I went to bed and fell straight asleep. What Stacey had said to me didn't seem to hurt me at all. Whether she had faith in me actually didn't matter. That was no longer anything I could control or trouble myself with. For reasons I can explain only by using the word "faith," I was at peace with myself and the situation despite the dire reality that I fully understood, and the likely outcome to what was unfolding.

Chapter 18

The returnable aluminum cans fetched twelve dollars and ten cents at the grocery store. I didn't hesitate to pour every nickel of it into my gas tank. I had about seven additional dollars that I had collected by running my loose change, collected in better days, through the store's coin-counting machine, which takes 8 percent of the money for the convenience of converting the rest to paper dollars.

I drove across town and presented myself, wearing a smile and a business suit, to an old friend who wanted to catch up on business and politics.

We had a great discussion about any number of subjects until I noticed the time thinning out for me to get to my next meeting. I glanced at my watch, and he noticed the gesture.

"Oh, hey," he said. "You said you had to go. It's been great catching up and all. I'm glad you're doing so well and you're still with Stacey and the kids."

We hadn't talked any shop, nor had I asked him for help with money or a job. It just hadn't ever seemed right to broach the subject, and I didn't want to force anything.

"Who are you going to see, anyway?" he said.

"Oh, Brad Parsons."

"Really?" he said, and his face broke into a tight smile. "That's a coincidence. I've been wanting to talk to Brad about a business deal between my interests and his. It's a big deal—big for both of us. I haven't been able to figure out how to bring it up with him, though. Just talking about it exposes me to a bunch of liability and gossip in the papers. Hell, I can't even trust my lawyers. I mean, I trust each of them individually, but law firms spread gossip worse than high-school girls."

He paused and glanced away from me in thought. His lips remained tight, and his shoulders hunched a bit. It was just a moment, and then he sat up straight and turned toward me, all in a fluid motion.

"I know: *you* can do it. You can tell him I want to talk to him. I trust you. He trusts you. I know we both had to talk to you about sensitive issues with tax policy and other things when you were Speaker, and I know you can be discrete."

"Sure, I don't mind," I said. "I'd love to help."

In my head, I thought doing this ordinary favor cost me nothing, and I was eager to be of some use to *someone*, job or not. Even with the wrenching changes that were happening inside me, it was still flattering just to be made to feel useful. At home and with those who took pleasure in beating me down publicly, it had become difficult to see what real use I could be to anyone. Thus, the simple offer to trust me with a task meant a great deal to me.

I thanked my friend for his time, and he generously paid for the coffee. I left and headed to my next appointment, which I had strategically planned nowhere near lunchtime, to avoid the embarrassment of not being able to pay for my own lunch.

When I arrived at Brad Parsons' business, I sat down comfortably across from his massive, dark-cherry, wood desk. The light beamed in from the windows behind him, lighting up his gray hair and glinting off his wedding ring and the picture frames adorning the wall.

Brad seemed glad to see me and launched right in with an ice-breaker to clear the air.

"That's some stuff you're going through. Sounds like you got it right, though: take your lumps and focus on your problem. You can't—nor should you—explain it further. You know what Henry Ford the Second said when he got the ride they're giving you?"

"No," I said.

"He got caught at, like, five a.m. driving around in southern California with someone who wasn't his wife in the car. He was dead drunk behind the wheel. When the press caught up with him, he turned and said, 'Never complain, never explain!' And that was all he ever said about it until he the day he died. You didn't have another girl, though?"

"No, nothing like that. For me, the booze was plenty. Good thing, too. Stacey is mad enough as it is."

"You two together?"

"Living together, yes. Happily married? That's developing."

"Things'll be fine," he said. "I'm sure of it. You were one of the best there is. I know that. I've seen them all. They come in here with their hands out. They all tell me how they're going to be the next governor, senator, president. You're smarter than any of them, and you did a great job. I can't imagine what you went through dealing with the all the other so-called leaders in Lansing you had fighting you every day. Besides, you're good in business and don't even need the politics. I can't wait to see what's next for you."

"Oh, it'll be something. I'm being patient on it. I didn't really have a purpose for coming, other than to check in and let some friends know I'm actually doing better than I was even before the arrests. But I have something else to pass on, and if I don't mention it straightaway, I'll forget. (It's how my mind works.)"

"Spill it, then. What's up?" Brad said in his endearing way. He must have had a million things in the world more important than meeting me, and he couldn't possibly know what I was going to say. And yet, he gave me patience and attention as if I were the most important person in the world.

"Well, I was just with our friend—I'll call him 'Bill'—and he wanted me to relay a message. But he said it was just for you. He said this wasn't for your staff, your lawyers, or even your wife."

"I'll bite. What's ol' Bill want?"

"He said—and I don't fully understand this—'I want to make the deal we talked about before happen now. It is what I believe to be the right timing and proper in principle, and I am ready to go through with it.'"

"Impossible!" Brad said. He stood upright and drew his thumb backward across his chin. He spun around to face the sunny glow radiating through the window.

About ten seconds passed in complete silence as he thought through what I had just told him. Slowly his shoulders relaxed from their statuesque pose, and his hand lowered from his mouth.

"Yes, I'm interested. What else did he say?"

"Just that he couldn't trust the big law firms in town. He said they gossip worse than schoolgirls."

"Don't they just!" Brad said, and beamed a warm smile toward me. "You should know that, Craig. You're perfect. I assume he trusts you, or he wouldn't have said any of this to you. I trust you, too. You can help us talk this through. I want the deal to happen, too, but it'll take some work, and we both will need your strategic brain. It's not that straightforward."

"I don't even know fully what it—"

"You'll learn about it—just business full of the usual entanglements and politics. Stuff you're good at. How much do you need?"

"What?" I said. I was dumbfounded. I hadn't thought for a moment about working an angle, asking for money, or even telling either of these men I needed help. I was desperate, and at the same time, I wasn't even thinking about myself, for probably the first time in my life. I just wanted to help them—just wanted to be useful again.

The pain and tension of my reality eclipsed my formerly reliable talent for diplospeak political babble. I groped for an appropriate answer, but they were miles away. I had only one number in my head: the number of how far behind my grand adventures in stupidity had placed me financially. I had done a spreadsheet, and the damage totaled $97,500 in debts, bills, and general obligations beyond our living expenses. This was an amazing number, but it was a reality I had accepted. I knew where every single mistake was made, contract signed, and item purchased.

"How much do you need to, you know, play liaison for the two of us?"

"I don't know what to charge you, but I know what I need, if that is what you're asking."

"They're one and the same, Craig."

"A hundred thousand."

"Good. That's fair. It's a big number, though, so I'll have to wire it. Is it okay if I wire on, say, Thursday?"

It was Monday.

"Yes, that's fine," I said. "I appreciate it. I hope I can help."

"I'm sure you will. As I said, you're the best I've seen," Brad said, and sent another warm smile across his desk.

I was able to get through the rest of the conversation despite the astounding magnitude of what had just happened. I got to watch an astonishing act of Grace as it was happening to me. There was no luck. I didn't have any fear. I wasn't overly excited. I just felt an inexpressible sense of peace. I wasn't in charge of the world anymore. That much was clear. The one who was in charge of the world was an amazing force indeed, though—a force beyond any words I can place here.

I arrived at home nearly penniless and with barely enough gas in the car to get to the bank when the money arrived in a couple of days. Our pantry was nearly bare as Stacey worked through the aged canned foods and noodle stores we had collected through our marriage. When I walked in, she was scrubbing a pan she had used to make "macaroni and cheese and green beans—again!"

"Stacey, I know you're mad still, and after everything you said last night, I'm not sure what to say except that I—"

"What? You're going to tell me about the next surefire scheme you have? How you're going to figure this out in a way I don't understand? Or are you going to go get a job?"

"If you would let me talk, I have something to say, I think and it's more important that you hear this. I think this should matter to you."

"What, then?"

"Well, the two guys I met with had some big business deal they've been cooking up for years, and the first one I talked to wanted me to ask the second one about it."

"I don't understand why—"

"Let me finish!" I snapped. "I knew them both from when I was in politics, and they needed someone they could trust to play go-between with them as business owners on a big deal. They have hundreds of millions riding on it and wanted me to help."

"Why would they want *your* help?" she said.

I didn't even have the time or the interest to feel hurt by the shot she fired my way. I just said, "I don't know why they want my help. Maybe they think I'm the least likely person in the world to screw them up in the press, seeing as I'm motivated to hide from the media. Thanks for the vote of confidence, by the way."

"It just seems weird. But what is the point? Are they going to give you a job?"

"No, but the second guy I talked to asked how much I needed. He didn't ask me how much I charged an hour to consult, or how much the deal would cost, like my other clients. He said, 'How much do you need?'"

"So?"

"So I told him. I said I needed a hundred grand."

"What'd he say?"

"He said, 'Fine. I'll wire into your bank on Thursday.'"

Stacey's mouth opened, and her eyes grew wide. The pot she had been scratching with a soapy brush was still in her hand, shoulder high. She had her back to the double kitchen sink, and time seemed to stop. She went completely still.

The handle slid in her grip, and the pan rotated toward the floor. Her eyes stayed on me, and she made no attempt to stop the metal pot from crashing to the wood floor and bouncing away. She kept her focus on me and, after a pause, gently bent down to pick up the mess.

I stood there, taking in her reaction and letting her process what had happened.

"It's a miracle from God!" she said.

I didn't hesitate after she said those words. Before I even realized it, I was speaking back to her. I said, "And you shouldn't forget it. I don't think God ordered this thing up for me today at all. Just so you know, I didn't pray for money or to get dug out of this mess. That isn't what I pray for anymore. I think maybe God didn't like what you said last night, and maybe He wanted you to see what He thought of your faith."

"But I can't explain it," she said, trembling visibly. "It had to be God. There isn't any other way to explain it."

"I wouldn't try to explain it any other way, either. There's no use in trying to explain it. I'm telling you, these things that God is doing are real. My prayers are real. I guess now you get to see it firsthand. God is being very good to me. To us. He is doing things I don't deserve. This is what I believe."

"So what about the . . . ," Stacey began, and then stopped speaking.

I let a moment pass and said, "I'll have the money on Thursday. Things will be fine. I have faith in this, and I pray you will, too. I'll pay all the bills. This is enough to get us back to square."

Chapter 19

It was about a month later that Stacey and I began attending a small group from our church. When she suggested we participate in a group that was forming to talk about strengthening marriage, I took it as a positive sign and not an insult.

Stacey hadn't ever really talked about what happened so unexpectedly and indescribably the month before. I'm not sure why, but I could imagine at least a couple of reasons for her fearing the reception she might receive.

About a month later, when Stacey and I were hosting the small group from church at our home, the topic came up. The question concerned Abraham's raising his blade to kill his son because God had commanded it. Abraham had the faith to carry out the command and stopped only when one of God's angels intervened. The question was, *Do you have this much faith in God?*

The group had about ten members, and we all were seated in the great room of our house. Stacey and I sat together on the couch with one of our guests. Two were on the love seat, one in our formal chair, and four on our dining room chairs. The group surrounded the large, square, leather-covered coffee table.

The question made its way around the circle as members answered from the home-study notes they had written over the past week. When my turn came, I said, "I'd like to think I have that much faith, but I don't know for sure."

My answer came in response to a couple of lukewarm responses about faith having limits and how it wasn't realistic to think in terms of such life-and-death decisions anymore. This troubled me. I felt there was something I was holding back. As I listened to more responses, the tension grew.

By the time everyone in the circle had given their thoughts on the topic, I raised my hand to the leader and asked for a second thought. He graciously accepted my gesture, and I could feel Stacey looking right into the side of my face. I'm sure she was nervous about what I might say.

"I have more to say about this," I said, "and I just felt this overwhelming urge to share it with you. Sorry for taking a second turn, but this is important to me."

"Go ahead, Craig," the leader said, and the others nodded their agreement.

"I kind of understand this question a little differently because of something that just happened with Stacey and me and the kids. Many of you know me from before and what I used to do for a living, and most know about the trouble I got myself into this summer, but none of you know the truth about some of the tests and work God has done in our lives since then. I always give off this image of being okay, even successful. Here we are, for example, in a really nice house."

I looked up at the cathedral ceiling and readjusted my position forward on the couch.

"The truth is, the actions I took and my arrest this summer wiped out *everything*. I lost my ability to earn an income, what money I did have went to legal and other bills, Stacey and I had significant issues in our marriage, and I had to figure out how not to drink anymore after being in and out of active addiction for twenty-nine years."

Stacey's hand now rested on my knee for the first time since the night I got arrested in this very house. I noticed the affection and also took it as a gesture toward restraint, reflecting her concerns about what I might say.

"Most of what happened I would share with you anyway since it touches on other questions, but I want to share something specific to this question. Our position wasn't one of comfort. In fact, just a few weeks ago, I was so broke I had to resort to using returnable cans, loose change, and even my kids' piggy banks to feed our family. You see, I've always been self-employed, so there isn't any unemployment insurance. My last W2 job was back in the legislature, so our family isn't eligible for unemployment and the like—one of the only benefits the legislature hasn't greedily given itself. We had no money, no plan, and no safety net. Our families weren't in a position to help us, either."

I paused before making the final point—a point I wanted Stacey to hear me make aloud. I wanted to express my gratitude in a positive way, for once, instead of using it as a defensive measure in our private quarrels.

"The backward thing, though—what I did differently—was that I kept paying our bills. This may sound weird to you all, but I think it pertains to this question. God had done so much in me when I surrendered this summer, and I could feel that I was supposed to keep paying the bills on the house and the other things. I had faith that what I was doing was following God's plan. It took away all our cash for food and living and caused an enormous divide between Stacey and me. I kept doing this until everything was gone, and I was living on canned green beans so the kids could eat the hot dogs and macaroni. Then, when everything was finally gone and I was truly surrendered to the reality of poverty, God restored our finances in *one day*, over two brief meetings in the most unexpected circumstances. I went to touch base with two friends and network for a job, and what God had planned was that they both asked for my immediate help on a project that I didn't even know existed. The beneficiary of the business interests asked me how much I needed. He didn't ask me how much I would normally charge for my time. I told him how much I needed before I could stop myself from saying such an inappropriately large number. Before I could even hedge myself, he had said, 'Okay, then. I'll send you the money in three days.'"

I noticed an intense interest from the crowd. They all were hanging on my words and gestures, and at least two in the room were crying. I noticed that Stacey had reclined out of my peripheral view, and I turned to acknowledge her. She was crying, too.

"So you see, for me, God is very real. He didn't ask me to raise a blade to my beautiful daughters literally, but metaphorically that is exactly what I was doing. Our marriage was over in many ways, and this house and our possessions were gone. I was okay with it. I got to the point where God's plan mattered more to me than my own. Then things got better. God's plan turned out to be a lot better than anything I could have devised or worked for with my own time and talent. All at once, everything to do with money and paying bills was fixed. I mean, I still have challenges with money and may have them the rest of my life, but God showed me His power again. Maybe this time, He showed it to me so Stacey and you all could see it. I know I didn't deserve what I received."

I stopped speaking and lowered my head. I silently said, "Thank you, God, for giving me that story to share."

Stacey pushed forward on the couch. She was wiping away tears and beginning to talk, and it was clear that she wanted to add her experience to the offering.

"I didn't really understand it when it was happening, and I don't really understand it now, but it is real," she said. "I was so mad at Craig. My friends and people I trust—some even in the family—said 'you should leave Craig' and 'you need to walk away from your house; everyone is doing it after the banks collapsed.' I admit I thought they may be right, and I thought Craig was risking everything and maybe being irresponsible, too. Our marriage wasn't good, and he had lied for so long about so many things, I didn't know if I could believe in him or what he was doing. But I do believe this wasn't Craig. This was God. There is no other way to explain it. Things happened just like Craig said. I am still stunned by it today. We were so broke. So poor. Just a few weeks ago, I had no hope."

Then, to my surprise, Stacey added, "And I told Craig I didn't believe in him anymore and that I lost faith in God—the very night before the business deal came through."

She stopped talking and attended to her tears. I could see happiness in her weeping. She wasn't in pain. She was experiencing joy and relief. My arm was around her shoulder, and I gently pulled her toward me for a hug.

"Grace," the leader said. "Unmerited gain. That is what God gave you for your faith."

"I just so . . . I'm so amazed by what you have said," a woman said from across the room. "I think most of us here know about you but never brought it up, because we were trying to be polite. You've been, like, Novi's number-one citizen for so long, and watching all your success and then not understanding what we read about you in the papers this year . . . and, well, to imagine the poverty. I couldn't have imagined you wanting for anything. Thank you for sharing that powerful story."

"Well, it isn't my story," I said. "I'm not proud of it, but I am eternally grateful for it. I don't mind telling people who I really am anymore, because I can tell them who God really is at the same time, and that's pretty cool. For me, the story is real and the lesson is real, and I guess I was afraid to share it the first time around, and thank you for letting me share it now."

We moved on and completed the week's lesson together as a group. After the discussion, I felt closer to everyone in the room, and I felt a growing warmth between Stacey and me as we saw everyone out of the house and cleaned up after the meeting.

Before bed, Stacey and I had our first real discussion since I was preparing to leave the legislature two years before. We talked about the miracle we experienced together, the happiness that sharing it had brought, and the practical steps we should take as a family.

In that evening, a breakthrough occurred between Stacey and me. We had been married for twelve years, and we started seeing each other and acknowledging the value in each other differently.

This change brought about hope, but the enemy is never far behind.

* * *

Within a couple of weeks, I returned home in a great mood on a Friday afternoon. Things were going well. I was busy and had had a decent day scrounging out solutions for my small client base.

I entered the house through the garage and was leaving my shoes on the mat when Stacey lit into me from the laundry room. The laundry is just across the service hallway in our home, near the garage, and her words traveled through the room, the hallway, and, I would imagine, the neighboring yards.

"You didn't run the dishwasher last night."

"I'll run it now," I said.

"Don't bother; I did. You didn't call your mom like I asked. You didn't send the check for the money I owe my sister. You told the kids they could have a sleepover. You're driving me nuts!"

I left my shoes on the mat, stood up, and walked into the laundry. Stacey was facing the wall and slamming the contents of clothes bins into separate piles with startling ferocity.

"Honey, I—"

"And I'm going to see a counselor, and I don't care how much it costs."

I was taken aback by her words. I thought we had made progress and were finally getting along better. My life was getting better. Sure, I didn't have any money, retirement, or life or health insurance, but I knew that things were going to be fine. God had shown us this.

"Well, okay," I murmured. "I want you to be happy. I would never tell you not to go to a counselor. Is it something I'm doing?" I cringed. My sponsors had been training me not to be selfish or defensive, and here I was, my imperfections on full display.

"No . . ." And she gave a little gasp that seemed to hold back a bigger cry. She turned to face the wall again and began shuffling clothes. "It's not you. It's me. All these years, I have been so mad at you—your lies, your drinking. Now I don't know what happened to you, but it's great. I like that you are changing."

She turned to face me.

"That's the problem. I am still angry even after things are getting better. I thought if you fixed your behavior, I'd be happy. Well, you have, and I'm not, and I don't understand it."

"Then you should go," I said. "I support it. I found the same thing within me. I thought it was just my drinking, and I had to learn that drinking was my *solution*, not my problem. I learned I had to deal with my problems of fear, resentment, and anger. So I get it."

"Well, I'm going. I start on Monday. And don't try to give me any of your A.A.-speak. I'm not an alcoholic, and I hear you trying it with those people on the phone that call you at night. You talk like you're some kind of guru now or something."

"Those people at night?" I said. "Do you know who they are?"

"No," she said. "I just thought you figured you had good advice and were an expert big shot now."

"Honey, those are my sponsors or people I sponsor. It's how the program works. I'm not giving them advice per se. We share 'pain points,' and the only thing I can really do is explain what worked for me. I can't tell them what will work for them. I'm not an expert."

"You're kidding me. What's the value in that?" She turned from the laundry and faced me.

"I don't know. You just said you liked what it did in me. God did it, but I think He works through others. I get a lot of good suggestions every day—stuff I wouldn't have figured out on my own or believed until I tried it."

"Okay. You do your thing; I'll go to counseling."

* * *

A month later, things were getting rapidly better and progressively worse in my brave, new life.

The sweet, crisp fall air in Michigan is unique and glorious. All the world around us here slowly dies as the temperatures drop, winds gather, and days shorten. The blazing palate of yellows, oranges, and reds stands out against what remains of the green in the endless tree lines.

There is no place you can travel in Michigan without being within six miles of a lake. And to be out on one of the Great Lakes in the fall is to feel the wild splendor of this earth—one-quarter of the fresh water on the entire planet, gathered together in one place to toss and churn under blustery gray skies.

Inland, the focus shifts from boats to hunting. Vacations have ended, school and sports begin, and there is a quickening in the blood.

In our family, Stacey had grown in confidence and happiness since visiting someone described as a "Christian counselor" through our church. I never bothered to tell her that the programming at recovery groups was, in fact, based on Christian teachings, though they left it, properly and in all humility, up to the Higher Power to name himself or even reveal himself to those who sought Him.

I wasn't making enough to survive, and I no longer much concerned myself with what might come next. Things were good, and small jobs kept popping up here and there. I had a great group of mentors. One in particular, whom I will forever be indebted to, was introduced to me quite unexpectedly.

He was late for a speech he was going to give to problem teens about how he, too, had problems in life and had to turn them around. Coming from this person of considerable wealth, it would be quite a story.

When his private jet was diverted because of weather, the coordinator for the event asked me to stand in.

I gave the talk, and when the speaker who had to cancel heard about it, he asked me how I had gotten involved in things like this. He said, "I'm surprised. I've known your work for years, and I never would have guessed!"

The irony of this immensely successful businessman saying he wouldn't have believed I had such issues was a rich experience.

He is someone I admire and look up to. He is also one of the humblest people I know.

He had advised me to stick to what I was doing: a kind of "fix-it" guy for major business deals and for business owners with tricky or intricate problems. It was good advice that served me well.

On the trial front, tension was growing. Every time I had a court date, it made the paper. Worse, the paper maliciously used each hearing—which was essentially just to change the date—to rerun the false allegations against me. It was driving Stacey and our families crazy.

Everyone I knew stood behind me on what I was facing, but I know they were actually beginning to believe what they read. I wasn't defending myself in the press, so they quite logically began to assume that it must be true.

The prosecutor used every opportunity, in the newspaper and on television, to say that I had recklessly endangered my kids' lives. Neither the reporters nor the prosecution even bothered to investigate the fact that my "friend" Mick, who was a good deal drunker than I, had a loaded gun in his house, had beat the crap out of me, and had left his kids unattended while he pursued his little adventure all night.

Mick had his own problems for sure. I mentioned earlier that he seemed to have more on his mind than just me on the night I was arrested, and the consequences were becoming real for him, too.

Matters of the heart can afflict and bind us stronger than any addiction. For Mick, on the night of my arrest, had a focus and a secret bigger than me. His beautiful and unassuming wife, Mim, remained in blissful ignorance. I am still shocked and saddened after learning all the facts of what happened in their lives following that fateful night. As the sequence of events unraveled, it became clear that Mick's fixation on the night I was arrested sparked a course of action that forced things to a head for better or worse in his marriage with Mim. The goal was to get the wives to abandon their trip and come home early from their mini-vacation on the shores of Lake Michigan.

My anger burned when I learned of Mick's using the police and me in the manner he did that night. I had been just a means to an end but at the same time, I was grateful I wasn't going to have to live through what he and those affected by his actions were facing.

Hidden in the shadows behind many big drinkers and addicts are spouses and partners who suffer. This is true of what I put Stacey through and for Mim it would be no different.

Even though, for Stacey and me, our world had been so publically and catastrophically upended in the media, the events of that night had led to a miraculously better life for us. But it was the cause of far greater damage elsewhere and for others the pain would continue relentlessly. In many ways I was grateful for the tornado that Mick had manifested into that night, which had only served to finally push me in the direction of redemption and freedom.

However, the reality was that I still had real cause for concern. Mick's behavior that night had been bizarre, unreliable, and predatory. So what could I expect if the prosecution called him as a witness in my trial? He was out spinning the story to all the neighbors who would still listen to him, about how he had saved me from imminent disaster and was a hero of sorts. I guess he wanted to get some last licks in on me before he moved back to Texas later that year. I didn't know how things would be reconciled, but my focus had shifted. I had surrendered my will when it came to my drinking and relationships and now business and yet I wasn't done fighting when it came to the looming charges against me. My mind would race, looking for solutions, and I would allow myself minutes, sometimes hours, to vent my anger and frustration mentally at the judge, the prosecutor, Mick, and others. I knew that it wasn't healthy, and still I couldn't let it go.

At least, I knew I must try to overcome it. Before, I would have fought it all the way through. As the days and weeks went by, I focused on letting go of my concerns about the trial, and I had made considerable progress. I would hardly think about it until my lawyer, Harold, called to go over things. Then I was back to the old me.

"So the judge thinks he has a great deal for you," Harold said.

"Great for who?" I replied.

"All right, smart guy. Great for you. He wants you to plead guilty and enter the Sobriety Court. You know what that is?"

"Yeah, it's an eighteen-month deal. I see a lot of people going through it. You know I'm doing that stuff already."

"That's the point. We aren't asking you to do something you haven't already felt you needed to do for yourself."

"Yes, you are. You're asking me to say I'm guilty and not possess a gun for the rest of my life. That is a big deal."

"Big deal to who? Don't start giving me this right-wing constitutional crap you say onstage. What do you care? You don't go to jail. My job is to defend you. I'm trying. You're still keeping quiet in the media, though, right?"

"Yes. I say nothing. I do nothing. I don't return calls. There is one thing I want to do, though. It's a little weird, but I got invited to be the guest speaker at what is called the Reconciliation Breakfast, in Lansing. The current governor, governor elect, current and newly elected legislators all get invited. No media, no staff. No one speaks about it outside the room. I have been to them, and people hold confidence well. I owe some people my apology, and I want to make it."

"Then do it. But nothing else. Let me keep working on this, okay?"

"Will do," I said.

* * *

Two weeks later, I drove to Lansing for the Reconciliation Breakfast. It was a cold November morning. I hadn't written much down, but I felt good about having the opportunity to share.

I gave the speech. It was the first chance I had to tell my story to anyone publicly. Stacey wasn't interested in hearing it. My sponsors had heard it unfiltered, including the sixty pages of things I had done wrong in my life and needed to repair, but I wanted to share the story to more people. I wanted to say who I really was, and the miracle of what had happened, because maybe it would help others like me.

The event was hosted in a Lansing hotel. The large room had over a hundred elected officials, sitting at round tables with white linen. The guests were well into their hot breakfasts when a state senator introduced me to the crowd. More than half the crowd were people I had served with before leaving the legislature two years earlier.

To break the ice, the senator said, "So, Craig, have you been up to anything interesting lately since you got out of the legislature? Maybe something you can share?"

His question got a laugh from everyone in the room. I laughed, too. It was perfect.

I don't remember everything I said, but later I heard from someone who thought it was one of the most remarkable things he had heard in his career in office. He said he loved my opening line. I asked him what it was, and he said, "You said, 'I have been dishonest with you all about some important things for a very long time.'"

I told him it sounded as though I was telling the truth. We had another good laugh.

I do remember getting to state some things plainly. I did understand what I had done wrong, and could accept it. I knew what I had been falsely accused of, and I was more concerned with the truth of what I got wrong than with trying to use others' lies to defend my indefensible behavior. I explained how cleaning up my side of what was wrong in the world was all I really had the power to do, and added that this might be good advice for those newly elected to office. I got to acknowledge and take responsibility for some important mistakes I had made. I had the chance to make some amends.

It was an amazing day. I was invited to stay around and catch up with more people, and I did.

I got to work through my list, making amends to several people through the day. I also got the chance to learn something important about other people and their lives. When I connected with my friends and political colleagues and they heard what I was going through, I got to see something unmistakable in their eyes. I saw raw fear. I saw it in nearly everyone.

I have thought about it since, and I believe that many in public life understand just how thin the barrier is between the ridiculous stories about a politician's real life and those puff pieces making us sound tough and smart. Tissue thin, really. Once the tissue had been torn with a public figure's first mistake, it is open season and it seems that I could be accused of almost anything by the press and anyone else who could say and do anything they wanted and it would be accepted as something that I had done.

Everyone has something that could be described by the media in a way to make the public believe that the leader is corrupt or crazy. Many journalists are past masters at this. The journalist implies the lie or half-truth, and the public then connects the apparent dots.

I wasn't still angry with the media's treatment of my case. I had accepted their work, damaging though it was, as necessary for me to overcome my enormous ego and pride.

For those I met and spoke with on my visit to the capitol, I wasn't so sure they understood this gift: the freedom that comes with honesty and true humility. I savor that gratitude, and I continue to pray each day for my friends and those I don't know in high office and public life.

About a week a later, I got invited to be on the radio. I decided to sneak in one radio show, called *Anything Is Possible!* with Jack Krasula, on WJR 760 AM in Detroit. I didn't mention it to my lawyer. This was not long after Charlie Sheen had his own run-ins and was being chased by the media.

WJR 760 is the leading station for talk radio in Michigan and in the country. It has a clear channel (no other station has 760 anywhere), so people in several states and Canadian provinces listen.

I sat in one of the backup radio booths, with the host across the desk from me. It was a small studio used for taping shows and not for live radio. I felt comfortable because I had been in the station for interviews many times before.

At a break in the show, I told the host, Jack Krasula, that I felt bad for Charlie Sheen because he has so much in his life—money, women, houses, fame—that it will be hard for him to find what I found. I told Jack I had to lose everything first, and with Charlie, losing everything was going to take years, since he was making about $100 million per year.

"Again I tell you, it is easier for a camel to go through the eye of a needle than for someone who is rich to enter the kingdom of God," Jack said to me. "That's Matthew 19:24, Craig."

The words struck me. He was responding to my take on Charlie Sheen's situation.

"Wow," I said. "I never thought of it that way." I paused before speaking again. Even though the interview was done, we were still in the recording booth. "I guess it is true, though. It wasn't just the money. I was rich in other ways—things that had to be removed before I could pass through the needle. Anyway, my empathy stands. I feel bad for other highly functional people like me and hope to help them someday."

Jack leaned forward in his chair and moved the microphone away from his face with a sweeping motion. "Craig, it is such a blessing to hear what happened," he said. "I am so thankful you shared it here. Who knows? Maybe somebody hears this out there in Radioland and it helps them. Amazing! Thanks for being on the show."

As I drove home from the radio station, I wondered what sort of response the interview would get when it played the next Sunday. I felt good about it. It was nice, for a change, to share something on the radio that wasn't intended to advance my cause or defend myself, but just to help others.

I wish there were something I could do for those who are rich with the markers of worldly success—marriage, money, homes, jobs, friends—to help them understand this. I still pray to be used in a way that helps people understand this counterintuitive key to happiness.

Chapter 20

Over the month that followed, Stacey had begun accepting me back. Something fundamental had changed, and we were now fighting from the same corner on things.

I felt hope and optimism for my ability to provide for the family and even to move forward. Stacey and I had big decisions to make, and she began to value my opinion once again.

I never mentioned it to her at the time, but these small gestures meant the world to me. With all that I had gone through and the respect I had for her intense anger and resentment, this seemed like the most meaningful approval I had ever received.

Still, even with the major victories, life was far from perfect. The kids were back in dance class, but I didn't have any regular work yet. I poured myself into helping other people because this gave me the strongest sense of purpose and yielded the most happiness in my new life.

Everywhere I turned, people were going through what I had experienced. Some were in better shape, others far worse. I learned not to try to help but just to be ready to serve, as I had learned to do. No one could have "fixed" me, but their willingness to share what worked in their own lives and personal adventures was my lifeline and my pathway forward.

The world and my relationships seemed to take on a whole new shape. I stopped watching the news so much. I didn't really care how the Red Wings were doing in the playoffs. I experienced it all as a stream of changes that came in the form of improvements in focus and attention.

My love for Stacey grew beyond anything I had known before, and I could spend all day with my children, even at their messiest. I felt comfortable in my own skin, and at the same time, I understood that I didn't have a reason that others could understand for the peace I felt. The things pending in my life included dealing with the remnants of a failed business, a trial and potential jail time, no real job prospects, no life insurance, no savings account, and an Internet with hundreds of stories related to my troubles. I knew that the answers would come, so I just stopped worrying about them—well, almost all of them. I wasn't ready yet to let the trial go. I needed some help.

The thoughts of going to trial haunted me. What would I say? Who knew what Mick was going to say as he kept making up war stories about his "heroics" that night? What if I had to plead to something I hadn't done?

I allowed myself to think this over and over in my head. I knew it wasn't good for me, but I let it continue far too long, too often. I had let go of my anger toward Mick and the police. I had even learned to pray for the people I was mad at. I also learned to pray for their relief. They were just the same as me: broken, flawed people. And I came to understand that whatever their failings were, I was capable of equaling or surpassing them.

I couldn't let my anger toward the court system go, though. The prosecutors were the ones who frustrated me. Why would they keep on after they had all the facts and I clearly wasn't breaking any laws? How did they get the power, and why would they use it in such a perverse way?

The prosecutor in my home county was described to me by a prominent lawyer as being "a couple of French fries short of a Happy Meal." I took this to mean she wasn't professionally as deliberate as one might expect. Around the year of my arrest, she had prosecuted a woman for murdering her husband, denied her even the right to attend the funeral, and found out weeks later that the man had died of an aneurysm in his aorta—something very difficult for the wife to have done to the person she was sleeping next to in bed when it happened.

Not to be outdone by this misadventure, the prosecutor had proceeded to bring felony charges under an antiterrorism statute for a man who logged into his estranged wife's e-mail account with a password the wife shared with him. The couple were going through a divorce. The prosecutor argued her case all the way up to national, prime-time news-magazine shows, only to leave the hosts scratching their heads.

I was her third strike on trying to bring her brand of justice to the mean streets of my affluent little hometown. The charge was possession of a firearm while intoxicated. If I got convicted, I would have had to pay a hundred-dollar fine. This wasn't the big deal. The real problem was that the charge would be my second criminal conviction and would lead to jail time or a long, stringent probation sentence—punishment that may have been warranted based on my own failings that night, whether they were against the law or not. My problem wasn't the punishment or the fine. The thing I couldn't get past in my mind was the collateral consequences—the things ordinary citizens don't know about criminal convictions until they receive them.

I would never be allowed to own a gun again. I would be permanently classified as a violent criminal despite the complete lack of violence on my part. I would not be able to hunt. I would not be able to own weapons for self-defense. Plenty of people might see this as no big deal, but to me it meant a lot.

My lawyer didn't put much stock in the idea of my caring about owning a gun. He would say, "So, what? Losing your guns is a small price compared to jail!"

Harold's plan was to show the prosecution that they didn't have a case, and then try to get the best deal possible. I'm certain his plan was sound, but I couldn't accept it. I had no one else to vent to outside of my recovery meetings, so Harold got it in spades.

"Don't you think you can argue this?" I would say to him. Or "I think you should go stronger with this type of approach."

He tolerated my abuse of our friendship personally and professionally as well as anyone could expect—for a while, anyway. But as the weeks went by, his patience began to run thin. He would keep steady and just disagree with me, tell me to focus on the future, and cut short our conversations.

Finally, in November, about four months after my arrest, Harold approached me with a deal. We were in the courthouse, and he had me stashed away in a small conference room to keep me clear of the media. He had returned from the judge's chambers after successfully securing a new trial date without needing me to be present.

"Craig, this is good," he said. "You're not going to like it. It is good, though." He explained that a deal had been offered while he was away in the judge's chambers. "I want you to listen to me and I want you to understand it."

"Okay, shoot," I said.

"You will plead guilty to drunk and disorderly. You weren't being disorderly, and the judge is upset about that part of it, and technically, you can't be drunk and disorderly in your own home, but the prosecutor is buying it. She needs a win. You're a big political figure, and her political party thinks you personally are the devil incarnate, so she doesn't have a lot of room. I think if we both—the prosecutor and I—stick together on this, we can sell it to the judge. You would go into Sobriety Court and be subject to daily drug testing, which you already do, but it would keep going for eighteen months. You would have the blow-thing breathalyzer to start your car. You would have all the other rules like random home inspections and things, too. I think you would be good in Sobriety Court. And it's a real public thing, too, and I think the media would follow you through it and see your life change."

I sat there for a moment, taking in what he said.

"What do you think?" Harold said.

"Man, I don't know where to start here, Harold. I get what you said. I understand all of it. I go to meetings with people who are in Sobriety Court. I get it. I don't know. Can I think about it?"

"Don't think about it too long, hotshot. You need to understand, this is good for you. I'm doing what you need done. Call me after you talk to Stacey about it."

Leaving the court and Harold, my mind raced a bit through all the facts and angles. How did I ever get in this situation, anyway? Now I had to plead guilty to being disorderly and go through a public sobriety process. How was this going to work? How could I even afford it? I knew that Sobriety Court cost nine thousand to twelve thousand dollars, depending on who I spoke with.

Fear returned. Anger surrounded me. I didn't let it in, though. I drove home. I prayed. I called friends, family, and sponsors and prepared to talk with Stacey.

In my focus on the pending trial, it had been two weeks of prayer for me at this point. I knew I was being selfish, and at the same time, I couldn't stop it. The third-step prayer in a recovery program says to pray for God to "relieve me of the bondage of self." I began to understand that I needed help on this, and I repeated this prayer often. I certainly wasn't capable of relieving my own selfish thoughts and motivations. They would constantly beat their way back into my head, repeating and recycling their efforts. Some days, the lure of anger and resentment was more than I could handle, and I would fritter away an hour or more dreaming of overcoming my situation with my own strategy or plan. I would let my thoughts run until I cooked up a lie or half-truth. Then I knew it was time to shut down the train of thought and refocus my energy.

Relieve me of the bondage of self, Lord. Relieve me.

"Honey, I have some news today from the court," I said to Stacey.

I was sitting across from her on a bar stool at the island in our kitchen. On the other side, Stacey was cutting in half the sandwich she had just made for lunch. She had her face down and proceeded with her work while we talked.

"That stuff is still going on?" she said. "I thought it was done."

226

"Well, the Saline stuff is mostly done, but this is Novi. I haven't done anything yet there, and the prosecutor won't back off. Harold has a deal he wants me to consider, and I wanted to share it with you."

I told her about the deal, including the specifics about Sobriety Court.

"Let me get this straight," she said. "You screw up, and not only do I get Child Services rummaging through my house like I'm a bad parent—thanks to the Novi Police Department calling them—but now they have the right to come in and inspect our house anytime they want, for *two years*? Is this America still?"

"It's for eighteen months, and the Novi Police will say they had to call Child Services."

"It doesn't matter. I've known the officers there for what, twelve years, and they accuse me of being a bad mom by doing it!"

"Well, this is all my fault, but—"

"And, you plead guilty to drunk and disorderly, and then I have everyone judging me more than they already do. Let me tell you what it's like for me. People think you were running around the house with a gun, because that's what the paper said. They look at me funny. People want to know why I stay with someone who would do tha—"

"I didn't do that."

"It doesn't matter what you did. People don't care about the truth. They only go by what they read. I can't even go into the grocery store without being judged because of you. My mom gets it, too. She hates this. She wants to write a letter to the editor in the newspaper saying you were acting okay and that she couldn't even tell if you were drinking."

"She can't. Harold said—"

"'Harold said, Harold said.' Does Harold know that if you plead guilty to something, the public will assume you actually *did* it? People will think you did *all* of it. They'll also think, if you cut a deal, that you got out of what you really did, because of who you are. They'll think you're worse than what you pled guilty to.

You won't be able to explain it. This will be the facts going forward, and your kids will have to live with it, and my mom and dad . . . . My mom gets asked why she doesn't insist I move home, like you're some kind of dangerous man. She'll have to go through it all again, and I don't . . . ." She quivered as her tears took away her words.

Stacey was crying now, and I couldn't help her with words. I knew she wouldn't want me to hug her, either. By taking a deal, I would be hurting her and her family. Her mom was there, so she would have to live with people thinking she was covering for me, even when she told the truth. How could it turn out that I was being selfish by trying to give up? The solution didn't work. The situation was intolerable, and I had made fresh wounds over those that had begun to heal in Stacey.

* * *

"Relieve me of the bondage of self, that I might do your will instead of mine in all that I say, think, and do today, Lord," I prayed when I woke up. I was on my knees next to the king-size bed in our bedroom.

I didn't know what to do. I wished things would wrap up so I could move forward. I didn't like how it all would shake out in the potential deal that had taken shape, but I accepted that there would be some punishment. I assumed that going to trial wouldn't be a viable plan.

Every night, I would drink at least twenty ounces of decaffeinated coffee or tea. The purpose in doing this was to have a full bladder. Each morning between six and nine, I would have to submit to a urine test for drugs. The problem was, I couldn't pee on demand. Having a guy in the room watching the act made it a struggle every time. It got to the point where, to force the action on demand and not violate probation, I had to hold it till I practically wet myself.

I would wake up each morning, try to open the drug-testing place at six, and then head to a seven a.m. recovery meeting. I used the time to pray, meditate, and focus.

Compliance with probation was a terrible, anxious burden to carry. The checklist of things I must do and not do wasn't so bad, but just the prospect of stepping out of line and doing three months in jail disrupted a lot of my thoughts during the day. The best thing I could get from it was the increased attention to detail that the mandates required, but I feel for those who go to jail literally because they cannot urinate on demand each day in the crudest facilities imaginable.

After some thought and discussion on the subject, I phoned Harold to discuss my predicament and the feedback from Stacey and my mother-in-law, Marsha.

Harold was sympathetic to Stacey and Marsha's concerns about my pleading guilty to anything.

"Look, I get it," he said. "You plead guilty to jaywalking, and the public thinks you got away with being a barricaded gunman. I understand that. Aren't we both guilty of judging others that way, too? I just don't see a way out of this. You go to trial, and you may win because the facts are on your side, but the prosecutor will destroy your character and that of your family. It's what they do. You can't avoid it. My recommendation stands."

"Well, there is another thing, too," I said. "I just don't get the Sobriety Court thing. I mean, *eighteen months*? And they make me do this whole thing with the car, and I wasn't even driving. I don't want to agree to that."

Our conversation had built over the course of several minutes. Harold was being as patient as he could, but my last demands were too much for him to take. My selfish requests met with silence.

Seconds ticked by.

"Hey, Harold, I just don't want to—"

"You don't want to, you don't want to. You don't want to *listen*, is what you don't want to do, you selfish son of a bitch. What, you want to do my job? Or maybe that isn't good enough. Maybe you'd rather tell the judge how to do *his* job. You're so-o-o smart. In fact, I think you're smart enough to handle this on your own. Tell you what I'm going to do. Screw you. I quit. Find another lawyer."

Click.

I was in my garage, and I concluded our conversation on the other side of the entry door from Stacey, who was doing laundry.

I stood there shocked, paralyzed by what Harold had said. He quit. He was mad. I had known Harold for years, and he didn't say things he didn't mean. I had seen it before in how he handled others.

The problem was, Harold himself was a newsworthy guy. As the lawyer to billionaires and sports figures, he frequently, even though reluctantly, found himself in the media.

His quitting would generate a new round of news coverage—the opposite of what Stacey and her mom wanted. I would also be that much further away from getting a deal, and I couldn't afford to pay a lawyer to get up to speed for a trial. I was pinched, and I knew it.

And yet, for some reason, after immediately reviewing these facts, a smile came to my face. It wasn't a normal smile. It was broad and deep—an expression of how I felt inside. It was the kind of smile I hadn't felt for a good long while. I was genuinely happy, and I knew why.

I opened the door and followed Stacey around the corner to the kitchen.

"Who was that you were hollering with on the phone?"

"Harold."

"What did he want? Why were you talking so loud?"

"We were talking. He got upset with me. In fact, he quit."

"What!" she said. She tensed and cocked also her head over at the same time. "Why are you smiling if he quit? You need him. Without Harold, you're screwed."

I paused and held her eye, and decided to go forward with an explanation of how I truly felt, instead of a sales pitch. I knew that Stacey wouldn't take either approach well, so I'd better err toward a genuine description of what was going on.

"I'm going to explain some things to you," I said, "and you may think I'm crazy, but I mean every word of this. My whole life, I have tried to control things, and to a lot of people, I probably looked wildly successful doing it. And I suppose I did get some big wins. But the truth is, doing things my way always blew up in the end. I always had to look over my shoulder. I may get my way, but it hurt other people or left me with fear, anger, or resentment. Sometimes, I had to be selfish to win. I always had to put my priorities over others'.

"I know that what I did hurt you. More than that, I know that what I've been doing throughout our whole marriage hurt you. I've been incredibly selfish. I've embarrassed your family. I can't imagine what your mom and dad, or mine, are going through. I know how they glowed with pride over each of my achievements, and now all those people they bragged about me to are scratching their heads and saying I'm an embarrassment or worse.

"I don't want to do any more damage. I don't want to try to manipulate this situation anymore. I didn't do what they say I did. I made a mess, and the prosecutor is out of control. I have to deal with it.

"The reason I'm smiling is, I have been praying for weeks for God to take away the bondage of my selfishness. I let it go with drinking, and I let it go with earning money. You remember when I let it go over money and you didn't think it would work? Well, it *did* work, for the same reason as why I don't need to drink anymore. But for some reason, I couldn't let this court case go. I had too much ego. I have too much pride. I still want to arrange things for my benefit.

"The truth is, anything I do will just screw things up. But anything I *let happen* will probably be just fine. I believe in God now. I know He is real. He keeps showing me these things.

"I know it may seem like a burden I'm putting on you if I take a deal or if I go to trial and get sent to jail, but I'm asking you to consider what I believe now. How do I know this isn't the perfect plan? How can I be sure the cell mate that I meet won't start a business with me and make millions of dollars? What if I'm there to save someone's life?

"I don't want to get in front of this path that is being laid out for me. It's better—magically better—than anything I would have dreamed up on my own.

"I'm asking you to let me call Harold back and tell him I will do whatever he says, and will accept any punishment that comes down, no matter what. I want to see what God has in store for all this, and I don't want to influence it at all. I think this is an opportunity to grow spiritually, and that's more important to me now than other things, but I don't want to do this if you think I'm being selfish."

Stacey swayed back and forth as she pondered the case I made. "Do you really think you can do that and not regret it?"

"I do," I said. The smile hadn't left my face. I felt great, and I'm sure this was being telegraphed to her in my speech and manner.

"Then you're tougher than me," she replied. "I don't think I could do that and be happy. I do hope the truth comes out, and I respect you for having faith that it will. I'm sure my mom will, too, but you need to call her."

She looked me square in the eyes and said, "I support what you're doing, even if you are crazy." She smiled.

I could feel the warmth of her smile throughout my body. This simple gesture meant the world to me. Our relationship was healing, and I could see it and feel it.

I wouldn't have predicted in a thousand years the outcome of discussing with her the possibility of going to jail and willingly letting my character be assassinated in public. I was amazed that it led to the two of us sharing a smile and loving understanding about moving forward together in life.

I believed every word I told her, and I knew without a doubt that it was the right thing to do. I felt great, and I called Marsha straightaway.

"Craig, I love you, and you know I don't care what people say," she told me. "I was there. You were a perfect gentleman. I couldn't even tell you were drinking. In fact, you were more polite than I would have been. You told them to leave the house about a hundred times, and they wouldn't listen, and you had every right to be a lot louder than you were."

"Well, there at the end, I did tell them to get the 'f' out of the house."

"You know what I mean. Even when you said that, you weren't being mean. They needed to leave. I just wish you had this behind you. I wish I could talk about it public and tell people what really happened. I can't imagine what you're going through, but I've seen what has changed in you over the past months, and it's beautiful."

"This means a lot to me," I gasped. I was unexpectedly gripped with emotion and barcly got the sentence out without crying audibly.

"Whatever you do, this is going to be fine. I support you. I think things are going to be fine. You're doing the right thing. I wish you didn't have to do a deal and say you did things you didn't. It seems backward to me, but what do we know? I'm here to support you, and if it goes to trial, I'll be there, too."

"Thanks, Mom," I said.

"You got it, kiddo. Just keep your chin up."

The call with Harold was the next order of business, and after my third attempt, it was clear he wasn't going to answer.

"Harold, this is Craig," I said. "I'm sorry. I know you're mad, so I'm leaving this message. You were right. I am wrong. I don't care about the outcome. I trust you and will do whatever you say. You have my authority to negotiate anything you think is best with the prosecutor and judge. I will accept it and I won't complain. I talked to Stacey and Marsha. They understand and appreciate your work. *I* appreciate your work. I hope you will reconsider working on my case."

I waited an hour and called Harold's partner, Steve Vitale. When I first met Steve, he made me feel at ease instantly. He could shift between talking to the prosecutor or judge and ordinary folks in an instant. His demeanor in court was jovial and direct. He had a Matlock-style way of turning on and dialing into the points he had to make, while still coming off as pleasant as could be in between his efforts.

"Yeah, Harold is really mad," Steve said when the secretary at their office passed me through to him. "I wouldn't try calling him again anytime soon."

"Well, how do I square up with him, then?"

"You don't have to. I understand where you are, and frankly, I was going to be the trial lawyer if it ever got there anyway. I used to be a prosecutor. Harold would be there, but I'm the one that plays lead in trial. I told him I was going to do your case even if he didn't pay me for it. He'll come around. I meant it. You don't have to worry. I'm sure Harold will come back on board, but if he doesn't, you have me. We'll keep you posted. I should know more in a couple of weeks."

Chapter 21

Time marched by, and it was getting close to Thanksgiving. Beautiful fall colors still graced the streets in Michigan, and the lake was clear of boats. The air had grown crisp, and life was beginning to feel normal again.

Stacey and I continued to grow in our relationship, and I even began to speak openly with my parents and brothers about what was happening. On Stacey's side of the family, personal invasions of space were the norm. With the DeRoches, things incongruent, inconvenient, or indiscreet were best left unsaid.

My brother Paul had taken to my new approach in life and was risking additional hours of his time advising me on my finances. He had given me the same advice over and over since we were in college together, only to see it disregarded.

I was grateful to him for giving me a final shot. I needed the help, and I wanted to dig out as quickly as I could.

Our discussions about addiction left him frustrated. He would come back to the same things again and again, clearly lacking any understanding of why Kirk and I had veered so wildly off track from the same experiences he had in adolescent drinking and debauchery.

He would return to the subject every now and then until the truth I shared frustrated him enough that he could move on. He, as much as my parents, would be repeatedly exasperated by the fits and starts we both had experienced in life. I'm certain that he saw something different in me and, at the same time, privately worried that it wouldn't stick.

Kirk, on the other hand, continued to live life at full throttle. He always did. Everything about Kirk was larger than life. The projects he undertook, the adventures he went on, how he ate, how he drank, the relationships he had, and even his job all represented extremes.

Kirk was going to head off to Afghanistan again. He had come home and couldn't find work in Michigan.

His unemployability had nothing to do with his credentials. He was certified as an EMT, Marine-trained firefighter, and hazardous-materials-certified frontline guy. He had served honorably in the Marines for four years domestically and overseas. When America went to war, Kirk was working the airstrip in Yuma, Arizona, for twenty-four-hour shifts, and he deployed from the base to go to war.

Kirk balanced his life, his young family, and his career on the point of a needle, in many ways the same as I had. Anywhere he went, he was the most affable guy in the room, even though he had a terribly stressful and difficult job.

Since my return from rehab, Kirk had taken the time to give me advice, for a change. At the time, he had been off booze for a couple of years at least, but his doctors were medicating him in other ways. This troubled me, and we would argue about it.

Kirk had experience getting arrested for drunk driving, too. I think he properly considered me lucky in an imbalanced way. Getting caught had helped him change his life and move away from booze. Not getting caught had let me keep returning to booze. And yet, because of the burdens he had carried in his life since, he still thought I was lucky for not getting caught sooner. When we were young, I behaved inappropriately the same as he did. He got caught; I didn't. His employment options narrowed as a result. Mine didn't. So I understood his take on things.

Now that the shoe was on the other foot, Kirk became my resident expert on strategy and legal tactics. I told him he could have the job because I no longer wanted to play in the game. We had good talks and, for the first time, had the chance to walk through our experiences in childhood, in college, and as roommates after.

He told me that the first time Paul and I let him drink with us, he was 9. I pretended not to remember, but I did. I wanted him to tell me the story.

We had collected some wine out of the enormous Gallo Brothers gallon jugs that my parents and neighboring parents bought in the 1970s, and we had given him a glass. He told me he had known immediately that he would rather have that feeling than sobriety. It was instant for him, and that was why it was so hard for him to give it up. He said there was never a second of in-between time in his life. I confessed that I had had a similar experience.

Thinking back, it is amazing that brothers can live their whole lives and not share thoughts like this until after bad things happen— probably something to chalk up to our "man code."

We differed on a great many things we discussed, but I was refreshed by the honesty and hearing the perspective of my own brother filling in the gaps in stories I had long forgotten. Kirk was living in Tennessee at the time. Paul lived just a few miles down the road.

Both brothers accepted my path and seemed to understand my logic in letting go of the legal drama. They both told me they weren't worried about the name we shared getting run through the mud and that I shouldn't let that influence my decision.

I had tough but important conversations with both of them. Kirk was going to leave again for another year and fight in Afghanistan. He had another baby on the way, and since he couldn't find a job at home in Tennessee, he feared he wouldn't be able to provide for his family any other way. Paul told me he would help where he could. I agreed to keep them posted, but assured them nothing was happening quickly.

The conversation with my parents was much easier. They were completely supportive of what I told them. Our relationship had opened up greatly since the arrest, both in the small things like hugging or saying "I love you" and in the bigger, deeper talks we had never had when I was growing up. They have always been my biggest cheerleaders. I can't imagine the burden on a mother to raise three wild boys. The worry she must have had all these years, the tough spots she saw us through, the emotional weight she had to carry since giving birth to each of us four decades earlier.

* * *

Two weeks passed, and I got a call from Harold. I was driving home from a business meeting. When I saw it was from his mobile number, I got nervous because I knew it would be him on the line. I caught my breath and then pushed the green button.

"All right, tough guy, you got your wish," he said. "You're going to trial." He wasn't mad. He was calling from his office and just giving it to me straight.

"What?"

"Isn't that what you wanted last time we talked? You didn't want to do things their way, and now you don't have to. The prosecutor backed out of the deal that had been more or less accepted before."

"She can *do* that?"

"Technically, yes. Practically is a different story. The rules of poker apply here. You back out of what you say you'll do in front of a judge, and bad things happen. So you have that going for you. The judge is mad. I'm mad. The prosecutor, if she's smart, should be mad. This whole thing is a mess, which is why they never should have arrested you. So I guess we're back where you wanted us to be. The bad news for you is, they're going to kill you on character. I want you to take that seriously."

"Harold, I didn't want anything. I told you I would go however you want me to. I gave up. I'm sorry this has been such a crappy case for you."

"Forget about it. I'm just venting. I'm not mad at you. I'm frustrated with the prosecutor. I don't have any facts to base this on, but some around her staff tell me this is politics. They say her base is up in arms about her pleading down a gun case and she could get a primary election challenger if she did."

"Good to see the justice system is objective and not political."

"Ha-ha, smart guy. How many ads did you take out attacking the prosecutor in the last election for the member of your caucus who was running against her?"

"Touché," I said. "I never said I didn't have it coming. Just disturbing how overt it is."

"So you'll get a trial date. It'll be after the holidays, and it will not move. This case is getting old, and they try to get them done within six months of the arrest so as not to screw up your right to speedy service."

"Is there anything I should do?"

"No. Enjoy the holidays and relax. Prepare to show up, smile, and keep your mouth shut. I'll try to keep you out of jail. You know I love you, brother. 'Bye."

I thought about Harold's words. *Enjoy the holidays and relax.* I wondered if that would be possible under the circumstances.

* * *

I awoke to the glow of reflected sunlight from the snow-covered roofs and yards nearby.

The billions of leaves, created in green and then fired with blazing colors, now lay scattered on the ground, leaving a cold and barren landscape. Without the thrum and riot of insects and birds, and with the waterways silent, the only sound was the faint crunch of snow as a lone walker ambled by outside.

By today, the day of my trial, I had come to some important realizations. First, the trial would not be delayed. Nearly six months had passed since my arrest. Second, I no longer worried about what would be done and said in the court. I was not afflicted by anxiety over the outcome, good or bad. In fact, I would describe my interest in the outcome of the trial as curiosity more than fear.

It had been a long road to find myself at this place mentally, emotionally, and spiritually. To let go enough to find peace in this situation, I had had to let everything be taken away from me. And yet, I wasn't numb; I was fully engaged. At the same time, I was an observer and no longer someone comfortable with trying to inflict myself on others. I had done a great many things wrong the day I was arrested. My assumption was that Harold's worst predictions would come true. I believed that wild stories would be embellished and left just short of perjury by the professionals who prosecuted for a living. I figured the facts would be parsed and reassembled to suit the strategies of the lawyers or the judge. I knew this would be a difficult day for Stacey, my parents, and hers, although they, too, had become resigned to its inevitability.

I drove alone to the courthouse. This was not punishment by friends or family. It was practical. We had been advised that the court would be overrun with reporters and news crews, so the plan was to appear in small pockets into the traffic of the court and assemble together in a holding room inside. Walking in together gave the cameras too easy a time cornering us.

When it was my turn to enter the court, I walked swiftly in the door and through the metal detector. I turned right and weaved through other families huddled together around their various beloved defendants. The plan worked, and I made it to the holding room without being accosted. But I did get a full view of what was being set up. This was not going to be fun.

Accepting a judge trial instead of a jury trial made perfect sense from a legal and political view. To find me guilty, the prosecution was trying to create a new interpretation of a very specific law. A judge would be far less likely than a jury to buy this rationale—particularly a jury evaluating the law as it applied to a loathsome politician. This I understood completely. What never occurred to me when making this decision was the unintended consequence of freeing up the jury box for the media to point their cameras from!

The hour or two it took in final prep to begin the trial was excruciatingly long. This took a toll on each family member assembled. In an effort to distance my friends from the drama, we didn't ask for friends to be there and, in fact, hadn't talked much about when the trial would be. My parents and Stacey had been formally asked to remain outside the courtroom, and Stacey's parents had been asked to do the same—until Marsha was to be called as a witness.

I know how hard this slice of time was for me. I can't imagine what it was like for the others.

I entered the court with my lawyers, Steve Vitale and Harold Fried, and I could hear the camera shutters snapping furiously away until we sat down. The others in the court seemed to be bored citizens awaiting their turn at justice, who, to pass the time, had stayed in their seats for the morning matinee. As I walked past them, they began to rise. I looked forward and noticed the judge entering the chamber.

"All rise!" the bailiff cried.

It took only a matter of moments to get through the perfunctory formal procedures identifying the parties and claims and laying out the ground rules. I entertained myself by noticing the venue's parallels to the beginning of a prize fight. I supposed, if I were a lawyer, I might see this part of the trial as much like that little talk by the ref before the first bell rings.

The way a criminal trial works in America is, the prosecution is called first. They have to make their case. From the moment of arrest, the defendant can be functionally treated as guilty by all those involved in the justice system, right up until the moment they get to stand before a judge (if they make it that far through the intimidation and pressures to plead guilty early). Once the defendant gets in front of a judge, the scales of justice seem to rebalance a little, and the discussion becomes more subject to orderly processes.

While awaiting my trial, I had the chance to observe the modern practice of the lowest-level, highest-volume prosecutors of criminal complaints. Their behavior seemed much like what I had observed in the insurance business. These good folks functioned more as claims adjusters than as advocates for any sort of justice. In most cases they worked on, the crime had no direct victim, so their incentives were to serve the state, not the victims. This is perverse because the incentives are based in such questions as cost of county versus state programs, the expense of prosecuting this type of claim, the politics of who the defendant is (something I learned firsthand), and, all too often, the worldview, egos, and competence of the staff prosecuting lawyer, who was granted great power and absolute immunity.

My lawyer stood up, shuffled his paperwork, and gave the thumbs-up to the young prosecutor sitting at his conference table. In addition to the prosecutor, there was an additional lawyer and the first witness for their side: the arresting officer.

"People of the State of Michigan call Officer Willard Conner to the stand," said the prosecutor.

I paused and breathed in. I prayed, *God, I am just here for the show. Let me see what you want from this.*

A young and visibly nervous Officer Conner took the stand. The prosecutor also seemed to be fumbling through his routine. Feeling the tension in the room, I thought it must be tough for both of them, too. They were here to do a job, and their superiors, both on the police force and in the county prosecutor's office, had done a disservice by ordering up this exercise and then leaving it to their lower-level staff to do their dirty work.

Through a series of crisp, short questions, the prosecutor and my lawyer, Steve Vitale, were walking the officer through the facts of the night. Their pacing was impressive. The officer could answer most questions with "yes" or "no." I believe this was by design.

The shape and design of the prosecution's case in the course of this questioning morphed from the story in the media to an actual account of what had happened that night. I recognized what the officer was saying, and could discern that he was, by and large, telling the truth.

I was stunned. My expectations of police giving testimony had been jaded from years of experience in seeing their efforts play out in politics, court cases, and insurance-related claims. My belief was that the officer would simply manipulate words, cast aspersions, and leave facts unsettled in an attempt to justify his behavior. He did none of this. In fact, he made my case from start to finish.

At one point, about twenty minutes into the testimony, when my lawyer, Steve, was doing the cross-examination, the judge called for a sidebar discussion.

He interrupted the proceedings and called the lawyers forward for an off-the-record conversation. Since I had hearing loss from a young age, I could lip-read his words. Afterward, Steve confirmed the accuracy of my lipreading when I asked, "Did the judge say to you, 'We are here to establish the facts in the case, not destroy the career of the police officer!'?"

After the sidebar, not much slowed down.

Officer Conner had to verify that he had had my gun, the weapon I was allegedly carrying, in his possession and that it had been unloaded at the time it was handed to him.

"Okay. And the reason you were dispatched was for the gun, and you already had that secured, correct?" said Steve.

"That's correct," said the officer.

"So when you asked Ms. Zoellner if it was okay to come in, you mentioned only that you wanted to come in for the purpose of retrieving the gun, correct?"

"Correct."

"You did not say you wanted to come in for the purpose of retrieving the gun and for the purpose of speaking with Mr. DeRoche, or Craig, correct?"

"I don't believe I said that, no."

"Now, at this point, there are three officers in the house, correct?"

"Hum-huh," the officer mumbled.

"That's a yes?" Steve pressed.

"Yes."

"You've already retrieved the gun, correct?"

"Yes."

"And I take it that at no time did you officers have a search warrant to enter Mr. DeRoche's house, correct?"

"No, we did not."

The tension in the room picked up measurably with this admission. I could see the judge's posture visibly tighten as he leaned forward.

The young police officer's eyes widened, and the prosecutors looked straight down at their notepads and scribbled furiously. Steve didn't miss a beat. He pounced forward with his questions in rapid order.

"Now, um, on the times that Mr. DeRoche told you, when you were in the house, that he wasn't coming down the stairs, or conveyed to you that he wasn't coming down the stairs, you had already retrieved the gun and secured it, correct?"

"Yes."

"Okay. And you did not leave the house, correct?"

"Yes."

"You weren't within close distance when Mr. DeRoche was at the top of the stairs?"

"No."

"So even up to the point of you admitting that you weren't going to leave until Mr. DeRoche came down the stairs, you still have no evidence up to that point, before he comes down the stairs, that he's had any drinks, correct?"

"We weren't speaking with him. We were speaking with him to find out what had occurred and what was going on. We weren't speaking with him with the respect of placing him under arrest. The decision was made afterwards, when all the facts were together, after everybody at the scene—"

"So the answer to my question should be no, you didn't see any evidence that he had been drinking prior to his coming down the stairs, correct?"

"That would be correct," the officer muttered, looking down.

The judge shifted in his chair again. Steve lunged deeper.

"And despite not seeing any evidence of his drinking before he comes down the stairs, you state that you're not leaving until he comes down to talk to you, correct?"

"Correct."

"And when you went back the second time and you spoke to Mick before you went up to the house, Mick actually told you, the second time you went to the house, that Mr. DeRoche was acting differently, correct?"

"Yes."

"He told you Mr. DeRoche was very calm, correct?"

"Yes."

"He told you Mr. DeRoche was not at all agitated, correct?"

"As I recall, yes."

"And you got this information before going up to the house and knocking on the door, correct?" Steve said emphasizing each word.

"Yes," the officer said.

Steve's demeanor was one of disgust as he rounded out his questions. I am quite certain he was pleased that his line of questioning yielded truth, and it was the truth that had upset everyone in attendance. The judge was now visibly angry. His face looked as if the cop had just keyed his car.

Steve wasn't done, though. He had one more point to make. "And all you officers were in full uniform at this time, correct?"

"Yes."

"All obviously carrying your duty weapons, correct?"

"Yes."

"I have no other questions at this time," Steve said. He was aggressive in his final delivery. I think this perplexed Officer Conner. On the final question, he was no doubt thinking that it was a good thing to be in the house with his shiny uniform, badge, and gun—maybe even a matter of professional pride. Only now was he just beginning to understand what he had done wrong six months ago.

The point wasn't lost on the judge. He was steaming. Three officers coming into someone's house without permission, a warrant, or any semblance of a reason. The prosecution hadn't even posited a theory during its forty minutes of argument and testimony, and it wasn't going to have a chance now. After a brief scramble by the prosecutors to try to bring things back in line with what they had sold to the media, the judge furiously interrupted.

"That's it. We're done here. Everyone in my chambers. Now!" He slapped his gavel down.

The court was dead silent. The judge got up from his chair and strode briskly out.

Steve looked at me and winked. "Well, I gotta go see what the judge wants. I mean, I think I know, but, well, let's not guess. Stay here."

"What am I going to—" I started.

"You stay right here. Don't say a word."

Chapter 22

Two weeks had gone by since the judge abruptly put an end to the trial. Time stood still for me.

Things seemed to go well. The police officer had told the truth on many things. Sure, at the end he threw in a couple of haphazard half-truths. He seemed terrified (I assume, of his bosses on the force) and said he didn't remember my telling him to leave the house. At the time, I was so delighted with the rest of his testimony, this didn't much bother me. I figured that at least he hadn't lied about what I said; he merely said he didn't remember that one sentence I had spoken over and over again for five minutes straight.

The next day, I was front-page news again, with full-color photos in multiple newspapers. Stacey and I kept this from the kids and, surprisingly, didn't argue about it much with each other.

I just wanted it to be over.

The judge announced to the lawyers that he was ready to rule on my counsel's motion to dismiss. He would rule not only on our motion based on my constitutional rights under the Second Amendment; he would rule on our Fourth Amendment argument saying the whole incident was an illegal search and seizure.

I wouldn't allow myself to imagine what the day would look like or what the ruling might be. At this point in my life, I had finally started to learn that thinking about the future was the surest way to make a wreck of it. Just letting the future unfold rather than trying to control it takes a lot less work, and expectations don't sour the successes, however small they may be.

The story in the news came and went. I spent the next two weeks working and staying involved with Stacey and the kids. I no longer worried about what would happen when court reconvened on January 27, 2010.

On that day, I awoke in my home, lying next to Stacey. I crawled out from under our thick comforter and knelt quietly beside the bed.

I took stock of the miracle it was to wake up sober in a beautiful home, still married to the woman I had hurt so deeply. I thanked God for the process I had been going through, and thanked Him for how long it had taken. I noticed that it was six months to the day since I was in the jail cell in Novi. Finally, I thanked God for what He showed me whenever I got out of the way of His work. I was still astounded by how He had enabled me to survive financially and, later, by the display in the courtroom. I promised God I would hold up my end of the deal and bear witness that others might come to know His power, grace, love, and way of life.

I went downstairs and took my home alcohol breath test, which the court had me install to comply with its orders. I went to the seven a.m. recovery group meeting in town. There, I told those in attendance that I felt I had grown a bit and that I looked forward to hearing what the judge had to say.

At home, Stacey and I got the kids ready and sent them off to school, bundled up in their hats, scarves, and thick, clunky snow boots. When nothing was left showing but their eyes, we sent them on their way. Phoebe, at 3, was too young to know or care what was happening, so she stayed behind with Grandpa Zoellner, who had decided—with a lot of encouragement—that his temperament and past heart problems weren't a good fit for the outing.

My parents, Stacey, and her mom all headed off to the court in separate cars. I told them I didn't know what to expect, but that I expected the press to be there and that we shouldn't give them any more than we had to. Everyone agreed to wait in the parking lot until they got the word that it was okay to enter.

I left first. I was wearing a suit and looked like an attorney going to court to work for someone else. I drove straight to the courthouse, still happy knowing I had been treated fairly in the hearing we were now about to conclude.

When I arrived at the court, the snow had been plowed from the asphalt parking lot, but it was still covered with ice spots, and blustery wisps of snow were snaking across it in the cold Michigan wind. The sky was bright blue, and everything on earth seemed to glow in the sunlight reflecting off the dazzling white blanket that covered every surface but the roads.

I breathed in the cold, fresh air and smiled. I could feel how tight the cold day made my face, and my hands felt the bite from the subzero chill.

I walked briskly into the courthouse and through the metal detectors and straight for the back room, where I saw Harold and Steve waving at me.

"It's a friggin' zoo in there, Craig," Harold said. "Don't go look. They're in the lobby, too. I feel bad for everyone else who had a case scheduled today. They got no idea what's happening."

He continued. "Sit down and shut up. You know the drill. I love you. You know that. You're doing good. You're gonna win. No matter what happens, you're gonna win. I think you'll be fine in there, but that isn't the most important thing. You've come a long way. You got nothing to look back for or be ashamed of. When we're in there, keep your head up and listen. Steve's gonna finish it. It won't take long. You're up first. The judge wants to get the media circus out of here, and he told us and the prosecution to be ready now. Get your family ready. We're going in."

"Crap, Harold! Seriously?"

"Do it. Everyone's ready."

I frantically called my parents on my cell phone. I had only moments. Then Stacey came back to the holding room and loudly said that she had seen my folks walking in with her mom, Marsha. Another lawyer who worked with Harold and Steve intercepted them and held them outside the courtroom. I had left the holding room and walked past them with Steve and Harold, through the huge wooden doors in the back of the courthouse. I waved and said to Stacey, "I'll be fine. This won't take long."

It was a weird moment for me. It seemed like those disjointed, dreamlike moments when you get wheeled back for surgery while still conscious. I didn't have time to think for long, because the doors in front of me were open, and I could now see the zoo in operation.

Gone was the dark, sterile, sedate room I remembered. People were shuffling everywhere.

To my right, I could see print reporters standing with their pads and papers. On my left, others were waiting for their day in court. Up front, the court officers were assembling near the bench, and to the right, television and still cameras were stacked three high, the entire width of the jury box. My decision to select a judge trial instead of a jury trial had yielded an unpleasant dividend. The jury box was so packed, I couldn't have fit my 3-year-old in there.

None of the reporters said a word, and the clicking of camera shutters was but a minor nuisance. They couldn't advance toward me, so I just had to keep walking and deal with it. I made a mental note not to chew my nails, pick my nose, or make any abrupt gestures.

I walked through the barrier and sat in a chair next to Steve and Harold.

Almost instantly, the shuffling and soft chatter ceased as the door opened and the bailiff commanded, "All rise!"

The court fell silent as everyone stood and then sat back down.

The judge began with a simple explanation of why we were here and the reason he had concluded the hearing on our motion to dismiss. He said he was ready to rule on the motion.

He paused. There was a faint clatter from the jury box as the camera crews made their final adjustments. I did my best to sit straight, keep my composure, and look straight ahead. My hands felt cold, and a film of cold sweat had appeared and dried in the moments I sat there mute.

What came next caught me completely by surprise. The judge began speaking again, this time with a notable rise in his tone and volume. He was angry, and it showed. The stern, directed comments that judges make when delivering a ruling or sentence are typically aimed at the defendant. Their profession develops them into masters at delivering succinct, cutting, extraordinarily clear pronouncements to their targets. By and large, they do it adequately, and they carry it off well far more often than not. It takes the judge a long time—the entire length of the trial—to get his or her turn to speak in judgment. They have to wait until the end. For me, this day was the end, or so I hoped. Today was the day for the judge to announce the findings of fact on who was right and who was wrong.

He ruled in our favor on the violation of my Second Amendment rights, saying it was not a crime merely to possess a gun somewhere in my home. Off the published transcript, he commented that owning a gun and being intoxicated would make criminals out of fifty million Americans each Saturday night and that the prosecutor might as well have tacked drunk driving on to the charges, because I also had the keys to my car, which was parked in the garage.

Tension still filled the room. The case was over, but the judge wasn't done. The prosecution stood there, taking in the loss. My attorney stood next to me. Everyone gazed forward, and nobody moved.

"And I'm not done yet!" the judge continued. "Three armed police officers entering the defendant's home and taking his possessions. When you don't have a search warrant, the fact that you have a badge on your chest doesn't make you any better than armed burglars. On the matter of the Fourth Amendment, violation of illegal search and seizure, this case is dismissed as well."

When the gavel dropped, the victory for my lawyers was complete. The court erupted into loud chatter as the judge moved forward in his docket and announced a brief delay while the media left the room. He looked at me and said I was free to go, released from any bond or compliance with court orders, and that my case before him was complete. He wished me well in life going forward.

I turned, smiled to my attorneys, shook their hands, and said, "I'd better get out of here."

"Go," said Harold. "Get going. You can beat the media if you follow me—I know a way out."

With that, we made our way through the side door and met the anxious faces of Stacey, my parents, and my in-laws. They were anxious, and they knew from the commotion that something big had happened. People were now beginning to pour out of the courtroom doors.

"What happened?" Stacey said.

"I won. We gotta go. Now. Please, I'll explain when we get out of here. We need to go, though. The media are all here, and they're going to try to corner me. Follow me. Let's walk."

This was clearly unacceptable to them. The small group of my closest loved ones had been barred from the courtroom, had no visual understanding of the throng of media in attendance, and hadn't gotten to hear a word of what happened in the trial or on the motions, or the outcome. They followed me but kept firing questions as we walked.

We made our way to the exit by the entry metal detectors, and I was ahead by several steps.

"Come on, we need to hurry," I said.

"I don't understand," my mom said. "Are you done now?"

"Pretty much, except the appeals will probably happen," I replied.

"You have to appeal?" said my father-in-law.

"No, I won. *They* can appeal and probably will."

"You're walking too fast," Stacey said. We were moving carefully along the frozen sidewalk after leaving the building. Between my mom and my mother-in-law, they had about seven surgeries on knees and hips, and they were hoofing it as best they could.

"I know, but I just want to avoid the media. I want to go."

"Too late," Stacey said from the rear. Behind her, I could see the cameramen bailing out of the exit doors and sprinting across the parking lot toward me. I stopped walking, encouraged my family to back away unless they wanted to be on the news, and stood ready for the unwelcome questions.

I knew the drill. I had done it countless times in my work in politics. You spend your career trying to chase up the cameras, and they're hard to find. Then, when you screw up or get beat on a political move, *they* find *you*. They come in with a force and energy that makes the paparazzi look like a bunch of slackers.

I turned and stood straight as the microphones were thrust under my chin and the wall of cameras formed up.

The reporters were looking for me to spit some venom at the city of Novi, the police, or the prosecutor. They asked, "Are you angry that they arrested you?" And "Do you expect to take action?" This was still America, after all.

The press understood the situation a little better now—a full six months after the night of my arrest. What they had reported before wasn't true. The media report most things in a win/lose scenario, and now the roles of winner and loser had been dramatically reversed. Now that I was the "winner," the reporters expected me to use the same aggressive, malicious language the police and prosecutors had used. Some even asked me, "What really happened that night? How did *they* get it so wrong?" I found the use of the word "they" a little bizarre. Here was a whole crowd of eager, excited people who hadn't even considered that their incorrect reporting made them part of the very group with egg on their faces.

After letting a couple of questions go, I answered them in a way that surprised everyone, including me. I didn't have anything bad to say about anyone. I was just relieved. I said, "What happened was far different from what was reported. So I don't have a great deal to be embarrassed about or ashamed of. You know, I can be happy with what I am doing in my own life, take the good out of this, and just move forward. Before, I had too much pride and too much shame to be honest and talk about my own drinking problem that I have had since I was a little kid. It wasn't something that just developed, and I can talk about that honestly now, so I have no problem coming forward with the truth."

This seemed to throw everyone off, and the questions died away quickly. I was relieved to see the reporters go. As we left—this time slowly and without warring camera crews and reporters in pursuit— Harold said he was particularly impressed that I didn't go back after the prosecutor in the media. He said most people would.

I simply told him, "I feel good about the things I said. I'm moving forward now."

"You should feel good about them," Harold said.

I saw my mother-in-law, Marsha, behind him, nodding approvingly. Stacey was there, too, smiling at me.

It was one of the craziest days I could have imagined having to live through, but it was over now. The trial had ended in spectacular fashion, and it felt good.

When we returned home, Stacey and I enjoyed our peace—until we started flipping channels at eleven p.m. and saw the news. We had known it would be there, of course, but didn't want to hear any more about it.

The reporters seemed to grope around in their explanations. To them, the template didn't fit. They had to say that the case appeared to be different from what they first reported. Then they quickly ended their segments with the warning, "The prosecutors said they already have copies of the judge's orders but are very likely to appeal this decision, saying that in their view, this was a very dangerous situation."

Stacey turned off the television and said, "How can they say that still?"

"Absolute immunity, honey. They can do whatever they want, even when they lose—and we pay for them to do it with our property taxes. Fun to know how it really works, isn't it?"

Chapter 23

The day after the judge dismissed the charges against me, I woke in a panic. My body lurched upright in bed even before my eyes opened.

The notion that I was going to miss my morning drug test had fired the adrenaline, revving my body into high gear before my higher brain functions were even awake.

"What are you doing?" Stacey said.

I looked at the clock. It was still before eight a.m., and I would have had until nine to get tested. But I didn't have to test today, and, God willing, I would never have to again. I reassured myself that all was well, said a prayer of gratitude, and tried to relax.

* * *

It was summer, months after the trial, when I caught myself running out of room with my finances and sense of peace. I was nowhere close to drinking. The desire was gone, removed the year before. I was doing more in recovery circles and practicing the five basics I had learned from the Dignitary Sympathy group. Still, I was wound up. I knew that my life was continually getting better, and at the same time, I wanted to resolve some big issues. I wanted to know what I should do with my time—how to provide better for my family with health insurance and cash. I earned some big paychecks, but it was still hit or miss, feast or famine. I craved some stability, and I was pursuing it through my own willpower, despite knowing that this tactic worked poorly and, at best, achieved temporary successes at oversize costs.

At the time, I had about three hundred thousand dollars in business deals owed to me for my work, and I was getting screwed over by the partner who had brought me in to help bail him out. I should have realized that helping someone out of a multi-million-dollar deal at a time when that someone was desperate might create too great a temptation to stick me at the end. Looking back, I was naive in not pinning things down. Chalk it up to experience.

For the previous two weeks, I had been calling the deadbeat businessman I had helped, who was now a deadbeat client. Then, in a moment of sudden clarity, I returned to what I had come to know of success: I worked to get out of trouble my own way, through prayer, meditation, and focused discussions. I asked for help and guidance. And I decided to let the debt go. I would get the money if it came. It was time to move on.

The same day, I got a call from a man named Ethan Nadelman, the president of the Drug Policy Alliance in New York City. He explained he was hosting a panel on drug addiction and public policy from a conservative perspective, for the benefit of a liberal audience he was convening in Washington, D.C. The idea was for us to speak about how our conservative principles seemed to match their liberal principles concerning the American criminal justice system. In the summer of 2011, this was a new discussion in Washington, and it was of interest to some leaders Nadelman had gathered for an event.

I was pleased to get the call and offered to attend. I told Stacey about the trip.

"Why would you take two days to go to Washington if they won't even pay you?" she said. "Do they want to be a client of yours?"

"I wouldn't take them as a client. I appreciate their work, but we aren't on the same page politically. I just want them to fund my trip down there. I'm going to try to schedule a couple of meetings and maybe prospect for clients. I'm also going to check in with some of my old gang who are now running the Romney campaign."

This was really all the thought I gave to the trip. I didn't do any preparation for what I would say, but I was ready to help.

On the panel with me was Grover Norquist, the controversial leader of Americans for Tax Reform, and author of the "no-tax pledge" that all aspiring conservative candidates seemed to be signing on their way into politics to show their fiscal, right-wing bona fides. David Boaz, vice president of the CATO Foundation, was there, and Pat Nolan, president of Justice Fellowship, joined by phone.

After the introductions, the purpose of the panel was clear to me. In the room was national leadership representing the three main conservative bloodlines in US politics. The Libertarians were represented by CATO, the fiscal conservatives by Grover, and the social conservatives by Pat Nolan. I was introduced as the person with experience in both addiction and running a conservative caucus. The liberal audience genuinely wanted to know what a conservative point of view looked like when it came to criminal justice reform issues. I answered them honestly, succinctly, and no doubt surprisingly on a number of their inquiries. It got to the point where the other panelists started commenting on what I was saying, and agreed with it, too.

When I left the room, all three panelists asked what I had been doing with my time and whether I was available to be more involved in this area of the conservative movement. I joked and said, "Didn't you hear me? I was out doing field research and getting arrested!" They laughed but encouraged me to follow up. In fact, all three of them encouraged me to meet a man named Chuck Colson, who ran the nonprofit where Pat Nolan worked.

At the time, I knew nothing of Chuck Colson except that multiple people had brought up his name after I told them how God had revealed himself to me in the rehab center. I wasn't running around hitting people over the head with my spiritual beliefs. But when asked, I always took the time to hold up my end of the promise and bear witness to what God had done in my life, so others would know that it was His work and not mine.

I told Pat Nolan I had been hearing a great deal about Chuck, and agreed I should come back to Washington in the next couple of months to meet him. I looked forward to the meeting but didn't think too much of it otherwise. It was July at the time, and we planned for me to visit in early October.

* * *

When I went to visit Prison Fellowship and Justice Fellowship, I was greeted warmly and was put up at their guesthouse on the corporate campus, in the D.C. suburb of Lansdowne, Virginia. It was a comfortable house with books everywhere. I had finally located a copy of the book *Born Again*, a runaway best seller that Colson had written in the 1970s.

Chuck Colson was President Richard Nixon's political right-hand guy—something like what Karl Rove was to President George W. Bush, or James Carville to President Clinton. He was a political legend who engineered the largest electoral victory in modern American history in Nixon's landslide reelection win in 1972. He was also part of the biggest presidential scandal in American history and went to prison for a crime he voluntarily revealed during the Watergate investigation.

Colson had hit his own bottom in life after realizing the emptiness of the power and success he had achieved in his career. Tired of the incessant Watergate inquiries and the burden on his young family, he had surrendered and let God redirect his life. And he made a most unusual offer to a federal prosecutor. He basically told the US attorney that he would tell him everything he was involved in and that it included a felony. He told them the downside was that they would never find anything about his involvement in Watergate, because it wasn't something he was involved in. He also wasn't interested in helping the prosecution by cutting a deal of any sort. He said his faith had made him see that it was more important just to come clean, knowing that from there, things would work out for the best.

I would have loved to be a fly on the wall in that discussion at the United States Justice Department. "Let me get this straight: this guy will tell us *everything*, including releasing a confidential FBI file, to smear an intelligence leaker named Ellsberg?"

Daniel Ellsberg was a government worker who was releasing damaging documents on the Vietnam War, which made a fool of President Lyndon Johnson. In doing this, he had, in Colson's view, damaged the country. So in a way, Chuck was snared. He would serve seven months in federal prison for showing an FBI file to a *Detroit News* reporter to save the image of a Democrat (President Johnson). Funny how the world works sometimes. When I was in my twenties, the first lady, Hillary Clinton, was believed to have misused over nine hundred FBI files, and the country responded with a collective yawn.

What was clear to me in learning of all this was that Chuck Colson had thrown all in with his faith. He didn't want what he once had, and was willing to pay any price to live and serve with a greater purpose. I found this admirable and immensely compelling. After reading his first book and a couple more of his later works in preparation for meeting him, I grew interested in seeking his counsel on my spiritual growth as well.

It was about ten thirty at night, and I was in the kitchen of the guesthouse, making myself a cup of tea, when Chuck Colson walked into the room. They had just gotten back from a dinner in Washington, D.C.

"Oh . . . hi," Colson said, putting out his hand. "I'm Chuck. How are you?" I was taken by how sharp this octogenarian was in his appearance, dress, words, smile, and all-around enthusiasm. He just pulled me right in. He was wearing these big Ray-Ban-style, plastic-framed glasses that had been popular in the 1950s, and he pulled the look off nicely. His full head of hair still had traces of the original brown. His suit looked as crisp as if he had just put it on, and his black shoes were so shiny they gleamed.

"This is Craig DeRoche," said Jim Liske. "He's down here to meet some of the crew. He was Speaker of the House when I was running Ridgepointe Church in Holland, Michigan, and building grassroots support for your work."

"Oh, that's right," Colson said. "I heard about you. It's nice to meet you. It's important that people of faith and conservatives start talking about addiction. We've been silent too long, and it's a serious problem. I'm glad you're here. Make yourself comfortable."

"Thanks Mr. Cols—"

"That's 'Chuck,' Craig. It's all I've ever gone by." He spoke with the remnants of a Boston accent acquired decades before.

"Thanks, Chuck," I said. "This place is beautiful."

"Well, it makes it easier to travel, and it costs a lot less than shelling out for hotels." He chuckled. "Hey, there is a thing I wanted to tell Jim. You should hear this, too, Craig. While we were leaving the restaurant, I'm just walking toward the door and I feel someone grab my wrist. I stop and look, and it's John Kerry. He says to me, 'Chuck, you know, I think I owe you an apology'—just like that. 'Man, with all the things we have said to and about each other, it would be great to put it all in the past.' I was so surprised. I guess God just went before both of us and irons these things out."

I was stunned. Here I was, talking to one of the more colorful characters in the history of our country outside of its elected officials, and he jumps right to this fascinating detail from his dinner. I thought about how long the two of them must have been at odds, going all the way back to when John Kerry was a war protester testifying before Congress, through his being the Democratic Party presidential nominee, and beyond.

"And there is one more thing, Craig," Chuck continued. "I need your help. I have something I've got to do tomorrow, and I talked with Pat Nolan and he isn't feeling well. Could you testify on our behalf tomorrow at the US Senate hearing on the renewal of the Second Chance Act?"

"Well, I—"

"I mean, if it isn't in the way of your schedule."

"No, it isn't that. I'm just not sure I'm up for doing it the way you want."

"Nonsense. You'll do great. You know what you're doing."

"Well, I know what I'm doing testifying in front of a committee, but I don't know that I can represent the Second Chance Act the way Prison Fellowship would have me do it."

"You know this better than anyone else who is going to be in that room tomorrow, because you've had to live it. Pray for guidance. You'll be great." He smiled. "Now, I'm going to go turn in. It's late for old guys like me. I'll see you when you get back to the office."

* * *

I went to bed fairly confident I could pull off what Chuck had asked me to do. I called Pat Nolan and talked it through with him and read everything I could on the Internet.

Pat was as enthusiastic as Chuck about sending me into the meeting. The hearing was going to be senior staff only and maybe some senators who would be coming and going. This took some of the pressure off.

I felt bad for Pat, who had some debilitating health issues that, he told me, were chronic and difficult to control. He had been traveling less and doing everything he could to keep the ball rolling without any real staff support. It was good to give him a lift and assure him that Justice Fellowship—the advocacy side of Prison Fellowship—would be served to the best of this volunteer's abilities.

The meeting went well, and I was specifically called on to explain to the conservative senators' staff members why the bill should be supported when it increased funding in a year (2011) when the government was heading toward a shutdown over a debt-funding dispute.

I explained to the Senate staff why the funding was conservative on an economic, practical-value basis, and suggested a method of including it in the deal that Speaker of the House Boehner and President Obama would later strike.

Something must have worked, because the bill was renewed and it included the funding in dispute, too. In a year when no new money was spent, new money was, in fact, spent. I am used to seeing considerable deviation between what is reported and what actually gets signed when it comes to legislatively approved budgets.

When I got back to the office, I made a circuit of meetings to get acquainted with the different areas of the work at Prison Fellowship. I was greatly impressed with the work they did. Later in the afternoon, I was leaning against the desk of Chuck Colson's assistant's cubicle when Chuck noticed me through the window to his office. He got up from his desk and came straight out to me. He walked up so close, I felt a little as if he were invading my space. I could tell immediately that he was fired up, but I wasn't sure what we were going to talk about.

"What are you doing?" Chuck said to me.

"Oh, just waiting for a few minutes and then heading to the airport to go home."

"No, I mean, what do you do at home?"

I never seemed to have a good answer for how I earned my money now. Should I say "political fixer"? "Behind-the-scenes choreographer"? "Bailer-out of troubled friends"? "Scavenger for the crumbs of big business deals"? Nothing sounded good, even though everyone I worked with, on all sides of the deals, was happy with my help.

"Not too much. Enough to pay the bills. I was focused on insurance, and now I—"

Chuck laughed. "Help me out here. I meant, what pays your mortgage?"

I paused and smiled at him. This guy was good. He had a great filter for nonsense, and it helped me avoid waffling anymore.

"I consult. I fix people's problems. I have one large client and three or four that roll through every couple of months. I'm doing okay."

"That's good to hear," Chuck said. "But I want to say something to you. I just feel that God has a bigger plan for you than what you're doing. I don't know if it's possible for you, and I have no idea if it works here, but I think you should be here. That's what I feel."

"Well, I would love to help as much as I can," I said. "My work affords me a lot of flexibility, and if you ever wanted me to speak or try to support your efforts, I'd love to volunteer."

"That isn't what I meant." He smiled again and put his hand on my shoulder. "Keep an open mind, okay? Think about it. Pray about it, all right?"

"I will," I said. "I promise. Thanks for sharing that with me—and for your hospitality, too. This has been great. My aunt and uncle, Diane and Carl Buttermore, love you and they are two of the people who told me I should read your books. They'll love that we met. I think it went well today at the Senate, too."

"Oh, it went *very* well. I still have my friends there. I can't say enough about it. I told you the Spirit would help you. Thanks for being willing."

"No problem, Chuck. Thanks again," I said as we shook hands.

He turned and walked back into his office.

I thought for a moment about what he had said. I knew at once what he was saying, but I wanted to turn it over in my mind.

In prayer, I often ask for God's help in making things clear to me. Since I had deflected all His help for so many years, I had lousy radar for picking up on help that was always at hand. This time, like the others, what happened could not have been clearer.

I was getting out of my own way, only to be invited to Washington and have this "chance" meeting with Chuck Colson. I felt that this was in response to my selfish prayer some fifteen months earlier, while in rehab.

I had prayed for God to tell me what He would have me do, and in my heart I was still thinking thoughts of "keep these things; buy more things; redeem my career." I heard the words clearly spoken in my head: "Who said I did these things for you . . . ?"

I knew what "these things" were, and I instantly had hope that the future would be clear even though it was nothing I would ever control. I also had a sense of purpose, without that purpose being any embodiment of a job, task, or skill.

The statement was clear. I had received a lot of things good and bad, and I was wrong to think they were done simply so that I might run for higher office or acquire more wealth. I had acquired my experience at great cost, and it was best used for the benefit of others.

I knew straightaway what Chuck Colson was saying. It was amazing. He was asking me to set aside what I was doing and join him in serving God instead of chasing after my own priorities. In that moment, I was certain this was the direction I should be going in. Everything in me felt good about working with Prison Fellowship, and I looked forward to what might materialize from the conversation.

After I returned from the trip and told Stacey what had happened, she showed her disinterest for the political side of the job, which I had grown accustomed to. She couldn't care less about politics. I remembered telling her I was going to be the person introducing Massachusetts Governor Mitt Romney onstage at the Henry Ford Museum in Dearborn, Michigan, the day he announced his run for president in 2007. She had asked me, "Why should I be there if you're onstage?" I had to laugh and tell her our kids and grandkids might think it was cool to have pictures in case he was president someday. This she understood, and agreed to come. Only once do I remember her really loving spending time with a politician she hardly knew. He was an aspiring leader in the US House of Representatives, named John Boehner. The future Speaker and I were golfing in the First Tee Pro-Am at Pebble Beach. We were the token politicians mixed in with the likes of Bill Murray, George Lopez, and others. At the time, I was smoking enough cigarettes that John and I were never far away from each other. The Speaker was a big smoker then. He always made sure Stacey got a glass of wine, and we went out to dinner every night. Stacey loved him and his daughter.

I knew the political history, and the importance of this work would be hard to explain to Stacey in a way that resonated with her. My spiritual growth (at least, I credit it to spiritual growth) had steered me clear of using my old spin and lies to sell my ideas, so I led with the harder side of what I saw as the truth about possibly going to work for Justice Fellowship.

"Stacey, I know you don't care much about what Chuck Colson has done," I said, "but I want to tell you how this feels inside to me. I hate to even bring this up, because I don't have an offer and I can't imagine they would pay me enough, and I would have to travel a lot and—"

"One hundred percent," Stacey said.

"What?" I said. "What do you mean, 'one hundred percent'?"

"I mean I support this a hundred percent. You should do it. I see what God has been doing in your life. I can't explain it. I don't understand what's happening, but you need to do this."

I started to talk and was overcome with emotion before I could complete my first word. I couldn't have imagined anything Stacey would ever say to me that meant this much. I collected myself, smiled, and said, "Well, let's see where it goes."

About a week later, I got a call from the Human Resources Department at Prison Fellowship, offering me a salary that was about a third of what I was making at the time. They asked if I needed to earn more, and said they would understand. I politely told them I was interested in working for them regardless of the money and just needed some time to pray and think on it. The greatest fear I had was of interjecting my ego, ambition, and old character flaws into a discussion I valued so highly.

A couple of days later, I was at a client's office. He was gushing with pleasure over the work I had just completed on his company's behalf, heading off a multimillion-dollar headache. The client was making plans for me to help them in 2012, and I interrupted him in mid pitch.

"Hey, I'm not quitting my work for you, or anything," I said, "but I have to be honest. You remember when I told you I gave a speech in DC this summer and got to meet Chuck Colson and was doing some more work in criminal justice and addiction recovery?"

"Yeah, I do. How's that going?"

"Well, that's the thing. I'm really happy I've been able to help you as much as I have, but to be honest with you, I'm hoping to be busy working for this ministry in 2012. I know it's just a couple of months away, but I feel that it's what I need to do and that I could help people there. I probably can't afford it, so don't fire me, either. I just wanted you to know that for me, I want to do more to help in criminal justice reform and less with the big business deals."

He looked across his desk and smiled. He let the pen in his hand slide through his fingers, catching the far end just before it fell, twirled the pen around, and let it slide down again. He paused and leaned forward in his chair, his expression growing brighter.

"Why don't I just pay you for next year at the same rate. You can take my calls if it doesn't interfere with your work, right? I mean, I'll probably only call you a few times all year."

I smiled and shook my head. "Look, I wasn't asking for charity. I was just trying to tell you—"

"*Charity?* I have three law firms and two lobbyist firms that don't do as much in three months of retainers as you do in a ten-minute phone call. It isn't charity. We need you, and your rate is a steal even if it is only for a few phone calls."

"Well, I'll let them know what I'd be doing, and if I have to come out here I'd have to take vacation time and all that. I just want everything on the table, in plain view."

I called the human resources department people back at Prison Fellowship and told them their offer was fine. The lady I spoke with said she wanted to raise the salary we had talked about. I told her I couldn't accept another dime, saying that God continued to go before me in lining things up. I told her I was looking forward to helping where I could.

* * *

It only took a month before I was working full-time for Justice Fellowship as its Director of External Affairs. The title was a bit grandiose because only three other people were employed there at the time. Justice Fellowship had suffered attrition for a number of reasons and had shrunk to a small corner office and two cubicles within the largest prison ministry operation in the country. I believe that the investments in operating Justice Fellowship had decreased because they weren't necessary while Chuck Colson was still active. It was always Chuck's opinion, endorsement, or explanation that was so highly coveted in the marketplace of criminal justice issues in America. The deeper staffing I would normally expect in the areas of research, policy, and communications would have been redundant as long as Chuck's still razor-sharp intellect and experience were available.

Things were beginning to change, though, and it was obvious to me. It wasn't a trade secret within the organization, either. Chuck Colson was making a very public passing of the torch. Pat Nolan, the president of Justice Fellowship, was unable to hold regular hours, because of his health issues, so I was looked to as a sort of utility infielder right out of the gate. Within a few weeks, they were putting me in front of things Pat couldn't get to, and I was taking the lead in the field.

It took my small team and me only about three months to see that big things were about to happen. When asked what our strategic plan would be for the next five years, we answered that we were going to "change the way America talked about criminal justice."

Some people in leadership thought this goal a bit grandiose for a few people to accomplish, but we already had our oars in the water and were rowing hard together. Almost immediately, big opportunities came up, and we began our work.

In the blink of an eye, it seemed I had gone from worrying about my marriage, finances, and possible jail time to helping advance what Chuck Colson had started thirty years before. It was a truly amazing time to serve, and I was loving every minute of it.

Chapter 24

It was April 14, 2012, and I was in Chicago to attend a closed-door discussion about the American criminal justice system with some national leaders from politics, academia, and the nonprofit foundation world. I sat next to Ben Jealous, CEO of the NAACP. At first, I was surprised that we would be seated next to each other, but I was very quickly amazed at how much we agreed on.

It was the second day of the discussions, and someone described the successes that Justice Fellowship had worked in the previous two months in a couple of states. The votes it sponsored had received unanimous support in both legislatures even though the underlying criminal justice issues were contentious and considerable political risk was involved. I was speaking when an accomplished professor from Harvard asked me to clarify the formula that led to success. He said, "How is it that you can get bipartisanship in such a partisan era?"

I told him, "I never said bipartisanship. Both parties voted for it, but your version of bipartisanship is where everyone loses except the people whose stock in trade is saying they brought compromise. I was a House Speaker, and I'll tell you a little secret: compromise isn't any fun at all, and it's what happens in eighty-five percent of the bills any legislature votes for. The news media just like to focus on the division, so they report the remaining 15 percent of the votes—the ones that follow partisan lines. Look at the voting records, and you'll be amazed at how many are compromises that receive the support of almost everyone at the end of the deal. This is different because neither side compromised. They are bills that have been locked in partisan division for decades until people started talking about their principles and values again."

The professor was clearly baffled. "You're telling me the criminal justice reforms happening today that you are helping craft *aren't* compromises? That doesn't make any sense to me. How come everyone supports it, then?"

Before I could answer, Ben Jealous put his hand on my shoulder and said, "Let me put it more plainly. The only people that get this politically are right-wing extremists like my friend Craig DeRoche—"

Ben paused for the laughter in the room to die down.

"I'm not offending you, am I, Craig?"

"Not in the least, Ben. Lay it out for him."

"Anyway, Tea Party types and Christians . . . and, well, I guess Craig is both, but the folks he works on don't care if their votes cost them the election. Neither do progressives, African-Americans, and liberals. So the far right and far left are leading with their principles. They get this. We (he pointed back and forth between us) agree on this, so we aren't compromising at all. If there is compromise, it's those folks in the middle who are scared of their shadow, who are the ones wanting to lock everyone up for the rest of their lives for fear a jaywalker will murder someone someday and they'll get blamed for it on TV."

The professor types and foundation researchers were now silent after the laughter from the Craig-and-Ben show. They didn't quite know how to understand or question what they had just heard.

I assured the crowd that the ability to convene discussions about principles and where they align has been discouraged in modern politics and the media. The government, federally and in the states, is set up where no one can win outright. This is done for good reason. To believe that compromise involves the disregard of principle is to feed on and encourage the worst human behavior possible for a person in elective office.

* * *

Later that evening, I was up in my hotel room and took a call from my accountant. It was bad news. The next day was tax day, and I owed about ten thousand dollars more than I had expected. I was beyond frustrated.

I took a quick look at our family checking and savings accounts and saw that I had about four thousand dollars to pay a bill that was due the next day with no wiggle room. I was shutting down my businesses and expected there to be some expenses, but this was extraordinary. In years past, I would simply have figured out how to raise the money with more work, more clients, and a bit of luck. But on this night, I was left with a different reality. I'd made a decision to go a different way. I'd been working for five months for Justice Fellowship, and things were going well. It really seemed that I was exactly where God wanted me to be, especially after the fun I was having with leaders like Ben Jealous in moving the cause forward.

I called Stacey and told her what was going on.

"What are we going to do?" she said, the worry in her voice clear.

"I'll just have to advance the credit cards. I don't have access to any other cash to shift, or invoices to move around."

"That sucks. How are we going to pay it back, then?"

"I don't have a plan on that, but we've been paying off the other debts from the last few years. I suppose this may be the last of them. At least, I hope it's the last of the surprises."

"Do we even have that much credit?" she said. "What about spring break? The kids are really looking forward to Florida."

"Yes. We can do it and still go Florida. I haven't been able to give the family a trip in five years, and I'm not going to screw this up. I believe things will be fine; I just don't know how or where they'll come together."

"Okay, but keep me posted."

"I will," I said. "Love you, honey."

"Love you, too," Stacey said, and hung up.

I was frustrated and curious at the same time. I was praying to God with a sort of wry laugh, as if to say, "You really keep things hopping, don't you?"

I took the hotel elevator downstairs and went outside to smoke. I had nothing but my lighter and pack of cigarettes. I even left my jacket in the hotel room.

The Chicago weather was crisp, and the wind was biting through my dress shirt, reminding me that winter wasn't leaving without a fight. I pressed my hands close and scratched the lighter wheel a few times before drawing in a lungful of smoke. I walked across the wide sidewalk toward the street so foot traffic could pass behind me. I was watching the cars pass when I heard someone on my right asking for money.

"Hey, man, you got any money? Can I get some help, please?"

I walked closer to the road and pulled in a full drag from my cigarette. My other hand was wedged deeply in my pocket to shield it from the wind. I didn't say a word or even turn my head. I just kept moving slightly away from the male voice, hoping to avoid a discussion so I could continue to run the numbers in my head between bills, debts, and, now, credit card advances.

"Hey, man, I need some help." The man spoke a little louder now. "You don't understand. I just got out of prison and I need some help."

I turned to face him and said, "What'd you just say?"

"I'm not gonna hurt ya. Don't get me wrong," he said, hands up in the air like a football ref's after a touchdown.

I walked toward him, and I could see the puzzlement in his eyes. I think he was contemplating running.

"I thought you said to me you just got out of prison."

"I'm Reggie, I *did* just get out of prison. I served three and half years. I have two more to go but got out on parole. The thing is, I have to get home by nine a.m. tomorrow or I violate. Man, I don't wanna go back. I prayed to God to turn my life around and I ain't gonna live that way no more, and I just can't figure out how to buy a ticket and get on a train to get to my sister's by morning."

He was shaking and looked emotionally spent. He was in decent clothes, including a jacket. I assumed he was wearing the clothes he wore when he was admitted to prison.

He reached into his jacket and pulled out a packet of papers that were triple-folded but far too thick to fit into an envelope. "Look at these. They're my papers. I'm tellin' you the truth. I just need help."

I read the dates and opening sentences and scanned the rest. He was telling the truth. He was just released from prison and was ordered to report to probation in a different county the next day. I felt a warm burning inside my body, pressing me forward.

"There's a church right down there. I can see the steeple. They can help you," I said, testing him. I had decided to help but wasn't sure what my role was going to be.

"Man, I went there. I can see that steeple. I went to another one, too. They shooed me away and said they couldn't help. They told me they could give me the address to a shelter. I told them I'm hungry, but I can wait. I gotta get home or I go back to prison for two years. They said they couldn't do anything."

"You have a problem with drugs or anything like that?" I said, buying myself time while, in the back of my mind, I prayed for help.

"No, man. Hell, I wouldn't even take one of them cigarettes if you offered it." He pointed to the Marlboro Light in my hand. "That stuff never did it for me. I got enough wrong. I made different mistakes, but I don't make excuses for them. I was never high or drunk when I did 'em. Now I decide I'm going to live my life different, and I ask for help and I just don't know what's gonna happen. I mean, I'm going to be back in prison tomorrow, looks like."

"Over what?" I said.

"Over not getting sixteen fifty to get a ticket on the train that leaves in an hour to my sister's town. I never panhandled, and I'm no good at it. I don't think it works."

I smiled. I looked him over again. He was pretty well put together considering what he had been through. His clothes looked okay, too. If he wasn't asking for money, no one would have assumed he was a beggar. In a moment, I knew what I wanted to do. It didn't make any sense to me intellectually, but it made perfect sense with how I felt inside.

"You know, Reggie, I was telling you the truth. I don't have a penny on me. I just brought my cigarettes down to smoke—which, by the way, you should keep avoiding." He was looking me straight in the eyes. I continued, "Do you remember what you said to get my attention?"

"What?" he said as he looked at me, still sizing me up.

"Do you remember what you said to get me to talk to you?"

The blank look continued.

"You don't remember what you said to me to get my attention?" I said.

"Nah, man. Maybe I said I needed money?"

"Nope. You said something different. You said I didn't understand and that you just got out of prison and needed some help."

"I said that?" he said in a higher voice.

"Yes. I was just wondering why you would go up to someone on the street and lead with 'I just got out of prison'!"

"Man, I can't believe I said that. I got no idea why I said that, but it's true."

"I know, but what is weird is, you said it to *me*. This town probably has five million people walking around it right now, and I can't think of too many who would spin around and pay attention to someone telling them that." He was still looking me straight in the eyes. I said, "You see, Reggie, I blew up my whole life about a year and a half ago, and God did some pretty special things for me. He brought people around me just when I needed them. I think it's important you know that. You said you prayed for help and weren't getting any. I'm here to help, though. I'm going to go up to my hotel room and get my ATM card and come down here and give you some money, okay?"

"Okay, I'll stay here as long as you need."

"It won't be long. I'll be right back."

I went up to my hotel room, got the ATM card, came down, and did a quick assessment of the issue. I said a little prayer and put the card in the machine. Once the money was dispensed, I walked out of the building and back over by Reggie, who was waiting nearby on the sidewalk.

"All right, Reggie. I got you some money. I'm not a rich dude, but this is what I got today. Here's a hundred dollars. I handed him the money."

"Nah, man, I don't need a hundred dollars, I need sixteen fifty to get home."

"I want you to listen to me. I heard what you asked for, but I have a different view. I wasn't in prison, but there were times I was a big burden to my family. I remember what coming home from jail and coming home from rehab felt like. The extra money is for you to eat some food and use a cab if you need to. I want your sister to be able to talk to you and see you before you're asking her for help with a ride or money. You said God wasn't answering your call for help, but I feel like He did. See, I think God was using me to help you understand that He has a bigger plan for you. I see it all the time where I work. I gave him my card that said "Prison Fellowship" and "Justice Fellowship.""

"Oh, thank God. You are a lifesaver. Thank you."

"You got it right. Thank God. It's a miracle *I'm* not the one asking for money today."

"I'm gonna pay you back someday."

"That's not how it works, Reggie. If you want to pay me back, remember to help someone else when they reach out in need. Remember today and where guys like you and I got to fight up from. I couldn't have made it without believing God would provide, and He does. You may just find He does the same for you if you give it a try."

"God bless you, man," he said. A tear ran down his cheek as he stuck the money in his pocket. He stood there silently, looking down at the sidewalk.

"You better go or you're not going to make the train," I said.

He gave me a quick hug, stepped back, and wiped away his tears. Then he quickly walked away.

Chapter 25

I peered through the side window to the door in the third-story office at Prison Fellowship Ministries headquarters in Lansdowne, Virginia. It was late April 2012, just a week or so after I met with Reggie on the wind-whipped streets of Chicago.

A group of about four men were gathered in front of the office, and the motion caught my attention out of the corner of my eye. I looked up and saw Chuck Colson talking with a huge smile and animated hand gestures. As he concluded, he saw me. His eyes brightened, and he headed straight for me.

"Oh, Craig, I'm so glad to see you here," Chuck said in his distinctive voice that seemed to parse out each word of the sentence. "You having a good time with your work?"

Chuck was no longer the CEO or even the chairman of the board. He was still the de facto leader, though. Much like Dave Thomas, the founder of Wendy's—no official title, but everyone still looked to him for any decision of consequence. And without Chuck's volunteer calls, the donors would not have welcomed the transition.

"You have no idea," I said. "I think God has me right where He wants me. Thanks for your confidence in me last fall."

"That's great to hear. I got so much I want to tell you. There is so much going on right now. I can't talk today, though. I just have the worst headache," he said, moving his hand up and down behind his head without touching it. "Will you be here tomorrow for the Wilberforce Weekend?"

"Nope, can't," I said. "I'm leaving soon this afternoon. I have to fly home and then drive my kids to Disney tomorrow. Should be a fun couple of days."

"No big deal. I'll tell you about it when you get back. Go have fun with your family. I'm going to go lie down and rest. I haven't been tired my whole life, but the last couple of days, I have been tuckered out by lunchtime."

"Okay, Chuck," I said. "Talk to you soon. Enjoy the weekend."

He gave me a big hug and walked away.

It was the last time I saw or spoke with Chuck Colson. When I got to our hotel in Orlando the next day, I heard the news. Chuck fell ill after giving a speech at the Wilberforce Weekend hosted by the Colson Center. About three hundred Christian leaders were in the audience, and somehow, he had marshaled the strength to show up and finish the speech. When he concluded, he sat down in a chair on the stage as the emcee introduced the next speaker. He looked out at the audience and smiled. Eventually, a staff member quietly approached Chuck and said the script called for him to leave the stage after he spoke. He said, "I know. I can't. Just give me a minute."

Within moments, it was clear that he needed more help, and he was taken to the hospital.

When the news reached me, I was shocked. This incredible mentor and wonderful man had fallen so quickly! At 80, Chuck was as vibrant as many a 50-year-old in work ethic, stamina, and contemporary relevance.

I felt helpless as I followed his instructions to stay away and be with my family on vacation. It was still an important part of our healing process, and I needed to be there for my kids and Stacey. I prayed a great deal, though, for Chuck and his family. I wondered, too, about what it all meant. And I thought about our first and last conversations and all those in between.

Chuck was conscious and resting in the hospital, receiving excellent care. He was surrounded by family and friends. I had known him for only seven months and savored every snippet of advice, instruction, and explanation he ever gave.

Two weeks later, he passed away suddenly. The news hit me hard, and I felt a sense of responsibility to help carry things forward, especially after our last conversation. I was at home and made plans to attend the memorial service at the National Cathedral in Washington, D.C.

* * *

Walking into the National Cathedral was an experience all its own. Approaching that imposing structure, I followed the points and roof lines that cut into the beautiful Washington sky on an especially hot spring day. With each step, the building absorbed more of the blue, until all I could see looking up was the elegant brick and concrete infrastructure.

I walked down the broad center aisle as people streamed around me toward their seats. In the middle of the church, chairs were set up so rows of people in three sections could sit, all facing the lectern.

Looking left and right, I saw captains of industry, television personalities, and current and former elected officials. And hundreds of others were here, too. I couldn't speculate on what Chuck had done in their lives, but I did understand something immediately. I had a sense I hadn't felt for several years.

I sat in my seat on a polished wooden pew to the left of center, away from the family-and-close-friends section. I listened to Chuck's many friends as they came forward and spoke of the man who had lived such a splendid personal transformation in plain view for all to see. Those who knew him well and those who only read his books and watched him on television would say the same things. Chuck had humbled himself before God and lived to serve from that day forward. He didn't miss an opportunity to advance the cause of "the least of these" in our midst, right up until the moment he fell ill.

When people began speaking about Chuck and his life, their message made clear the feeling I recognized when I first sat down in the cathedral. They spoke of Chuck being a civil rights leader and a prophet—two titles I may not yet fully understand to this day, though I immediately made the connection in my experience.

It was seven years earlier, in 2005, when I sat in the front row at the funeral of another unexpected leader in American history.

When Rosa Parks died, I was invited as part of the official delegation for the state of Michigan, and I was the only Republican leader in the room. Even though it was hard to get there and even harder to get in, I wouldn't have missed it for anything. That day, thousands of people were overflowing into the halls and surrounding the church.

I was doing my best to make my way politely through the frustrated and impassioned mourners trying to enter through doors that had been closed. It wasn't until Detroit Police Chief Ella Bully Cummings saw me and pushed me through the crowd that I had a chance to enter at all.

Inside that cathedral in Detroit, I got to spend some hours taking in the words of leaders such as President Clinton, Mayor Kilpatrick, and my friend Governor Jennifer Granholm. Sitting there in the audience, I learned a great deal about what a civil rights leader is, even though I didn't fully understand much of it until seven years later, when I sat listening to people describe Chuck Colson.

The greatness of those who advance the cause of justice is not measured by the bills they pass or the tributes they received. The truly extraordinary, those who put everything on the line in the name of justice, are so rare, their lives are best described by who they were rather than just what they did.

I suppose that by the time Chuck died, God had eased my selfishness enough that I could recognize why the memorials for these two giants were so different from the pomp and circumstance of other funerals I have attended, where the departed's accomplishments are totted up like a checklist for those mourning their loss. It was a joy to experience—twice now—a celebration of how a person can live in such a way that they make a small glimpse of God's Kingdom visible for ordinary mortals to behold in wonder.

It was a gift to know Chuck Colson. It was a blessing to understand in retrospect what I had felt at Rosa Parks's service seven years earlier. What an inspiration they both were for me to want to serve, even in some small way, today!

Leaving Chuck's funeral, I felt an upwelling of gratitude to God for the gifts He had given me already—gifts I could explain only through grace. I was now living a life of unmerited rewards.

Chapter 26

Summer came and went, and I continued to plow forward with family, faith, work, and service projects. I was active, busy, and everywhere things were on the mend.

My life had transformed externally nearly as fast as on the inside. Only two years had gone by since my arrest, and many daunting hurdles had been removed from my path.

Stacey and I were growing in our marriage, and my greatest delight was to watch my three girls, now 11, 9, and 5, grow, learn, and play soccer. I loved the soccer. I could watch them play all day, and many days, when overlapping tournaments resulted in four or five games, that was exactly what happened.

The distance I had come, the difference between what I had been and who I was becoming, was nothing short of astounding. And the problems I had obsessed over for so many days and weeks had washed away with no apparent effort—with me scarcely even noticing the change.

The criminal appeals were continuing, but I had left my concerns behind. I honestly wasn't worried about the outcome either way as the prosecution flailed away, burning the taxpayers' dollars in the vain effort to save face. The first appeal, to the Circuit Court in Oakland County, went down in flames. The judge wrote a twenty-three-page opinion just to make her point. She did me the kindness of making it clear that not only was there no probable cause for the police to enter my home, but no crime had even been committed or contemplated.

Still, the prosecutor would hammer away and appeal the case again, as it is the state's right to do. I was learning just how much leeway and how little accountability for their lack of discernment prosecutors can actually have.

My marriage was growing, and I had fallen in love with Stacey in a way I never had before. This new love I felt for her was much greater and, in many ways, unexpected. I had always been attracted to her physically. And I loved her humor and her ability to get to know people and genuinely care for them. I loved the way she noticed the little things. I loved the way she let me go off and pursue grand adventures whose outcome was anything but guaranteed, and the way she balanced both my priorities and hers so easily. She never got wrapped up in what I thought was important. She gave a meeting with a presidential candidate or a sitting US senator the same respectful attention she would give a schoolteacher.

Now, though, I could not imagine my life without her. I looked forward to seeing her and talking with her about the little things in her day and mine, and the big adventures we might share in life. I had a new love for her hopes and dreams. I wanted to provide for her. I could submit to her without resentment or anger and be happy just seeing her smile. I began to love even the little things we might never resolve. With Stacey, I no longer cared about winning but could enjoy the give-and-take in a way I couldn't have imagined in the first thirteen years of our marriage.

It became clear to me that I had, in fact, married a beautiful woman who could do so much better than the sorry treatment, commitment, and resources I had provided. Moreover, I was married to a woman who loved me through her fears and anger and despite the betrayal my life had been on so many days. I loved her for this and still, to this day, refuse to allow even our worst days to tarnish the gratitude and joy I have in being her husband.

Our marriage was by no means perfect, yet we began to work together without organizing the effort, and it was succeeding. Paying the bills was still a serious challenge because the money boost God had blessed us with had diminished and we couldn't adjust fast enough. Rather than complain, though, Stacey kept working with me, chipping away toward the bright financial future that we felt would come in the proper time.

Things were going well by the time the kids got back in school and I returned to Washington for some management meetings at the Justice Fellowship home office. I was traveling a lot now because the organization's mission was growing exponentially. A movement in criminal justice reform had begun in the states and was spreading nationally. By this time, work was growing in the federal government, too. I balanced my time the best I could, but I had to make more than 140 flights that year just to keep up and manage the growth of our budding advocacy efforts. I began calling Justice Fellowship a "thirty-year-old start-up" because it had shrunk till it worked on a just a few things a year, and was now growing fast in the Christian and conservative political movements.

When I was away from town, I tended to work late in the office since I was away from my family. Besides going to the recovery meetings and the occasional first-run movie, I didn't have much to do on the road other than working and sleeping. September 12, 2012, didn't appear to be any different from any other travel day.

Some tension was beginning to build on the so-called Benghazi incident, and coverage of the attack on the US embassy and the murder of the ambassador was dominating the news cycle. I was trying to avoid following it on television at the time. The media were covering the horrific events as though the whole thing were a chess move in the presidential election that would play out two months later. It was disgusting. I thought about calling Kirk to get his take on things, but I didn't want to get myself worked up.

As the evening progressed, I pulled my focus from everything but finishing the old to-do list so I could go back to the hotel and crash for the night. It was after eight when my phone rang.

I looked down and saw "Kirk DeRoche Mobile" on my screen. I thought about breaking off from work and taking the call, but I had just two more e-mails to send. I thought I would just call him in a few minutes when I was done, and we would talk foreign policy. I let the phone go to voice mail.

I clicked away at the remaining work, and the phone rang again. This time, "Stacey DeRoche Mobile" called.

My gut tensed. For me to get two phone calls from family this late in the evening, something must be wrong. I answered at once.

"Hi, what's up?" I said. Stacey and I had already talked about the day and said good night, as is our custom whenever I travel. I figured that her calling back meant some news worth sharing—my gut feeling was surely just nervous overreaction.

"It's Kirk," she said. "It's bad. Have you talked to Paul or your parents?"

"What's bad? He just called me."

"It wasn't Kirk; that was Ken [Kirk's father-in-law]. He has Kirk's phone. You better call him back. He'll be—"

"Honey, sorry to be rude, but I'm going to hang up now. I'm calling Ken."

I hung up and caught my breath. A wave of dread washed over me. I knew Kirk's life. I had grown up with him, and we were roommates after college. I saw the best in him and the bad days, too, from the front-row seats. Nothing about the situation sounded good.

I scrolled to the missed call and clicked to call back.

"Hello, who's this?" said Ken. His voice was quiet and shaky. He sounded muffled, too, as if he was talking into one of his hands.

"This is Craig. What's going on?"

"Hi, Craig. This is Ken, Kirk's father-in-law—"

"Of course, Ken. What's going on? Stacey said something's happened."

"I'm afraid it has. That was me that just called you. I didn't know what else to do."

The tension inside me grew with each word of painfully dragged-out explanation. "Okay, what is happening?" I said.

"It's Kirk. Craig, when Kim and the kids got home from dinner at the church, he was on the floor next to his computer and, well . . . he was nonresponsive."

"What do you mean, 'nonresponsive'?"

"He wasn't breathing, and he didn't have a pulse. They didn't know how long he had been out, and Jenny, Kim's sister, worked to revive him. We think she might have brought him back, and maybe the EMTs did, too, but we aren't sure. I just want you to know it didn't look good. It *doesn't* look good. I wanted your family to know what's going on, since you're all up in Michigan."

Silence filled the phone line.

"Are you still there, Craig?"

"Um, yeah," I said, barely loud enough to be heard.

"I'm so sorry to tell you this. Kirk and Kim went to the hospital in the ambulance. I'll keep Kirk's phone with me. Please call your parents and your brother. I spoke with Stacey, and she said she would—"

"I'll call you back, Ken."

I hung up and threw myself back in the chair. The news hit me like a mule kick to the gut. My body and mind were on high alert. I couldn't believe what was happening, and yet, I had to dial my parents. If I had taken a moment to think, I wouldn't have had the courage to dial the numbers.

"Dad, have you heard?"

"Yes, son."

"What's going on? How is Mom?"

"She isn't doing good, Craig. She fears the worst. I can't even talk to her. I'm worried about her. This situation is awful. Do you have any updates?"

"I just hung up with Ken. He has Kirk's phone. He told me I could call or he'd call me with updates. Have you talked to Paul?"

"Not yet."

"What do you want me to do, Dad?"

"I don't know," he said. I could visualize my dad standing there stoically, trying to keep his composure while my mom fell to pieces behind him. They were at home in Michigan, I was in D.C., and Kirk was in the hospital in Knoxville, Tennessee.

"I'm going to call Ken from my office line. I'll keep you on my cell. I haven't left the office yet."

I dialed Ken and kept one phone to each ear.

"Ken, what's going on?" I said. "I have my mom and dad on the other line. Do you have any news?"

"Nothing yet, Craig, except that they're going to call when they get news."

"Okay, Dad, they don't have any—"

"Wait!" Ken said in my other ear.

"Yeah . . . Ken?" I said into one phone. "Dad, hold on," I said into the other.

"They're calling from the hospital. Hold on."

There was a pause, followed by gasps and rumblings behind Ken.

"Craig, he's gone," Ken said. "He didn't make it."

I was silent on the phone. He repeated, "Craig, did you hear me? Kirk's gone. I'm so sorry to tell you this on the phone. Kirk was pronounced dead at the hospital. Kim is with him now."

"I heard you, Ken. I'm on the other line with my dad. I'm going to have to call you back. Thank you for calling me earlier."

I hung up that phone and took a deep breath. "Dad, Kirk is gone. He's dead. They just announced it at the hospital."

"Hold on, son," my dad said. I could then hear him trying to muffle the phone a bit as he got my mother's attention. I could hear him say, "Anne, they just got news. Kirk didn't make it, honey—"

He didn't get any further. In the background, a wail erupted unlike any I had heard from her or anyone else in my life. Raw emotion came shrieking out of her in such an overpowering way, I could hear her through my dad's attempt to muffle the phone with his hand and over his appeals to me to stay on the line. She sobbed and sobbed, saying, "No . . . no, it can't be!" Then the unintelligible guttural wailing returned. I wished with everything in me that I could be there with them. I wanted to hug her and just be present. I couldn't have offered any assurance that things would be fine, or any other such condolence. I just wanted to be with her and my dad and with Paul, too. Overcome with emotion, she was emptying herself, and she and my dad had no option but to handle the tragic news over the telephone.

I listened and occasionally reassured my dad that I was still on the line with him. I reflected on all that the three of us boys had put my mother through with our many harrowing misadventures. Kirk was 39 years old at the time. I believe that my mom had probably worried about him every night since he was 9 years old. That is how much she loved him. That is how much she loved each of us.

Her worst fears realized, my dad and I were left to listen and wait. I wished I could speak with her.

After a few minutes, my dad said she wasn't going to be able to talk, and told me he wasn't doing much better. He asked me to call Paul and then call them back later.

* * *

Our family doesn't talk about health or money. We don't mention death. We rarely reveal an emotion, and this has been my experience my whole life.

Relatives don't die, either. It's a rare occurrence, and they're very old by then. In our family, there was no precedent for what was happening, and the situation brought unspoken fears to the fore. We shared grief awkwardly at best.

We all made it through the night and, after several conversations, agreed to a loosely assembled plan. Our goal was to support Kim in the unbearable task of preparing Kirk for his funeral, and we agreed that the family would go to Tennessee in force.

I got on the first available flight home from D.C. the next day and arrived just as my girls were coming home from school. The news devastated Carley and Zoe. I could only imagine their fears that I, too, might up and die someday because I took the wrong drugs. Phoebe was too young to grasp death and took in the news mostly with curiosity.

My coworkers at Justice Fellowship could not have been more supportive of what I needed to do. My schedule was cleared so I could focus on my family.

In no time flat, we were in two cars headed to Tennessee. Paul and Jill and their kids, Kyle and Courtney, our family, and my parents loaded everything up for the trip. At the last moment, we made a decision. Jill and Stacey suggested they ride with the kids in one vehicle and let Paul, our parents, and me ride together. It would give us some time to talk.

It was a small and wonderfully selfless gesture, and it yielded the most unexpected and important discussions with my parents in my entire life. We got to share the truth about how I had lived my life. We talked about Kirk and how he had lived his. Paul recounted his own decisions in life and worked to reconcile with us why the evils of addiction had passed him by. Hard truths were shared and old mysteries explained.

We got to tell our own stories of human struggle, for a change. I suppose, the things of this world had kept us from sharing honestly and plainly, right up until the worst events imaginable forced us.

Kirk was gone, and none of us had seen him much since he moved to Tennessee. We hadn't seen him much even when he lived in Michigan. He would go on tours of duty for at least six months at a time. As physical distance separated us, my fears for Kirk and his family grew. We would share our lives as best we could on the phone, and I would make it a point to try to corner him when we were together.

We would argue history, religion, and politics because those were the things Kirk was passionate about. He would advise me about what I should be doing and where I had left a chink in the armor of my argument.

After his death, our arguments about religion were first and foremost in my mind. Just months before he passed away, Kirk had gone from calling God out by name in anger to telling me he had made his peace with God. I sorted our conversations in my mind and worked to reconcile things. There wasn't anything I could do, and at the same time, it was important that I remember every word, every conversation. I revisited them in my memory, and it was as if I were playing back tapes of our childhood right up through adult life. My reminiscences were often interrupted by emotions that would sweep in and overtake the memory I was reliving.

On the ride to Knoxville, our biggest fear remained unspoken at first. Then it was out.

"What do we think killed Kirk?" and "Do you think he took too many drugs or was using other drugs or alcohol?" We needed to voice the thought that dominated our minds and our concerns, and once the ice was broken, we assembled every detail we knew from the night he died.

Kirk had gone to the doctor that day. He was home from Afghanistan, on disability leave from an American defense contracting company, where he led a squadron of surveillance blimps. The work he did there was deadly serious, and the decisions he made and witnessed caused him a great deal of stress. My understanding was that he had come home because of a back injury he incurred as a marine, working on the airstrip. And he had come clean with his doctors about the post-traumatic stress he was suffering after years of service in the Marines and his four previous tours as a contractor.

Kirk had told me it was nearly five years since he last drank alcohol or took drugs other than as prescribed. I believed him, but at the same time, I worried because the volume and strength of the drugs provided by the Veterans Administration seemed excessive. I knew of Kirk's own struggles with addiction since we both were young. Neither of us had managed our use of drugs and alcohol well, and for a long time we toggled back and forth about who was perceived to have a better grip on things. This is something sober people do, too, and we addicts let them do it because it makes us feel better about ourselves. We like to compare ourselves to others and say or think, "Well, at least I'm not as bad as . . . ."

We learned that Kirk had gone to the VA specifically to tell them he thought the drugs they prescribed to him were "giving him heart attacks." The VA doc gave him a pat on the head and said the drugs were not giving him heart attacks, that he was having panic attacks because of his post-traumatic stress disorder. The doctor made this assessment without examining Kirk for anything beyond the usual blood and urine sample to make sure he was taking his drugs at the prescribed levels and wasn't introducing other substances into the mix. I later reviewed the doctor's order and saw that it tested for amphetamines, alcohol, cocaine, and some other drugs along with his prescription drugs. The urine test is nearly immediate, so I presume the doc saw that Kirk wasn't taking additional drugs, and sent him on his way. He told him to keep taking the drugs as prescribed and to "play video games to take his mind off what was happening."

That night, Kirk stayed home from dinner because he was still not feeling well. Kim and the kids went to a dinner their church was hosting in town. When Kim was at the dinner, Kirk phoned her, but in the noisy crowd, she didn't hear it ring. He left her a message saying that "it's happening again," that he had "been playing video games like the doctor said for half an hour," and that he was "scared." He said he was going upstairs to take a shower or lie down, and to look for him to be in bed when she got home.

Kim didn't get the message immediately. When she returned home, she found Kirk on the floor next to the computer and the chair where he had been playing video games. From all later accounts, he was probably already gone.

None of us wanted to assume anything, and yet, it was important to put it out there. Did Kirk take something else or take too much? We wished we had the answers, but none came.

We all agreed—Kim, too, once we got to Knoxville—that it was important to know, though not our primary concern. We were trying to help plan the funeral events and still give Kim and her family room. We needed to let our kids be with their cousins for mutual love and support while still letting Kim have her alone time with them. It was necessary and nightmarish at the same time.

Kim's dignity and strength amazed all of us in the Michigan DeRoche contingent. She had a poise and focus that none of us could have imagined having at such a time.

For the days between Kirk's death and the memorial service, we ran an exhaustive schedule of planning, coordinating, and balancing tasks and familial relations. My mom and dad seemed at times to have been stunned numb. At other times, they showed love and leadership that brings tears to my eyes even today.

It was an awkward convening of families that, because of the geographical distance between them, didn't know each other well. We muddled through it as best we could. Meanwhile, on the Internet, another observance of mourning was playing out. It seemed to mirror what I have experienced personally at funeral homes and gatherings surrounding the death of a loved one, friend, or family member. The difference was the extent to which people shared, and how many could convene.

Kirk was loved by a great many people. The Facebook pages lit up with a stream of remembrance and celebration of life. What began with shock gave way quickly to honoring his memory and his service to his country and to others. Later, the downright amusing gestures and comments of friends and family through every stage of his life provided a much needed break in the days immediately following his death.

We had to accept that Kirk was gone. His death was not entirely unexpected, and I couldn't shake this haunting desire to learn the truth. Kim had me preserve his voice mail. In it, he said he had told the doctors that the drugs were literally killing him, and "the doctors didn't care." He planned to go in the next day to see the doctors and demand action.

But he didn't make it to the next day. He was snatched away from all of us who loved him, and there appeared to be a direct nexus between the drugs and his death.

It wasn't until I was preparing to leave for home after the memorial service that Kim showed me his collection of prescription drugs. When I looked at the names on the bottles, I was stunned.

Kirk was prescribed the narcotic Vicodin with the incredibly dangerous opioid drug Fentanyl, alongside the powerful muscle relaxant and sedative Klonopin. Astonished, I shuffled frantically through the bottles. I needed to know more. I wanted to know everything immediately. I couldn't believe it as I read. Kirk had *eight* other prescription drugs to be taken at the same time, all prescribed by the same team of doctors at the VA. I was looking at a cocktail that could be lethal for nearly any human, and there was my brother's name, on every one of them. The prescription dates were all current within the previous month. My mind raced. The awareness of what I was seeing hollowed me out and filled me with pain all at once.

I asked Kim if I could count the doses, and she gave me permission. She said she believed the police had done the same thing since they needed to rule out an intentional overdose.

I made room on the kitchen counter and began counting doses back from the date of Kirk's death to the prescription fill date. In every case, Kirk had from three to seven days' more pills still in the bottles than he would have had if he were taking the full dosage as prescribed. In other words, he wasn't taking too many drugs—he wasn't even keeping up with the dosage the doctors prescribed. What he was prescribed, though, was unbelievable. The pain inside me now shifted to disgust. It made me sick that something like this could occur.

I looked up at Kim and decided in an instant that it was more important to keep my composure for her sake than to tell her what I really felt. There was already enough anger, guilt, and fear in the room, and I didn't want to confuse her or stoke the resentments and anger that she and my mom in particular were feeling against those charged with Kirk's medical care.

How America treats its veterans had already been exposed as a national scandal. In the weeks before Kirk's death, I read that there were twenty-two suicides a day among veterans of the Iraq and Afghanistan wars. I had heard of the backlog of care for those seriously injured, and the bottlenecks in dispensing even the most basic psychological care. None of this was new to me. When I was in office, I actively helped World War II veterans receive their medals for service nearly sixty years after they returned home. But even then the human cost of it all seemed distant. I had just assumed that Kirk would get the care he needed, and couldn't have imagined a circumstance where any veteran would be so lightly regarded and doped to such a high level of toxicity.

Five weeks later, we learned from the postmortem blood tests that Kirk had, in fact, taken his drugs at the prescribed levels. He died unnecessarily on September 12, 2012.

What I have learned since is that this continues to happen each day at the VA. If I am not hearing about it from the loved ones of someone lost to an overdose, I'm reading it in the paper. In many of the recovery meetings I attended, I heard similar stories of doctors trying to medicate away the pain inside the soldiers coming home. This approach seemed outrageous, even criminal. For Kirk, it was lethal. Coming to learn of this injustice and official callousness toward human life was more than I could stomach.

I resolved for Kirk's sake to do something about it. My prayer was and is, first and foremost, to help Kim and my nieces and nephew. Beyond that, I hope that Kirk's experience may someday help another soldier who is full of pain and fear. For this cause, I will become a soldier. I never volunteered to serve overseas like Kirk and other heroes. But with Kirk's death, I learned that not every soldier dies on the battlefield. Their cause must be ours, though. It's the least we can do after what they have done for us.

Chapter 27

In January 2013, things in my life had settled in quite a bit. My work took off in a way I could never have predicted. United States senators, representatives, governors, and other state leaders began speaking of criminal justice and addiction issues without anyone's prompting. After forty years of failed policies in the drug war's lock-'em-up logic, which had swelled America's prison population to numbers unseen by any country in human history, an awakening seemed to be on the horizon.

It had taken a long time to get to this point. The leaders who promoted the failures and the government growth in prisons, police, and prosecutions had all the right intentions. I was right in there with them on many votes while in the legislature. In retrospect, it is amazing that the conservatives who gave so much scrutiny to food stamps, welfare, and the postal service would overlook a prison system with a 67 percent failure (return to prison) rate. Conservatives had finally come to question the notion that the government could fix human behavior.

In America in 2013, 1 in every 104 adults was in prison on any given day. One in thirty-three was incarcerated, on probation, or on parole. On any day, one in nine African-American kids in the K-12 school system had a parent in jail or prison. For white Americans, the rate of incarceration as a percentage of the population was roughly the same as the percentage of blacks in prison in South Africa under apartheid. More than sixty-five million American adults have a criminal record today.

The drug war raged on with all its tanks, helicopters, and surveillance equipment even as majorities began to vote in states to legalize certain drugs. The same big-government conservative types would rail against the use of marijuana and disregard the 136.5 million legal prescriptions for Vicodin written in America in 2012. But the voters—particularly Christians and Tea Party conservatives—joined the loud voices of progressives and liberals in seeking change.

There isn't a person I know who would want a dangerous person free on the streets after they commit a crime. At the same time, the majority of prisoners in America and those under correctional control are nonviolent offenders. We punish them for their "crimes" by paying top dollar for their housing, television, food, health care, and education. Until recently, few leaders who thought the novel concept of accountability, restitution, and victims' rights should supersede government's arresting the biggest money drivers for its operations: poor, inadequately represented, primarily minority young men. The current practice drives up the arrest rates and the conviction percentages, which lead to more staff, stuff, and buildings. A vicious self-feeding government budget problem had begun to metastasize. No one paid attention to the fact that none of the spending and massive government infrastructure was working in the way that was being sold to the taxpayers. Even worse, there was no accounting for how much the criminal records and lack of restoration to full citizenship was costing America in welfare, Medicaid, Medicare, Social Security, and other benefits. The worst findings had begun to show that much of what nonviolent offenders experienced while in the criminal justice system would actually make the community less safe when the offenders were eventually released.

It felt clear to me early on that my work would be important, though I would never have predicted the size and the scope of the opportunities for change. They began to materialize faster than our organization could keep up with them. The seeds that Chuck Colson had been planting all those years were now busting out and growing like bamboo.

In the midst of all this, I found my voice, and it continues to be joined by many in the highest posts in government, along with victims, offenders, and the families affected. I know that the changes needed are well beyond my ability to mend on my own. My role began with simply explaining to people that my life experience running a state, a conservative caucus, and large political organizations could be used alongside my personal experience in addiction, failure, criminal prosecution, and loss. Both were essential ingredients to the national and state debates. Unlike the others in the movement to change our justice system, heal our communities, and move people toward success, safety, and self-sufficiency, I had something unique to give. I wasn't just talking about "those people." I was *one of them*.

I realized all this fully when I returned to my office in Washington, D.C., after a family vacation. That day, I had a new office. It was the office that Chuck Colson had walked out of the day he asked me to leave what I was doing and serve alongside him. My name was on the door now, and I paused before walking in.

When I sat down, I took an inventory of what had just happened in the previous two and half years. My life propelled by ambition, talent, and design fueled by self-will had destroyed everything I had built over thirty-nine years. On the day this story I am sharing began, I hurt a great number of people, embarrassed many more, and left nothing standing. I surrendered my will completely, and God met me where I was, and changed me. And He has held my attention ever since. I am far from perfect. There is no rational explanation for everything that has occurred, and yet, it all was very real. In many ways, what happened is paradoxical. I make amends for the wrongs I have done whenever I can, but I don't live in the past, and I know that without the mistakes, I wouldn't be who I am today.

While I was out of town on the family vacation, the board of directors of Prison Fellowship Ministries named me president of Justice Fellowship. I was now running the largest and oldest conservative and Christian criminal justice reform organization in America. In Romans 8:28, Paul, who was Saul of Tarsus, a persecutor of believers, who held the coats of the men who stoned the Christian martyr Stephen to death, said, "And we know that in all things God works for the good of those who love him, who have been called according to his purpose."

Amen.

The dismissal of my case by the Michigan Court of Appeals was announced in a published opinion the same month. *Michigan v. DeRoche* is actually case law today and should give future overzealous prosecutors and police pause before they break into people's homes without a warrant. The Novi police quietly returned my property to me after holding it for two and a half years and losing three court cases.

My political experiences taught me not to expect any corrections to the stories that will live forever on the Internet. I have since observed this to be true. Most of them are still out there today. My belief, though, from the start through the end of this story, is the lesson that God wastes nothing. Without the media, I wouldn't have been properly motivated to share this story with you, my beautiful daughters. I love you completely and unconditionally, and it is for you that I wrote this book. I wanted you and your children to know and understand what my life has really been, and I pray that you will come to know God as I have. If I had my way, your lessons would come without the pain, but God is in charge of that, too. I am just blessed to have lived to share this experience—and my love—with you. My prayer is that reading the lessons I lived will attract you to the true solution for your problems, instead of the shortcuts of this world, which lead to such unfulfilling, even tragic, ends.

May God be with you and with all those who share this story I have written to hold up my end of the deal. I prayed in earnest, "God, I offer myself to you, to build with me and to do with me as you will. Relieve me of the bondage of self, that I may better do your will. Take away my difficulties, that victory over them may bear witness of your power, your love, and your way of life to those I might help. May I express your will in all that I say, think, and do."

My prayers were answered in a delightful and peculiarly perfect way. Yes, my end of the deal was to bear witness, and with the tale of these adventures, I submit for your consideration what I believe to be a demonstration of God's power and boundless love.

Author's note

Writing this memoir was a very difficult yet therapeutic exercise; something that would have been impossible without the help of a great many people, starting with a very special nudge.

Back in 2013, I was in a hotel in Orlando, Florida and decided for no particular reason to rent clubs and head out for a round of golf by myself. I hadn't played in years and had no equipment or shoes with me. Across town, Dr. Mark McKinney was laying poolside on "holiday" as he calls it in his home in Northern Ireland. He told his wife quite definitively that "God was telling him to play golf at a resort he had never been to."

Quite skeptically, but lovingly, his wife of many years teased him such a grandiose excuse was unnecessary.

Mark and I connected on the third hole and became a twosome. A few holes later we had shared what God had done in both our lives. In amazement that we were drawn together in such a strange way, we agreed to continue communicating. Mark also said my story would make a great book, and that he and some others had invested in a small Christian publisher called MySong.

So when it came time to write this, there was nowhere else to look but what had been arranged for me. Mark and I had become good friends and he welcomed the idea of telling this story. In MySong, I met a wonderfully talented and gifted team who saw this story from draft to final copy helping me express my experience better than I could have done on my own. Along with all of this,

Dr. McKinney's friends and business associates at Ashes to Gold made this a truly wonderful experience.

And to you for reading this book, I am truly grateful for the time you have shared with me. I believe that sharing what God did in my life has helped others, and I have had the privilege of seeing the gift I received pass on in greater measure to others. My prayer and hope is that you too will share your gifts so that others can break free of the slavery of addiction. If you personally need help, or are in a position to use your experience, strength and hope for the benefit of others – I would like to connect with you.

Addiction wrecks lives, families and relationships. Many, many families are torn apart and don't know where to look for help when facing the everyday reality of living with addiction. Many "Highly Functional" types like myself may feel they need to talk to someone "like them" to get started on the path to healing. I hope you come and visit with me at craigderoche.com so I can share what I have learned with you.

Maybe you have friends or loved ones struggling to adjust after their service to our country, you too can find help at craigderoche.com.

Finally, I hope you will join me in visiting the prisoner. If you feel called forward to action, let's join together to change the world for those affected by the justice system. Together we can advance toward "a more perfect union" and a justice system that restores the lives of those harmed, those who have harmed and the communities affected by crime.

I look forward to meeting you soon at craigderoche.com.

Join me on Twitter@craigderoche

Follow on faccbook.com/craigderoche

www.craigderoche.com

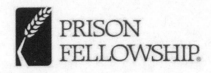

PRISON
FELLOWSHIP.

Restoring those affected by Crime and Incarceration.

I invite you to join us in pursuing justice and changing the lives of the most forgotten among us by contributing your time, talent and treasure to help the mission of Prison Fellowship.

prisonfellowship.org

justicefellowship.org

angeltree.org

colsoncenter.org

**Prison Fellowship
44180 Riverside Parkway
Lansdowne
VA 20176**

**Prison Fellowship works to make communities safer
and healthier through a restorative approach to
prisoners, former prisoners, and all those affected
by crime and incarceration.
Its programs reach prisoners, ex-prisoners,
and families of prisoners as well as policymakers,
judicial and administrative officials throughout the
United States and other parts of the world, through
Prison Fellowship International.**